Living Green
The Missing Manual®

Living Green: The Missing Manual

BY NANCY CONNER

Published by O'Reilly Media, Inc., 1005 Gravenstein Highway North, Sebastopol, CA 95472.

O'Reilly books may be purchased for educational, business, or sales promotional use. Online editions are also available for most titles (*my.safaribooksonline.com*). For more information, contact our corporate/institutional sales department: 800.998.9938 or corporate@*oreilly.com*.

Editor: Dawn Frausto
Production Editor: Nellie McKesson
Copy Editor: Alison O'Byrne
Indexer: Ron Strauss
Cover Designer: Karen Montgomery
Interior Designer: Ron Bilodeau

Print History:

August 2009:   First Edition.

100%

Printed on Rolland Enviro100 Book, which contains 100% post-consumer fibers and is manufactured in Canada by Cascades using biogas energy.

ISBN: 978-0-596-80172-4

[V]

Contents

Part 1: Living Green Begins at Home

Chapter 1

Chapter 2

Chapter 3

Part 2: Greening Your Lifestyle

Part 3: A Greener World

The Missing Credits

About the Author

 **Nancy Conner** holds a Ph.D. from Brown University and is the author of numerous books, including *Quick-Base: The Missing Manual* and *Google Apps: The Missing Manual.* She lives in Ithaca, NY, recently named one of the greenest U.S. cities, where she shops for organic produce at the local farmers market and browses second-hand stores. Each day, she commutes up the stairs to her home office, where she works as an author, editor, and distance educator. Read Nancy's Living Green blog at *www.missingmanuals.com*.

About the Creative Team

Dawn Frausto (editor) is assistant editor for the Missing Manual series. When not working, she plays soccer, beads, and causes trouble. Email: *dawn@oreilly.com*.

Nellie McKesson (production editor) lives in Brighton, Mass., where she makes t-shirts for her friends (*http://mattsaundersbynellie.etsy.com*) and plays music with her band Dr. & Mrs. Van Der Trampp. Email: *nellie@oreilly.com*.

Alison O'Byrne (copy editor) is a freelance editor from Dublin, Ireland. Alison has provided editorial services for corporate and government clients at home and internationally for over eight years. Email: *alison@alhaus.com*. Website: *www.alhaus.com*.

Ron Strauss (indexer) is a full-time freelance indexer specializing in IT. When not working, he moonlights as a concert violist and alternative medicine health consultant. Email: *rstrauss@mchsi.com*.

Willis Brown (tech reviewer, Chapters 3, 6–11) is a founder and the president of Michler & Brown, LLC, an ecological restoration company based in Madison, WI.

Farhad Ebrahimi (tech reviewer, Chapters 1, 2, 8, and 9) is the founder of the Chorus Foundation in Boston, MA. When indulging his narcissism, he plays exceptionally loud music in his bands Summerduck and Big Bear. Email: *farhad@thechorusfoundation.org*.

Don Willmott (tech reviewer, Chapters 2 and 3) is a New York-based writer and editor specializing in Internet, consumer electronics, and environmental topics.

Michele Brogunier (tech reviewer, Chapter 5) is a mother and family practice physician in Madison, WI.

Vivina Boster (tech reviewer, Chapter 4) is a Realtor and green-living consultant who lives and works in Portland, Oregon and New York. You can read more of her thoughts at *www.spaceforinspiredliving.com*.

Photina Ree Brown (tech reviewer, Chapter 3) tutors math and sciences at Madison Area Technical College and enjoys drawing and painting in Wisconsin.

Acknowledgments

A book like this requires the knowledge, skills, and talents of many people to take it from initial idea to finished product. I was fortunate to work with a world-class team. Pete Meyers helped me shape the outline and offered invaluable feedback. Dawn Frausto worked with me every step of the way, editing with care, extraordinary attention to detail, and a much appreciated sense of humor. Because this book covers such a broad range of topics, I needed the expertise of quite a few technical reviewers. Thanks to Willis Brown, Farhad Ebrahimi, Don Willmott, Michele Brogunier, Vivina Boster, and Photina Ree Brown for their suggestions, comments, and corrections. Thanks also to copyeditor Alison O'Byrne for rooting out typos, inconsistencies, and other mistakes, and to Ron Strauss for writing a great index.

As always, my husband Steve Holzner was loving and supportive throughout the many long hours it takes to write a book. (He's written more than 125 books himself, so he knows better than most what the process requires.) Thanks to him for hand-holding, back-patting, and steady supply of pizza on the weekends. He's the best!

—*Nancy Conner*

The Missing Manual Series

Missing Manuals are witty, superbly written guides to computer products that don't come with printed manuals (which is just about all of them). Each book features a handcrafted index and cross-references to specific page numbers (not just "see Chapter 14").

Recent and upcoming titles include:

Access 2007: The Missing Manual by Matthew MacDonald

AppleScript: The Missing Manual by Adam Goldstein

AppleWorks 6: The Missing Manual by Jim Elferdink and David Reynolds

CSS: The Missing Manual by David Sawyer McFarland

Creating Web Sites: The Missing Manual by Matthew MacDonald

David Pogue's Digital Photography: The Missing Manual by David Pogue

Dreamweaver 8: The Missing Manual by David Sawyer McFarland

Dreamweaver CS3: The Missing Manual by David Sawyer McFarland

Dreamweaver CS4: The Missing Manual by David Sawyer McFarland

eBay: The Missing Manual by Nancy Conner

Excel 2003: The Missing Manual by Matthew MacDonald

Excel 2007: The Missing Manual by Matthew MacDonald

Facebook: The Missing Manual by E.A. Vander Veer

FileMaker Pro 8: The Missing Manual by Geoff Coffey and Susan Prosser

FileMaker Pro 9: The Missing Manual by Geoff Coffey and Susan Prosser

Flash 8: The Missing Manual by E.A. Vander Veer

Flash CS3: The Missing Manual by E.A. Vander Veer and Chris Grover

Flash CS4: The Missing Manual by Chris Grover with E.A. Vander Veer

FrontPage 2003: The Missing Manual by Jessica Mantaro

Google Apps: The Missing Manual by Nancy Conner

Google SketchUp: The Missing Manual by Chris Grover

The Internet: The Missing Manual by David Pogue and J.D. Biersdorfer

iMovie 6 & iDVD: The Missing Manual by David Pogue

iMovie '08 & iDVD: The Missing Manual by David Pogue

iPhone: The Missing Manual by David Pogue

iPhoto '08: The Missing Manual by David Pogue

iPhoto '09: The Missing Manual by David Pogue and J.D. Biersdorfer

iPod: The Missing Manual, Seventh Edition by J.D. Biersdorfer

iWork '09: The Missing Manual by Josh Clark

JavaScript: The Missing Manual by David Sawyer McFarland

Living Green: The Missing Manual by Nancy Conner

Mac OS X: The Missing Manual, Tiger Edition by David Pogue

Mac OS X: The Missing Manual, Leopard Edition by David Pogue

Microsoft Project 2007: The Missing Manual by Bonnie Biafore

Netbooks: The Missing Manual by J.D. Biersdorfer

Office 2004 for Macintosh: The Missing Manual by Mark H. Walker and Franklin Tessler

Office 2007: The Missing Manual by Chris Grover, Matthew MacDonald, and E.A. Vander Veer

Office 2008 for Macintosh: The Missing Manual by Jim Elferdink

PCs: The Missing Manual by Andy Rathbone

Photoshop CS4: The Missing Manual by Lesa Snider

Photoshop Elements 7: The Missing Manual by Barbara Brundage

Photoshop Elements 6 for Mac: The Missing Manual by Barbara Brundage

PowerPoint 2007: The Missing Manual by E.A. Vander Veer

QuickBase: The Missing Manual by Nancy Conner

QuickBooks 2008: The Missing Manual by Bonnie Biafore

Quicken 2008: The Missing Manual by Bonnie Biafore

Quicken 2009: The Missing Manual by Bonnie Biafore

QuickBooks 2009: The Missing Manual by Bonnie Biafore

Switching to the Mac: The Missing Manual, Tiger Edition by David Pogue and Adam Goldstein

Switching to the Mac: The Missing Manual, Leopard Edition by David Pogue

Wikipedia: The Missing Manual by John Broughton

Windows XP Home Edition: The Missing Manual, Second Edition by David Pogue

Windows XP Pro: The Missing Manual, Second Edition by David Pogue, Craig Zacker, and Linda Zacker

Windows Vista: The Missing Manual by David Pogue

Windows Vista for Starters: The Missing Manual by David Pogue

Word 2007: The Missing Manual by Chris Grover

Your Body: The Missing Manual by Matthew MacDonald

Your Brain: The Missing Manual by Matthew MacDonald

Introduction

Earth is home to a magnificent, interconnected series of ecosystems that maintain an astonishing variety of life, from microbes to elephants, from algae to eagles, from fungi to your next-door neighbor. But the planet—and its inhabitants—face some major challenges. Climate change is making the seas rise and the weather change, and threatening biodiversity. There isn't enough clean water in many parts of the world. Natural habitats like forests and wetlands are disappearing. Mountains of trash are piling up at an alarming rate. And people are being exposed to toxic chemicals in their homes and at work.

These threats are caused by people who have put their economies, technologies, and convenience first—and the Earth is paying the price. But more and more folks are starting to recognize the importance of living in harmony with the earth rather than exploiting it. They want healthy, natural foods and products instead of those laden with chemicals and toxins. They're trying to conserve resources by reducing consumption, using energy more efficiently, and finding renewable energy sources. And they're doing things with an awareness that we're stewards of the earth—not just for ourselves, but also for other creatures and for future generations.

This book takes a look at how things got this way. And, more importantly, it tells you specific things you can do every day to live a greener life.

Saving the Planet, One Step at a Time

When you look at the mess humans have made of the planet, it's easy to despair. What good does it do, you may wonder, to carry reusable shopping bags or sort recyclables when factories continue to belch out more pollution each day than you cause in a whole year?

Doing your part makes a difference because there's power in numbers. As more people take steps to save the environment—reducing consumption, recycling and reusing, wasting less, becoming more energy efficient, insisting on renewable energy and sustainable industry—the effect builds. Think globally, but act where you can: at home, in your community, at work, and by joining or donating to environmental groups. Educate and encourage others, as well. The more people who work together to protect the environment, the bigger impact they'll have.

The planet didn't get this way overnight: It took lots of small steps to create these huge environmental problems. Fixing them won't happen overnight, either. But everything you do to live a healthier, more responsible, greener life is a step in the right direction.

What's a Carbon Footprint?

You've probably heard people mention carbon footprints, but you may not quite know what that term means. Your *carbon footprint* is the amount of greenhouse gases released into the atmosphere because of things you do. (As page 264 explains, greenhouse gases trap heat in the earth's atmosphere and cause global warming.) You may already think about emissions when you drive your car or pay your utility bills, but there are many factors that contribute to your carbon footprint:

- The size of your household.
- How energy efficient your home is.
- How much you travel and how you get there (plane, car, and so on).
- What you eat and how that food was produced.
- How much waste your household produces and how you deal with that waste.

Even factors like your age and where you live contribute to your carbon footprint. For example, according to one U.K. study, people aged 50–65 have bigger carbon footprints than people in other age groups.

So how do you find out how big your carbon footprint is? The University of California at Berkeley can tell you. Point your browser to *http://coolclimate. berkeley.edu* to use the school's Cool Climate Carbon Footprint Calculator.

Spend a few minutes telling the site about your household, energy use, and consumption, and it'll figure out the size of your footprint and how it compares to similar households, your country's average, and the world average.

Once you know your carbon "shoe size", you can take action to mitigate it by changing your habits (walking or taking the bus instead of driving, for example), consuming less (it takes energy to make the products you buy), and doing things to offset the carbon emissions you cause (like planting trees or investing in clean energy; page 259 tells you more about carbon offsets). Throughout this book, you'll find lots of suggestions and tips for saving energy, money, and the climate.

About This Book

Ever since Rachel Carson's 1962 book **Silent Spring** sounded the alarm about the effects of pesticides on the environment, countless books have been published that show how human behavior is taking a toll on the planet. Taken together, they present a convincing argument. But even if you want to start living a healthier, more environmentally responsible lifestyle, where do you begin?

That's where **Living Green: The Missing Manual** comes in. Although this book gives you plenty of reasons to think about your impact on the planet, its real focus is practical suggestions for making your impact a positive one. These pages are packed with tips, ideas, and instructions for greening in all areas of your life: at home, on the road, at work, at the grocery store, and beyond.

You probably picked up this book for one of two reasons: Either you're wondering what all the environmentalists are so worked up about (and what it has to do with you) or you're committed to living more responsibly and looking for more ways to put your ideals into practice. Either way, this book is for you. You'll get both the **whys** and the **hows** of greener living, and learn things you can do today to make the world a better place for everyone—now and for generations to come.

About the Outline

Living Green: The Missing Manual is divided into three parts, each containing several chapters:

- **Part 1, Living Green Begins at Home** helps you find ways to start living a healthier, greener lifestyle. Individuals don't have a lot of control over government policies or corporate practices, but you're the undisputed ruler of your home (well, unless you have a cat—then everyone knows who's *really* the boss). These chapters help you make your home a greener, healthier place to live:

    — **Home Green Home: Creating a Safe, Earth-Friendly Place to Live (Chapter 1)** gives you a tour of the hazards that may be lurking in cupboards, closets, and other parts of your home. You may be surprised to learn how many seemingly innocuous products could be harming your family's health. But don't worry—the chapter is packed with recipes and tips for healthy, natural alternatives. And you'll also find tips for growing a lawn that's both lush and nontoxic.

    — **Save Energy, Money, and the Earth (Chapter 2)** is all about energy efficiency. This chapter shows you how to do a home energy audit (or hire a pro to do one for you), how to choose energy-efficient appliances, and how to avoid wasting energy and increasing your bills. Saving energy means reducing your carbon footprint, so you can save money *and* help the planet at the same time.

    — **Reduce, Reuse, Recycle (Chapter 3)** takes a familiar mantra—the new three Rs—and shows why it's important. This chapter also offers fresh thinking on how to reduce consumption (and waste), find new uses for old items, and recycle just about everything, including stuff like electronics and worn-out tires.

    — **Building and Remodeling (Chapter 4)** explains the principles of green construction and shows how to put them to work for you, whether you're building a new home or remodeling an existing one. You'll learn about LEED certification (what that means and why you should look for it) finding a contractor you can work with, and hazards to watch out for when remodeling.

- **Part 2, Greening Your Lifestyle** looks at greener ways to do everyday things. Whether you're playing with the kids, giving the dog a bath, eating a cheeseburger, or shopping for a new t-shirt, these chapters help you find more earth-friendly ways to do them:

  — **Raising a Green Family (Chapter 5)** looks at how to ensure a non-toxic environment for your baby, get through the first couple of years of a baby's life without adding a mountain of diapers to landfills, teach your kids respect for the earth, and encourage teens to take responsibility and get involved. There's also a section on green pet care.

  — **Eating Green: It's Not Just Spinach Anymore (Chapter 6)** explains how food is produced in the modern world—and how you can choose food that's made without toxic chemicals or iffy farming practices. Whether you're growing your own food or buying it at the store, you'll learn what organic means and why it's good for you. You'll also find tips on eating healthy when you go out.

  — **Responsible Shopping (Chapter 7)** helps you feel better about the purchases you make by pointing out earth-friendly options. You'll read about fair-trade goods, organic and natural clothing, and non-toxic health and beauty products. You'll also learn about environmentally friendly gifts and companies that give something back.

  — **Going Green: Transportation and Travel (Chapter 8)** explores traveling in ways that don't leave giant-sized carbon footprints all along your route. Get tips for minimizing driving—and getting better fuel efficiency when you do go by car. Find the most fuel-efficient car so you can save money at the pump and reduce greenhouse-gas emissions. And if you're taking a longer trip (whether for business, pleasure, or a little of both), you'll find tips for getting there greener.

- **Part 3, A Greener World** moves beyond the home and personal spheres to the big, wide world. Whether it's in your community, your country, or across the globe, you can join forces with others to improve the quality of life on earth:

  — **Green Business Is Good Business (Chapter 9)** shows that making a difference and making a profit don't have to conflict. This chapter begins with ways you can green your workplace, from reducing waste to starting an office recycling program. It also looks at green-collar jobs, predicted to grow throughout the next decade and beyond. And it finishes with ways that companies can go greener, by purchasing carbon offsets and donating to earth-loving charities.

— **Alternative and Renewable Energy (Chapter 10)** peeks into the future of energy, looking at technologies that are currently in use, under development, or on the horizon to produce power that's clean, renewable, and sustainable. The chapter covers wind, solar, and geothermal energy; hydropower; biomass; and hydrogen fuel cells.

— **Getting Involved (Chapter 11)** suggests ways to use your time, efforts, and money to make a difference and help the earth. You'll learn about starting a grassroots project in your community, finding likeminded environmentalists online, and participating in national and international efforts. The chapter also covers environmentally responsible investing, so you can do good in the world while funding your nest egg.

Up To Speed

Tiny URLs

This book mentions lots of great websites where you can learn more ways to be green. But sometimes that info is on a very specific part of a site, and the Web address that takes you to that spot can be awfully long.

The geeky name for a Web address is a *URL* (that's short for Uniform Resource Locator). For example, *http://www.google.com* is a URL—it tells your Web browser how to get to the Google home page. But not all URLs are as short as that. To learn about Amazon.com's Frustration-Free Packaging program (page 92), for instance, you have to go to *http://www.amazon.com/gp/feature.html/?docId=1000276271*. That's a lot of gobbledygook to type in, and you have better ways to spend your time. That's where TinyURLs come in.

In 2002, a guy named Kevin Gilbertson started the website TinyURL.com. The site's mission is simple: to shorten ungainly Web addresses. All you do is copy the address you want to shrink, head over to *http://tinyurl.com*, and then paste the address in the box. Click the Make TinyURL button and voilà—the site gives you a much shorter address (which starts with *http://tinyurl.com*) that takes you to the same exact spot as the long one.

Throughout this book, you'll see TinyURLs used in place of giant, clunky ones. To get to the Amazon page mentioned earlier, for example, you can use *http://tinyurl.com/59b7kn* instead. Just type that address into your browser and your computer will get you to the right place. Better yet, head to this book's Missing CD page at *www.missingmanuals.com*, where you'll find clickable links to all the sites referenced in this book.

About MissingManuals.com

At *www.missingmanuals.com*, you'll find articles, tips, and updates to this book. In fact, we invite and encourage you to submit such corrections and updates yourself. In an effort to keep this book as up to date and accurate as possible, each time we print more copies of it, we'll make any confirmed corrections you've suggested. We'll also note such changes on the website, so you can mark important corrections into your copy of the book, if you like. (Go to *http://missingmanuals.com/feedback*, choose the book's name from the pop-up menu, and then click Go to see the changes.)

Also on our Feedback page, you can get expert answers to questions that come to you while reading this book, write a book review, and find groups for folks who share your interest in green living.

We'd love to hear your suggestions for new books in the Missing Manual line. There's a place for that on missingmanuals.com, too. And while you're online, you can also register this book at *www.oreilly.com* (you can jump directly to the registration page by going to *http://tinyurl.com/yo82k3*). Registering means we can send you updates about this book, and you'll be eligible for special offers like discounts on future editions of *Living Green: The Missing Manual*.

Safari® Books Online

Safari ••> When you see a Safari® Books Online icon on the cover of your favorite technology book, it means the book is available online through the O'Reilly Network Safari Bookshelf.

Safari offers a solution that's better than e-Books. It's a virtual library that lets you easily search thousands of top tech books, cut and paste code samples, download chapters, and find quick answers when you nee the most accurate, current information. Try it free at *http://my.safaribooksonline.com*.

1 Home Green Home: Creating a Safe, Earth-Friendly Place to Live

Living green is all about reducing pollution and creating a safe, healthy environment for you and your family, not to mention all the other critters on the planet. There's no better place to start your quest for greenification than at home—after all, that's where you have the most control.

Turns out there could be some pretty scary pollution right in your own house:

- The air in your home is probably more polluted than the air in the industrial part of a big city.

- Many common cleaning products contain toxic substances.

- The average American home contains 63 synthetic chemicals, which add up to about 10 gallons of hazardous stuff.

Yikes! Almost makes you want to up and move to a log cabin in the woods.

Luckily, you don't need all those nasty chemicals in your home. And, as you'll learn in this chapter, getting rid of them doesn't mean giving mildew free rein over your bathroom. Nope, you can easily and cheaply replace potentially harmful cleaning products with simple, natural alternatives. Same goes for your lawn: You can keep it healthy without feeding it synthetic fertilizers; the last section of this chapter teaches you how.

Before you can banish harsh chemicals in your home, it's important to learn about them and the problems they can cause so you can dispose of 'em properly. So this chapter starts with a rundown of common chemicals and the health problems they can cause. But don't lose hope: Keep reading to learn how to keep your family healthy without hurting the earth.

The Chemicals You Live With

Your home is your castle, your sanctuary, the place where you raise your family and relax at the end of the day. But rather than being a safe haven, many homes are a minefield of chemicals that can affect your health and harm the planet. In fact, the U.S. Environmental Protection Agency (EPA) has called the typical American home "the number one violator of chemical waste per capita" because many of those chemicals get tossed in the trash or go swirling down the drain. Let's take a tour of a typical home to see what chemical hazards may be lurking within its walls:

- **Throughout the house.** Paint, carpet, draperies, upholstery, and furniture may contain *volatile organic compounds*, or VOCs. The box on page 12 explains what VOCs are and why you should avoid them.

- **Kitchen.** Cleaners are the culprits here. Oven cleaners and drain uncloggers are loaded with lye. Dishwasher detergents may contain lots of chlorine—the leading cause of childhood poisoning—and phosphates, which pollute rivers and lakes. And many antibacterial cleaners contain a potentially harmful chemical called triclosan.

> **Note** The next section includes a table that tells you exactly how the chemicals mentioned here can affect you—see page 13.

- **Bathroom.** Here you'll find toilet-bowl cleaners (which get rid of gunk with corrosive ingredients like hydrochloric acid and oxalic acid), lye-filled drain uncloggers, and tub and tile sprays that go after mold and mildew while releasing sodium hypochlorite and formaldehyde into the air. And air freshener sprays may contain formaldehyde or phenol, neither of which you want to breathe in.

Note When you open the cabinet under your kitchen or bathroom sink, a characteristic smell wafts out. You may associate this smell with a clean house—but it comes from chemicals you don't want to inhale. VOCs (page 12) can escape even from closed containers, making the air under the sink some of the most polluted in the house. That's a good reason to use the green cleaning products discussed later in this chapter.

- **Laundry room.** The chlorine bleach you use to get your whites white is strongly corrosive, so you don't want it anywhere near your eyes, skin, mouth, or nose. Detergents and fabric softeners may contain chemicals and fragrances that can irritate skin or, worse, get *absorbed* through the skin and harm your health—not what you want on your family's clothes, towels, and bedding. And dryer sheets may contain chloroform or pentane.

- **Living and dining rooms.** The furniture polish or wax you use to clean your wood furniture may contain phenol or benzene. Upholstery and carpet shampoos are likely to have perchloroethylene or ammonium hydroxide in them.

- **Bedrooms and closets.** Bedrooms are often heavy on fabrics and upholstery: bedding, drapes, carpeting, and so on. These materials, especially when new, can emit VOCs (page 12). And more VOCs are waiting in your closet. Dry-cleaned clothing, for example, may give off benzene or contain perchloroethylene. Permanent-press clothing may be full of formaldehyde, and the fibers in fleece easily absorb VOCs from the air—and then re-emit them. Dust mites and pet dander can also cling to your clothes and cause breathing problems. Most closets aren't very well ventilated, so your walk-in closet may have some of the most polluted air in your home.

- **Home office.** Love the smell of fresh markers? Hold your breath! Markers, including felt-tip pens, permanent markers, and dry-erase markers, contain solvents that help the ink dry fast. Those solvents get into the air and into your lungs. Copiers and some printers release ozone, VOCs (including formaldehyde), and *particulates* (teensy particles that come from materials like paper, ink, and toner). To breathe easier, make sure your office is well ventilated, and get an ozone-filtered laser printer.

Tip Markers labeled "low VOC" or "low odor" don't release as many fumes. When you use a marker, put its cap back on when you're finished with it. Better still, use colored pencils or crayons to avoid fumes altogether.

- **Basement and garage.** If you have old paint cans sitting around, you're storing a source of VOCs that the EPA calls one of the top five environmental hazards. You don't want the ingredients in paint anywhere *near* your family: benzene, toluene, xylene, formaldehyde, even lead if the paint was made before 1970. That's why some states, like California, define certain kinds of leftover paint as toxic waste and have special rules for disposing of it (see page 86). If you wear contacts, the lenses can absorb these VOCs and trap them against your eyes, where they can cause irritation and get absorbed into your body. Other stuff you may store in your basement or garage—like paint strippers, varnish, lacquer, pesticides, glues, and sealants—also give off VOCs. Car soaps, waxes, and products that help you remove tar and bugs from your car contain petroleum distillates that can irritate your skin and respiratory system.

> **Note** Fortunately, you can buy low-VOC paints. Page 137 tells you all about them.

That's a scary list! The next section goes into more detail about health problems associated with these chemicals. But don't lose hope: Starting on page 16, you'll learn that you don't need all those nasty things in your house. There are all kinds of easy ways to avoid harmful chemicals while keeping your house clean and healthy.

Frequently Asked Question

VOCs and You

What are VOCs and how can they affect me?

VOC stands for *volatile organic compound*, a type of chemical. Unless you're a chemist, that's not very illuminating, so let's break it down:

- **Volatile** means the chemical evaporates easily at room temperature. That's why when you use a spray cleaner on the kitchen counter, for example, you smell the fumes. VOCs' volatility is the reason they're behind so much indoor air pollution.
- **Organic compound.** Wait a minute—organic is good, right? Not always. It's good when it describes how fruits and vegetables are grown (page xx6), but in chemistry, an *organic compound* is a chemical that has carbon in its makeup. Some organic compounds, like carbohydrates and vitamins, are beneficial. But others, especially synthetic chemicals, can be harmful. Many organic compounds are irritants that can affect your eyes, skin, and breathing. Others, like formaldehyde and benzene, can cause cancer. When such organic compounds are volatile—that is, when they get into the air—you obviously want to avoid inhaling them.

How Household Chemicals Can Affect Your Health

The following table spells out health problems that common household chemicals can cause.

> **Tip** Household products are packed with potentially harmful substances, so this table can't cover them all. If you want to learn about a specific product or ingredient, check the Household Products Database from the U.S. Department of Health and Human Services at *http://hpd.nlm.nih.gov*. Search for a product by name to see possible health effects and safe handling instructions. Search for an ingredient to get a list of products that contain it, along with links to information about its toxicity.

Chemical	Health Effects	Found In
Ammonia	Eye, nose, and throat irritation; skin problems; aggravation of asthma symptoms	Cleaning products, paint stripper, adhesive removers, some fertilizers
Ammonium hydroxide	Eye, nose, and throat irritation; aggravation of asthma symptoms	Cleaning products, disinfectants, metal polishes, car care products, carpet and upholstery cleaners
Benzene	Cancer	Adhesive removers, degreasers, interior paints, dry-cleaning solvents
Chlordane	With long-term exposure: kidney, liver, and central nervous system damage; cancer	Flea powders, pesticides
Chlorine bleach	Eye, nose, and throat irritation; skin problems; aggravation of asthma symptoms	Cleaning and laundry products, toilet-bowl cleaners
Chloroform	Central nervous system damage; possibly cancer	Dryer sheets; adhesive removers
Cresol	With long-term exposure: kidney, liver, and central nervous system damage	Antibacterial cleaning products, disinfectants, deodorizers, pesticides
Dichlorophene	With long-term exposure: kidney, liver, and central nervous system damage; cancer	Flea powders, pesticides
Ethylene glycol	Dizziness; heart, brain, kidney, liver, and central nervous system damage	Antifreeze, de-icers, brake fluid, adhesives, paints
Formaldehyde	Eye, nose, and throat irritation; aggravation of asthma symptoms; headaches; nausea; fatigue; memory problems; possibly cancer	Adhesives, sealers, paint, caulk

Chemical	Health Effects	Found In
Glycol ethers	Infertility	Water-based paints
Hydrochloric acid	Eye, nose, and throat irritation; aggravation of asthma symptoms	Cleaning products, toilet-bowl cleaners
Lye	Blindness (from direct contact with eyes); skin irritation	Drain uncloggers, oven cleaners, dishwasher detergents
Methanol	With long-term exposure: kidney, liver, and central nervous system damage	Antifreeze, de-icers, car care products, shellacs, adhesive removers, paint strippers
Naphthalene	Cataracts (with long-term exposure); nausea	Carpet cleaners, car care products, paints, insect repellants
Oxalic acid	With long-term exposure: kidney, liver, and central nervous system damage	Toilet-bowl cleaners, car care products, cleansers, metal polish
Ozone	Respiratory system damage	Given off by printers and copiers
Pentane	Eye, nose, and throat irritation; skin problems	Solvents, dryer sheets, fabric softeners
Perchloroethylene (also called tetrachloroethylene)	Dizziness; headache; nausea; skin irritation. With long-term exposure: kidney, liver, and central nervous system damage; possibly cancer	Adhesives and sealants, car care products, polishes, spot cleaners; dry-cleaning solvents
Perfluorooctanoate and perfluorooctane sulfonate	Infertility in women	Pesticides, stain-resistant upholstery, adhesives, nonstick cookware coatings
Phenol (a.k.a. carbolic acid)	Skin irritation. With long-term exposure: kidney, liver, and central nervous system damage	Antibacterial cleaning products
Sodium hypochlorite	Eye, nose, and throat irritation; aggravation of asthma symptoms; skin irritation	Cleaning products, disinfectants, drain uncloggers
Toluene	Eye, nose, and throat irritation; dizziness; nausea; central nervous system damage; cardiac arrest	Adhesives, solvents, paints, car care products.
Triclosan	Liver damage	Antibacterial soaps and cleaning products, pet shampoos
Trichloroethane	Dizziness; liver and central nervous system damage	Adhesives, lubricants, furniture cleaners
Xylene	Dizziness; eye, nose, and throat irritation; respiratory problems; nausea; kidney, liver, and central nervous system damage	Adhesives and sealants, car care products, paints, pesticides

The kinds of symptoms you have depend on the type of chemical, how concentrated it is, and how long you're exposed to it. For example, people whose work exposes them to high levels of VOCs, like painters and cleaners, are most likely to suffer health problems. Over time, even low-level exposure can cause problems, especially in kids, the elderly, people with existing conditions such as asthma or allergies, and folks who are extra sensitive to chemicals.

If you use products that contain any of the chemicals in this list, buy small quantities so you won't have to worry about disposing of leftovers. Also, be sure to work in a well-ventilated area (fresh air reduces the concentration of VOCs) and follow the manufacturer's directions. **Never** mix different kinds of cleaning products: Mixing ammonia with bleach, for example, creates chloramine gas, which is highly toxic—and often fatal—when inhaled.

Tip Because VOCs can leak from closed containers, don't keep old, half-empty bottles of cleaning products, paint strippers, or other VOC-filled chemicals in your home. But don't just toss them in the trash, either—read on to learn how to get rid of them safely.

Disposing of Household Chemicals

By now, you're probably ready to gather up all your cleaning products and dump them in the trash. Not so fast: While it's a good idea to remove harsh chemicals from your home, you need to dispose of them safely. The earth will thank you for it.

To get rid of household chemicals, don't throw them in the trash, pour them down a drain, or burn them. If your community has a day designated for hazardous waste pickup, unload them then. If you're not sure how to dispose of hazardous waste where you live, call your city's waste department or your garbage company or go to *www.earth911.com*. This helpful site lets you type in the kind of stuff you want to get rid of (such as *paint* or *household cleaners*) and your Zip code, and it finds a disposal facility near you.

Tip Head to this book's Missing CD page at *www.missingmanuals.com* for a list of all the websites mentioned in this book.

When it comes to health—yours, your family's, the environment's—you don't want to take chances. Luckily, you don't need to expose your family to harmful chemicals and indoor air pollutants because there are simple, healthier alternatives. As the next section explains, you can make your home greener and healthier in no time.

Clean and Green: Environmentally Friendly Cleaning

Nontoxic, earth-friendly cleaning products are nothing new. That's how people kept their homes clean before companies sold cleaners packed with synthetic chemicals. Your great-grandmother probably used vinegar and baking soda to scrub her house. This section shows that you don't need mass-produced chemicals to keep your home sparkling.

Here are the basics you'll need to green your cleaning:

- **Baking soda.** Sodium bicarbonate (that's baking soda's chemical name) is a nontoxic, inexpensive, multipurpose cleaner. Many people keep an open box of it in the fridge to absorb odors, but you can use it in every room of the house. It's a cleanser, stain-buster, and all-around deodorizer. Try putting some in the cat's litter box to absorb odors. Or to freshen up a smelly carpet, sprinkle a layer of baking soda over it, leave the baking soda overnight, and then vacuum first thing in the morning.

- **White vinegar.** Vinegar is all-natural and all-safe—and an excellent all-around cleaner. Like baking soda, it deodorizes and cleans. It's also a natural ant repellant: Spray or wipe vinegar along doors and window sills where ants come in to keep them out. And a half-vinegar, half-water solution will make your windows sparkle. (If the half-and-half mixture leaves streaks on the glass, try adding a drop or two of liquid castile soap, mentioned later in this list.) Be sure to use *white* vinegar; other kinds like cider vinegar may discolor what you're cleaning.

Tip Get two empty spray bottles; fill one with pure white vinegar and the other with half-vinegar, half-water. Use the full-strength vinegar for tough cleaning jobs, such as around the toilet and in the bathtub. Use the diluted vinegar to clean counters and windows and spot-treat carpet stains.

- **Lemon juice.** When life hands you lemons...use 'em to clean your house! The mild acid in lemon juice makes it great for cutting grease and getting stains out. A mixture of equal parts lemon juice and water in a spray bottle cleans your kitchen and bathroom and leaves them smelling wonderful. (You can also add a few drops of lemon juice to your water-and-vinegar cleaner to make it smell less vinegary.) No need to squeeze endless lemons, either—bottled lemon juice works just as well as fresh squeezed.

Note Lemon juice can spoil, so put this mixture in the fridge to keep it fresh. Or simply mix up a new batch whenever you're cleaning.

- **Club soda.** Not only does club soda make a good mixer, it also removes stains from fabrics and carpets, and does a great job of cleaning stainless steel. Pour a little on a cloth, and then dab at stains or wipe away fingerprints and smudges.

- **Borax.** This white powder is a naturally occurring mineral that dissolves easily in water and removes dirt. It also kills fungi and works as a deodorizer. You can find it by the detergents in most grocery stores. You'll learn several ways of using borax later in this chapter.

Note Borax is a natural substance, but it still requires some common-sense care when you're handling it. Borax can be toxic if swallowed, so *don't* store it where kids can get at it. Some people report that borax irritates their skin after prolonged contact, so wear rubber gloves when you work with it, especially if you'll be scrubbing for a while.

- **Olive oil.** You've probably read that olive oil is good for your heart, but did you know it's also good for your wood furniture? To clean wood without using chemical polishes, combine three parts olive oil with one part white vinegar. Or, if you like lemon-scented polish, try two parts olive oil to one part lemon juice. Use a soft cloth to rub a small amount of polish into the wood, and then buff it with a clean cloth.

- **Castile soap.** This soap is made with vegetable oil (olive, coconut, or jojoba, for example) instead of animal fat or synthetic chemicals, and it comes in both bar and liquid forms. You can find it in health-food stores and some grocery stores. It's gentle, versatile, and earth-friendly. Use liquid castile soap for washing dishes and clothes; dilute it with water to use it as a spray cleaner.

- **Coarse salt.** This stuff is great for scouring pans and cookware. Mix coarse salt (like sea salt) with vinegar (try one part salt to four parts vinegar) to remove stubborn coffee and tea stains from cups, rust stains, and bathroom soap scum.

> **Tip** To polish copper, brass, or silver, mix a teaspoon of coarse salt into a cup of vinegar, and then mix in enough flour to make a thick paste. Apply the paste to whatever you're polishing and leave it there for at least 15 minutes. Then, rinse with warm water and use a soft cloth to make the metal shine.

- **Hydrogen peroxide.** This mild bleach (which you can find at any grocery or drug store) is much safer than chlorine bleach: it breaks down into just water and oxygen. It fights bacteria and removes stains, including blood stains. Use a 3% hydrogen peroxide solution for cleaning (check the label to find out the percentage).

- **Essential oils.** Not only do these smell great, they can also kill bacteria. These oils—which include thyme, peppermint, lavender, bergamot, clove, basil, pine, lemon, lemongrass, eucalyptus, and tea tree—are antiseptic and antibacterial. Just a few drops will do it: Choose a scent you like, mix 10–20 drops of the oil into a spray bottle full of water, and spray the mixture on surfaces to zap germs and bacteria. You can buy these oils at health food stores and shops that sell aromatherapy products. Look for the phrase "pure essential oil" on the label.

- **Cleaning cloths.** To save some trees, recycle old clothes and towels by cutting them into squares and using them to clean instead of paper towels.

- **A squeegee.** Rather than using fistfuls of paper towels to clean your windows, copy the pros: Use a squeegee to get your windows crystal clear and streak free. Squeegees are also great for cleaning mirrors and shower doors.

- **A plunger.** To clear clogged toilets and drains without resorting to caustic chemicals, use a plunger and some good, old-fashioned elbow grease. Page 23 has more tips for unclogging drains.

Recipe for an All-Purpose Cleaner

Equal parts white vinegar and water mixed in a spray bottle is a cheap cleaning solution that gets the job done. But some people don't like the smell of vinegar, which *can* be a bit nose-wrinkling when you spray it (the smell dissipates quickly). Lemon juice smells better but costs more.

Here's a recipe for a good, all-purpose cleaner that works throughout the house. It cuts grease, cleans glass, disinfects countertops and other surfaces, removes soap scum from sinks and tubs, and leaves your home smelling great—all without hurting the planet:

1 cup water

1 cup white vinegar

1 drop liquid castile soap

4 drops grapefruit seed extract or eucalyptus oil, both of which are disinfectants. Undiluted eucalyptus oil can irritate the skin, so handle it carefully.

10–12 drops essential oil(s). Choose scents you like to boost disinfectant power and leave a fresh smell. Lavender is a good choice, as is lemon or tea tree oil. Or try a combination, like six drops of lemon oil, three of orange, and three of lime to make your home smell clean and delicious.

Mix all the ingredients in a clean 32-ounce spray bottle. Spray on, and then wipe with a soft cloth. That's it!

Note This mixture can separate if it sits for a long time, so be sure to shake the spray bottle before you clean.

Go ahead and tweak this recipe to find the ingredients and proportions that work best for you. You might try different essential oils, on their own or in combination. You can also add half a cup of 3% hydrogen peroxide solution to boost cleaning power. (If you don't like the smell of hydrogen peroxide, add a few more drops of essential oil.)

Conveniently Green

I barely have time to clean the house, let alone whip up my own cleaning products. What are some good, earth-friendly commercial cleaning products I can buy?

As consumers have become more interested in using safe, easy-on-the-environment cleaning products, companies have responded. If you don't have the time or inclination to cook up your own laundry detergent (page 25) or air freshener (page 24), check out some of these companies:

- **Biokleen** (*http://biokleenhome.com*) makes laundry and dishwasher detergents, as well as general cleaning products. All its products are biodegradable, nontoxic, and not tested on animals.

- **Ecos** (*www.ecos.com*) mostly sells kitchen, bathroom, and laundry products, with some others for the rest of the house. Ecos has a "Freedom Code," a long list of chemicals—including many of those mentioned earlier in this chapter—it *doesn't* use in its products.

- **Ecover** (*www.ecover.com*) makes products from renewable vegetable and mineral resources and specializes in dishwashing and laundry products, along with soaps and other household cleaners. Ecover also make earth-friendly cleaners for cars and boats.

- **Method** (*www.methodhome.com*) makes a complete range of cleaning products using nontoxic, biodegradable ingredients. You can find Method products at places like Target, Costco, and grocery and drug stores.

- **Mrs. Meyer's Clean Day** (*www.mrsmeyers.com*) combines cleaning power with aromatherapy—on the website, you can browse products by fragrance or cleaning task. The company also makes baby products and aromatherapy-related gifts.

- **Seventh Generation** (*www.seventhgeneration.com*) takes its name from the Great Law of the Iroquois: "In our every deliberation, we must consider the impact of our decisions on the next seven generations." The company's website has a store locator to help you find where to buy its laundry and dishwasher detergents, cleaners, and other products.

A Green Kitchen Is a Healthy Kitchen

For most families, the kitchen is the heart of the home. It's where you do your cooking, eating, chatting, laughing, coffee-drinking, homework, and so on—in other words, it's where life happens. So you want it to be safe for your family, your friends, and yourself. This section gives you green cleaning strategies for the room everyone uses most.

For all-purpose cleaning, try the recipe on page 19. Use this cleaner on countertops, stovetops, walls, inside and outside the fridge—everything up to and including the kitchen sink! For more specialized cleaning, try these approaches:

- For a good **mildly abrasive cleanser,** dampen a sponge and sprinkle on some baking soda, scrub away, and then rinse. Two tablespoons of baking soda dissolved in a quart of warm water shines up chrome and stainless steel sinks and stovetops without damaging the finish; simply apply the mixture, and then rinse it off.

- If you need a **nonabrasive cleanser,** mix a quarter-cup of borax with enough liquid castile soap to form a paste. If you want, add a few drops of lemon oil to make it smell good and add germ-fighting power. Use a damp sponge to apply a small amount of the mixture to the surface you're cleaning, and then follow up with a rinse.

- **To remove fingerprints from stainless steel,** dab a small amount of olive oil on a soft cloth, and then rub away the prints. To brighten stainless steel and protect its finish, dampen a cloth with white vinegar *or* club soda and use it to buff the surface to a shine.

- **When you run the dishwasher,** use a phosphate-free detergent. The trouble with phosphorus (which shows up as phosphates in detergents) is that, after it's gone down the drain, it runs off into rivers and lakes. Plants love phosphorus—it's an important nutrient for them. So when too much phosphorus gets into a lake, for example, it makes the algae grow like crazy, which upsets the lake's balance, making the water cloudy and stinky and harming aquatic plants and animals. Dishwasher detergents can contain as much as 4 to 8 percent phosphates, so look for brands that are phosphate-free, like those made by companies in the box on page 20.

- **To clean and deodorize the microwave,** combine half a cup of white vinegar with a cup of water in a microwave-safe glass bowl. Put the bowl in the microwave and heat it on high power until the mixture boils. Turn off the microwave and leave the bowl inside with the door shut for 5 to 10 minutes. This gets rid of odors and loosens zapped-on food splashes and stains so you can wipe them away with a damp sponge or cloth.

Tip Another way to clean the microwave and get rid of old food smells is to use a bowl of lemon slices floating in water. Microwave it on high for a minute or two, let it sit, and then wipe down.

- **Cleaning the oven** is a special challenge when you've banished harsh chemicals from your home; it can be tough to loosen baked-on gunk. The first line of offense is a good defense: Try to prevent spills by putting a sheet of aluminum foil on the oven's floor, under (but not touching) the heating element. Change the foil as needed (be sure to recycle it).

  If something bubbles over and you need to clean it up, sprinkle coarse salt (page 18) on the fresh spill while the oven is still warm but not hot (don't burn yourself!). If the spill is already dry, you may need to dampen it first with water. After the oven has cooled completely, scrape away the residue, and then clean the oven with your all-purpose cleaner.

  Another thing to try is baking soda. Dampen the oven, and then cover the area you're cleaning with baking soda. Let it sit overnight (don't use the oven in the meantime). In the morning, wipe away the baking soda with a damp cloth or sponge, and then rinse the oven. If necessary, use a steel-wool scrubber to (gently) scour off tough stains.

  One more option: Combine two teaspoons of borax with two tablespoons of liquid castile soap in a spray bottle, then fill the bottle with water and shake it up. Spray the mixture onto oven stains, and then scrub the stains away.

- **To clean wooden cutting boards,** rub them with lemon juice, leave 'em overnight, and then rinse in the morning. (Lemon is a great deodorizer.) If you're in a hurry to clean the board, wipe it with white vinegar.

- **To deodorize your kitchen,** use baking soda or white vinegar. An open dish of either one works wonders in the fridge. Sprinkle baking soda at the bottom of your garbage can to absorb odors. To get smells out of your sink, pour a cup of vinegar down the drain, wait an hour, and then rinse.

Tip If you've been working with strong-smelling foods like onions, garlic, or fish, rub some vinegar or lemon juice on your hands to neutralize the smell.

- **No-wax floors** get clean when you add a cup of white vinegar to a gallon of water and mop as you normally would. Another floor-cleaning recipe is to put a quarter cup of borax, a half-cup of white vinegar, and a gallon of water into a bucket. If you need to get scuff marks off, try sprinkling some baking soda over the mark, and then wiping the spot with a warm, damp, soft cloth.

Battling Bathroom Grime the Natural Way

Nobody likes a grimy bathroom. But despite what TV commercials would have you believe, you don't need harsh chemicals to keep yours clean and fresh-smelling. Especially when safe, natural alternatives are so easy to use and give you such good results. Try these in the bathroom:

- There are several recipes for green **toilet cleaners:**
    - Use the all-purpose green cleaner on page 19. (It also works on the toilet's seat, lid, and tank.)
    - Mix one part 3% hydrogen peroxide with one part water.
    - Combine one part borax with two parts lemon juice.
    - Combine an eighth of a cup of borax with a quart of water and add a few drops of liquid castile soap.
    - Whichever one you choose, shake the mixture before you use it, spray or squirt the cleaner into the bowl and under the rim, let it sit for several minutes, and then scrub with a toilet brush and flush to rinse.

- If **mold and mildew** are taking over your bathroom, fill a spray bottle with water and add several drops of grapefruit-seed extract. Spray, wait a few minutes, and then wipe. Or try adding equal parts borax and white vinegar (start with a half of cup each) to a bucket of warm water. Use the mixture to scrub mildew away.

- For **tub and tile cleaning**, try the all-purpose cleaner on page 19, or use baking soda to scour the tub and shower.

- To **clean tile grout,** make a paste using three parts baking soda and one part water. Spread this paste on the grout, scrub it in with an old toothbrush, and then rinse.

- To **keep your drains clear,** rinse them out (carefully!) with boiling water once a week. If a drain backs up, bust the clog with a combination of baking soda and vinegar: Pour half a cup of baking soda down the drain, and then follow it with half a cup of white vinegar. This is the same mixture that middle-school kids use to simulate volcano eruptions, so don't be alarmed when it foams up. When the fizzing stops, flush the drain with warm water. If the drain is still slow, use a plunger to break up the clog, and then repeat the vinegar-and-baking soda procedure.

> ⓘ Baking soda and vinegar can also unclog your kitchen sink, but this combination can damage some garbage disposals, so read your disposal's owner's manual or check with the manufacturer before you try it.

- **Mirrors and shower doors** shine up beautifully with a half-and-half mixture of vinegar and water. (If you get streaks, add a drop or two of liquid castile soap.)

- The **lime scale** that coats faucets and plumbing fixtures dissolves in the mild acid of vinegar or lemon juice. Soak a cloth in white vinegar, and leave the wet cloth on the fixture for about an hour. Wipe, and then rinse. Or cut a lemon in half and rub the cut surface over the fixture. Be sure to rinse thoroughly.

- **Air freshener** doesn't have to come from an aerosol can—or contain chemicals like phenol and formaldehyde. You already know that an open dish of baking soda or vinegar absorbs odors. If you want to do more than neutralize odors, here are a bunch of sweet-smelling options that won't hurt your respiratory system or the environment:

  — Open the windows! Nothing freshens the air like fresh air itself.

  — Combine equal parts lemon juice and water in a misting spray bottle or a clean, empty perfume atomizer (a bottle that sprays a fine mist).

  — Combine a few drops of your favorite essential oil (page 18) with water in an atomizer.

  — Make potpourri. Ask your local florist for flowers that they're going to throw out, or choose sweet-smelling flowers from your garden. Lilac, lavender, and roses work well, as do herbs like rosemary and lemon balm. Lay out the petals in a single layer on an elevated screen or hang stemmed flowers in small bunches—the idea is to let air circulate freely around them. (It takes a week or two for the flowers and leaves to dry out completely.) When it's dry, put the mixture in an airtight container (add cinnamon sticks, vanilla beans, or cloves if you like) and let the scent develop for about a month. When it's ready, pour your potpourri into a bowl or dish and place it where you want to freshen the air.

  — Use a cotton ball to soak up a teaspoon of pure vanilla extract or a couple of drops of your favorite essential oil, and then hide the ball in an inconspicuous place in the bathroom.

Clean Laundry, Clean Earth

A greener lifestyle doesn't have to mean dingy laundry. You can keep your whites white and your colors bright without sending nasty chemicals down the drain (and from there into lakes and rivers). Here are some earth-friendly tips for the laundry room:

- When you buy **laundry detergent**, look for products that are biodegradable, free of petroleum-based ingredients, and that don't contain bleach. To reduce potential irritants, pick detergents without dyes and fragrances, as well. (Check out detergents made by companies listed in the box on page 20.)

Tip If you want to know *exactly* what's going into the wash with your clothes, make your own laundry detergent. To do that, you'll need to get some *washing soda*, which is sodium carbonate, often used as a water softener. It's available in the detergent aisle of most grocery stores.

Here's what you do: Grate a bar of pure soap, like Ivory or Fels Naphtha, using a grater or by feeding it to a food processor in small chunks. Put the grated soap in a saucepan and add enough water to cover it. Stir it over medium-low heat until the soap dissolves.

Meanwhile, heat two-and-a-half gallons of water. Pour the hot water into a bucket. Add the hot, melted soap to the bucket and stir. Mix in half a cup of borax and a cup of washing soda (*not* baking soda). Let the mixture cool (it'll gel), then cover the bucket and keep it near your washing machine. To use the detergent, stir it to break up the gel and add half a cup to each load of laundry.

- **Wash in cold water**, not hot, to save energy and lower your utility costs. Sometimes you may *need* to wash in hot water—for example, to help hydrogen peroxide whiten, as explained later in this list—but make it the exception, not the rule.

- **Hang clothes outside to dry** whenever possible instead of running the dryer, which is a major energy hog. Air-dried clothes smell better, too—without chemical perfumes.

- Use inexpensive **wooden drying racks** for indoor drying.

- **To whiten whites**, switch from chlorine bleach to 3% hydrogen peroxide, which is the basis for oxygen cleaners (like OxiClean). Add a cup of hydrogen peroxide to loads of whites, and wash with hot water. Another option is lemon juice: Add half a cup to the rinse cycle, and then hang the clothes outside to dry.

- **To brighten colors**, add half a cup of white vinegar to the rinse cycle. Three-percent hydrogen peroxide is also safe for most colors (test it on a small, inconspicuous spot first).

- **To deodorize** smelly socks, dirty diapers, and sweaty t-shirts, add a half-cup of baking soda to your laundry detergent. (This will also whiten and brighten the clothes.) A sprinkle of baking soda in the hamper or diaper pail helps deodorize between laundry days.

- There are lots of ways **to banish stains** besides chemical stain removers:

  — Spot-treat blood stains with 3% hydrogen peroxide solution. (If you're cleaning colored fabric, test an inconspicuous spot first.) Put a little hydrogen peroxide on the blood stain and blot it. Then rinse thoroughly to avoid bleaching the fabric.

  — Sprinkle some baking soda or borax onto a damp stain, rub it in, and then wash.

  — Use baking soda and water to make a thick paste and apply it to grease stains. The grease should come out in the wash.

  — Try white vinegar on food stains like wine, coffee, jam, and ketchup. Rub in the vinegar, and then wash.

- White vinegar is a natural **fabric softener**. Put half a cup of it in the rinse cycle to soften clothes (add a few drops of your favorite essential oil to make your clothes smell heavenly, too). Or replace commercial fabric softener with the homemade kind, using this recipe:

  Put one cup of baking soda in a one-gallon bucket, and then add two cups of water. Stir the mixture as you slowly add a cup of white vinegar. (When the vinegar hits the baking soda, it'll fizz, so take your time.) If you want, add a drop or two of an essential oil. Transfer the mixture to a clean bottle or other closed container. When you're ready to use the fabric softener, shake the bottle, and then add one-quarter to one-third cup of the mixture to the wash cycle.

- **To make laundry smell fresh**, add a teaspoon of lemon juice with your detergent.

Nontoxic Furnishings

Your brand-new living room set looks great—but did you know it may be polluting the air in your home? Just like cleaning products, new furniture can give off VOCs (page 12), thanks to *off-gassing*, which means giving off the chemicals used to make the product. For example, your new sofa's cushions and the chemicals that make them stain- and fire-resistant all emit VOCs. So do the glues used to make furniture, including the glue that holds particleboard together. So while you're sitting in your living room watching the tube, you may be breathing in formaldehyde, benzene, dioxins, and other VOCs. (They say watching TV is bad for you, but it doesn't have to be *that* hazardous.)

You may also want to think about how your furniture was made and what impact that had on the environment. Take that new sofa, for example. The foam in its cushions is made of polyurethane, a petroleum-based material that isn't exactly earth-friendly. To make just one pound of polyurethane foam requires nearly a pound of crude oil, half a pound of coal, and 400 gallons of water—and spits 4.5 pounds of carbon dioxide into the atmosphere. Also, unless the cotton used to make the couch's fabric was organic, the cotton was sprayed with pesticides. In addition, up to half of the dyes and other chemicals used to treat the fabric got washed back into the environment as waste. And where did the wood for the sofa's frame come from—a well-managed, sustainable forest or an at-risk one?

Your buying decisions make a difference. Use your wallet to vote for furniture that's both healthy and environmentally responsible by considering these options:

- **Buy used.** Whether you go to a fancy antiques store, the local thrift shop, or check the classifieds, buying used furniture has several green advantages. Because it's not new, the furniture has already done its off-gassing, so you're not bringing VOCs into your home. Buying used also saves the energy that would have gone into manufacturing brand-new furniture and keeps perfectly good, usable furniture out of landfills.

- **Buy recycled.** You can find beautiful furniture made from *reclaimed wood,* salvaged lumber that comes from old buildings like factories, warehouses, barns, and houses. If you need new carpeting, look for carpet with recycled content (page 136), which does less off-gassing than traditional carpet.

Tip Reclaimed wood is also an earth-friendly source for flooring and paneling, as page 135 explains.

- **Buy handcrafted.** When you buy furniture directly from the artisan who made it, you can ask questions about how it was made or commission a piece that fits your needs.

- **Buy floor models.** Furniture that's been on display in a showroom has already done most of its off-gassing, so it'll release fewer VOCs into your home.

- **Buy natural.** When you're buying drapes or upholstered furniture, insist on natural fabrics like organic cotton, linen, hemp, and wool. Page 213 tells you more about what to look for when buying organic fabrics.

- **Buy certified.** Wooden furniture looks good and is made from a natural material, but you want to be sure that the wood was harvested responsibly. Wood is a renewable resource, and the Forest Stewardship Council (FSC) is committed to promoting sustainable forestry worldwide. When you buy an FSC-certified product, you know it came from a responsibly managed forest. Check out FSC's website (*www.fscus. org*) and do a product search.

If you do buy brand-new furniture, carpets, or drapes, open the windows! Increasing ventilation lets VOCs out and fresh air in. Use fans to get the air moving and bring in as much fresh air as possible. A few days with the windows open will greatly reduce the levels of off-gassed VOCs in your home.

If you can't open the windows (you live in the snow belt and had your new carpet installed in January, say), climate control is the second-best way to reduce off-gassed VOCs. These chemicals love warm, humid conditions, which make them evaporate faster. Keep the temperature cool and the air relatively dry to make them off-gas more slowly.

Tip Stainless steel furniture looks sleek and contemporary. It won't off-gas—and it's likely to be high in recycled content.

A Greener Lawn

You already know about the types of chemicals in your home, but what about just outside your door? Many homeowners take great pride in their lush lawns. Yet acres of thick, bright-green grass cost far more than a few bags of fertilizer and some weed-killer:

- Pesticides and fertilizer get into homes and run off into lakes, rivers, and drinking water supplies like wells. Some of these chemicals are harmful to humans and animals.

- Watering lawns uses a *huge* amount of precious water: up to 60% of all the water people use in arid climates.

- Yard waste (such as grass clippings and tree branches) accounts for nearly 20% of the solid wastes in landfills.

- Gas-powered lawn mowers, weed trimmers, and leaf blowers emit more greenhouse gases per hour of use than most cars.

You don't want to harm the great outdoors while you're enjoying it. Read on to find out what's bad about chemical lawn treatments and learn natural alternatives you can try.

The Trouble with Pesticides

Pesticide, insecticide, herbicide, fungicide: The suffix *–cide* comes from *cida*, the Latin word for "killer." The chemicals that kill lawn pests like insects and weeds can also be toxic to people and pets. That's why you see those little plastic flags warning you to stay off recently treated grass.

Every year, people in the U.S. dump more than 100 million pounds of pesticides on their lawns and gardens. Suburban lawns and gardens actually get more pesticides per acre than most agricultural areas. And those pesticides can get tracked into your house or blow in through open windows as you enjoy the breeze on a nice day.

Pesticides get into your body in one of three ways:

- **Through the skin.** You might want to think twice before you walk barefoot through the grass or lie down on a shady lawn. And pesticides can get into your house on shoes or clothing. Then, when you walk barefoot through the house or pick up clothes to toss into the washing machine, they can get on your skin.

Note Some parts of the body absorb pesticides more readily than others. The eyes, ear drums, and scalp are all fast absorbers. And if you have a cut or scrape, pesticides can get into your body much more easily than through healthy skin.

- **Through inhalation.** You can breathe in pesticides in dust, fumes, or mist from a spray. Particles can travel in the wind, so your neighbor's pesticide use can affect your health. Larger particles tend to stick to your throat and nasal passages, but smaller particles can get into your lungs and from there into your bloodstream.

- **Through the mouth.** Nobody in their right mind would munch on pesticides, but ingestion is a common way for pesticides to get into the body. Pets may eat grass or lick pesticide-coated fur. And if people have pesticide on their hands and don't wash it off, it can get on their food.

In a recent study of more than 9,000 people across the country, the U.S. Centers for Disease Control and Prevention found pesticides in *everyone* who had both blood and urine tested. And the average person had evidence of 13 pesticides out of the 23 the CDC tested for. Pesticides have been linked to a range of diseases, including cancer, birth defects, liver and kidney damage, neurological and hormonal problems, and infertility. And they're not just toxic to humans—pets and other mammals, birds, fish, and bees are also at risk. Common symptoms of pesticide poisoning include a burning sensation in the throat, coughing, rash, diarrhea, vomiting, dizziness, and headache. If you suspect you've been overexposed to harmful pesticides, see your doctor.

> **Note** Pesticides also kill the earthworms that aerate and mix the soil and help make *humus* (a rich form of dirt that's made up of decomposed organic material, like dead leaves and worm poop—not to be confused with hummus, the tasty Mediterranean dip), all of which is good for your lawn. But if you use chemical pesticides, you can kill up to 90% of the worms that naturally make your soil healthy and fertile.

The chemicals in pesticides also run off into rivers and lakes, contaminate groundwater, and leach into wells. From there, they can kill aquatic plants and animals and get into drinking water.

> **Note** The National Coalition for Pesticide-Free Lawns educates people about the dangers of pesticides and promotes safe, healthy, environmentally friendly lawn and landscape care. Learn more or get involved at *www.beyondpesticides.org/ pesticidefreelawns*.

If you use pesticides, use them safely. Buy small quantities, store them in their original containers, and dispose of any leftovers according to package instructions and local ordinances. But fortunately, as you're about to learn, you don't need these dangerous chemicals to have a healthy lawn.

Keep (Chemicals) Off the Grass!

Whether you're discouraging weeds and other pests or encouraging your lawn to grow, you can do it without using harsh chemicals. This section describes how to care for your lawn the natural way.

The grass is greener...when it's the right kind

The first thing to do when you're switching to natural lawn care is to take a good look at what you're growing. Is your lawn the best kind of grass for your area? In warm, dry climates, for example, you want a grass that can tolerate drought conditions and recover quickly after an extended dry spell. Temperature range, shadiness, rainfall, humidity, wear—all these factors affect which variety of grass grows best in your region. And knowing which one works best can save you water and cut back on the time you spend caring for your lawn.

> **Tip** For recommendations about the kind of grass best suited to your climate and conditions, visit *www.american-lawns.com/lawns/best_lawns.html*.

When choosing a grass, keep in mind that fine-bladed varieties and the older types of Kentucky bluegrass (like Kenblue and Park) need less water and fertilizer than perennial ryegrass or many of the newer varieties of Kentucky bluegrass. Or go with a "no-mow" lawn. That's a bit of a misnomer—you'll have to mow, oh, once a month or so, starting in June. No-mow lawns are made up of low-maintenance grasses, mainly fescue. Prairie Nursery (*www.prairienursery.com*) and NoMowGrass.com (*http://nomowgrass.com*) sell low-maintenance grass seed blends.

> **Tip** Groundcover plants, such as juniper and ivy, are truly "no-mow" alternatives to grass. Check with your local garden center to find groundcover that's suitable for your area. Some kinds can be aggressive, so make sure the species you pick won't take over the neighborhood.

Go Native

Another option is to rethink the whole concept of lawns. Many homeowners are replacing grass with gardens of native plants, like wildflowers and ornamental grasses. Native plants already thrive where you live, so they require less care than grass and other plants that don't grow there naturally. You can replace your whole lawn with such a garden, use native plants for decorative borders, or design a more complex landscape.

Tip The U.S. EPA has a website devoted to landscaping with native plants: *www.epa. gov/greenacres*. The site has all kinds of helpful stuff like suggestions for getting started, landscaping and maintenance tips, and how-to videos.

Prepare your lawn for natural care

If you decide to stick with grass rather than native plants, it's important to set yourself up for success. Whether you're planting a brand-new lawn or caring for an existing one, there are a few simple ways to keep it green and lush.

If you're starting from scratch and planting grass seed, it's a good idea to:

- **Check the topsoil.** A lawn needs at least four inches of topsoil to thrive. Eight inches—or more—is even better. If you can only dig an inch or so into your yard before hitting rock or solid clay, buy topsoil to give your grass something to take root in. To make rich soil your new lawn will love, mix the top four inches of dirt with an equal amount of compost before you sow the seeds.

- **Test the soil.** To test your soil's pH—that's its level of acidity—buy a do-it-yourself tester kit or hire someone to test it. Ideally, the soil should be slightly acidic to neutral, with a pH of 6–7. If the pH is lower than 6, add lime to make it less acidic; if it's above 7, add gardener's sulfur to make it more acidic (you can buy both at any nursery). Sulfur is also a good natural fungicide.

Tip If you have a pro test the soil, ask him to check for the major nutrients: nitrogen, phosphorus, and potassium. That'll help you choose the best fertilizer for your lawn. And if you know your soil already has enough of those nutrients, you can avoid overfeeding your lawn: When you give it nutrients it doesn't need, the extra nutrients run off into lakes and streams and make algae go nuts.

Once your grass seedlings are fully grown (they grow up so fast, don't they?), here's how to keep them happy and healthy:

- **Enrich the soil.** Make sure your dirt is full of the nutrients that will make the grass thrive. If you enrich the soil with compost, you only need to spread the compost once a year—if that often. (Page 191 explains what compost is and how to get started composting.) Aim for up to 1 cubic yard of compost for every 1,000 square feet of grass (that works out to a layer that's about a third of an inch thick after you've spread it). Use a shovel to spread compost, and use a broom to sweep the compost off the grass and into the soil. Then water the lawn to help wash the compost's microbes into the soil.

- **Dethatch.** As grass grows, a layer of woody stems builds up under the blades and above the soil. This layer is called *thatch*. When it gets too thick, air, water, and nutrients have trouble reaching the grass's roots, so it's a good idea to get rid of thatch when it gets more than about half an inch thick. Get a rake with strong, stiff tines (garden stores sell dethatching rakes), and sink the rake into the thatch. Strike hard enough to get the thatch up but not hard enough to pull up grass blades. If your thatch is particularly thick and hard to get up, consider using your lawn mower's thatching blade (if it has one) or renting a power dethatcher. Toss the thatch you dislodge onto your compost pile (see page 191).

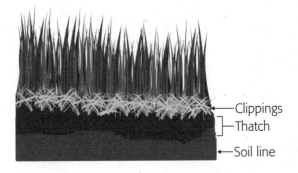

Clippings
Thatch
Soil line

- **Aerate.** Another way to help air and water reach your grass's roots is to use an aerator that removes plugs of turf, loosening up dense or compacted soil. You can buy a manual aerator, but these can be tricky to use, especially if you have a big lawn. Other options include renting a power aerator, hiring a lawn service, or buying earthworms to aerate your soil for you.

Tip The best time to aerate your lawn is before you apply fertilizer.

Get smart about fertilizers

Fertilizers promote plant growth, making your lawn lush and green. But what's in that stuff you're feeding your lawn? Both natural and artificial fertilizers contain elements that help plants grow—like nitrogen, phosphorus, and potassium—but they get those nutrients from different sources:

> **Tip** Look for low- or no-phosphate fertilizers. As mentioned on page xx1, phosphorus is a plant nutrient, but there's probably already enough of it in your soil to feed your grass. (Have your soil tested if you're not sure.) The phosphorus in fertilizers can run off into rivers and lakes and make algae go nuts, which can choke off healthy bodies of water. Some areas with at-risk lakes have banned fertilizers with phosphates.

- **Natural fertilizers** use organic materials to enrich the soil and provide nutrients for your lawn. (Here, *organic* means that the fertilizer came from a living thing, whether plant or animal.) Grass needs a lot of nitrogen, so these fertilizers contain protein, which can come from stuff like ground corn, soybeans, bone meal, or seaweed. The protein gets eaten by friendly microbes in the soil that then expel nitrogen, which your grass absorbs through its roots. It takes about three weeks of letting the microbes to do their thing before you start to see a difference in your lawn, so be patient. Page 191 tells you more about natural fertilizers.

> **Tip** Here's an advantage of using organic fertilizer: The microbes that eat the fertilizer will aerate your lawn and soften the soil, making watering more efficient. So if you care for your lawn the organic way, you shouldn't have to aerate it. (Microbes eat thatch, too.)

- **Inorganic fertilizers**—also called chemical, mineral, or artificial fertilizers—don't come from living sources. They may be mineral in origin, such as limestone and mined phosphates, or synthesized, like ammonia-based nitrogen fertilizers. A significant problem with these fertilizers is that they can suppress the bacteria in the soil that produce nitrogen, making you increasingly dependent on inorganic fertilizer to enrich the soil with nitrogen. This kind of fertilizer can also wash off and get into surface water, making plants grow like crazy and harming water quality. Finally, current methods of producing these fertilizers aren't sustainable: Potassium and phosphate fertilizers use up already limited resources for those minerals, and the process for making nitrogen fertilizer uses fossil fuels or natural gas—resources we can't afford to use thoughtlessly.

Note Producing ammonia, the main ingredient in artificial nitrogen fertilizer, currently accounts for 5% of the world's natural gas use.

Spring and fall are the best times to fertilize. If you're using a commercial organic fertilizer, apply between 10 and 20 pounds of fertilizer per 1,000 square feet of lawn.

Note What about using compost to fertilize your lawn? Compost, by itself, isn't a good fertilizer. Compost supplies the soil with healthy microbes, but they then need protein to thrive and produce the nutrients that help your grass grow.

Say goodbye to weeds

If weeds seem to like your natural lawn-care program as much as the grass does, you don't need to poison the weeds to get rid of 'em. Instead, try these approaches:

- **Deep watering.** As page 37 explains, when you water your grass deeply, you encourage the grass to grow long roots. This means the grass will be more deeply rooted than the weed seedlings that want to take up residence. When the top inch or two of dirt dries out, the weeds dry out and die. But the grass, whose roots go deeper, can still reach damp soil and survives until the next watering.

- **Frequent mowing.** Grass grows from the bottom up, adding new cells to the bottom of each blade. Most weeds, on the other hand, grow from the top, adding new leaves at the top of the plant. So if you mow frequently with the mower blades set high, you cut off the weeds where they grow and leave the grass unharmed.

Tip High mowing also makes the grass taller than weed seedlings, so your grass hogs the sunlight and shades the weeds.

- **Good, old-fashioned digging.** One sure way to get weeds out of your lawn is to dig them out. At the start of your region's growing season, grab a hoe and dig up weeds while they're still small. Later in the season, use a trowel to dig out dandelions and other weeds at the roots. (It's easiest to dig up weeds when the soil is damp.)

- **Suppressing new weeds before they grow.** Corn meal gluten is an organic fertilizer that also prevents seedlings from growing healthy roots (but doesn't harm the roots of full-grown plants), so it's a good, natural way to control weeds. After you dig out a dandelion, for example, sprinkle corn meal gluten around the spot where it was to keep any seeds that got away from turning into new dandelion plants.

> **!** Don't use corn gluten meal for weed control or as a fertilizer if you're growing new grass from seed. It'll mess up grass seedlings' roots just like weed seedlings' roots.

- **Zapping weeds with vinegar.** Vinegar tastes great on a salad, but growing plants don't like it. Although you can get high-concentration vinegar (10, 15, or even 20% acetic acid) from garden-supply stores, household vinegar (5% acetic acid) is both cheaper and safer. (If you go for high-concentration vinegar, protect your skin, eyes, and lungs from possible irritation.) Simply spray undiluted household vinegar on weeds, saturating their leaves; the leaves should wither within a couple of days. This works best on young plants (older weeds can regrow from their roots), and you may have to repeat the process every couple of weeks until the weeds are gone. Be aware that vinegar isn't picky—it kills grass, too—so this method works best when you have a patch of weeds you want to get rid of.

> **Note** Vinegar lowers your soil's pH, making it more acidic, but only for a couple of days. The acid in vinegar breaks down in water, so don't spray it on weeds if there's rain in the forecast.

Give Your Lawn a Drink

Many people water their lawn more often than they should, which wastes water and doesn't help the lawn. When you practice natural lawn care, you don't need to water as frequently because the well-aerated soil soaks up water and holds it like a sponge.

Tip The best time to water is in the morning. Watering in the evening can make your lawn vulnerable to fungus.

Here are the two most important things to know about watering:

- **Water infrequently.** Watering too often encourages thatch (page 33), while less frequent watering makes the grass push its roots deeper into the soil. How do you know when to water? Watch your grass. It lets you know when it's getting thirsty by curling its blades. Water when the blades start to curl (but before they turn brown). Another way to check is to walk across the grass; if you turn around and see your footprints, the grass is getting dry and it's time to water. Or grab a trowel and dig about three inches into the soil. If the dirt is damp at that level (even if it's dry on the surface), you don't need to water.

- **Water deeply.** When your grass gets thirsty, give it a long, satisfying drink. Place a cup in the area you're watering; when there's an inch of water in the cup, turn the water off. This may seem like a lot of water, but when you water deeply, you don't have to water as often.

Tip Oddly enough, a good time to water is after it rains. If a rainstorm drops half an inch of rain on your lawn, for example, you can give your grass the deep watering it needs while using less water—another half an inch, and you've done the job. And you don't have to wait for a rainy day to give your lawn a drink of rainwater— page 68 explains how to collect rain and store it for later.

Making Gray Water Green

Gray water is the water that comes from your home's sinks, showers, bathtubs, dishwasher, and washing machine. (Toilet water is *not* gray water—water that contains sewage is called *black water*.) You can recycle gray water and use it on your lawn. Think about it: Instead of using fresh, drinking-quality water to care for the grass, you save money and resources by reusing water. Given that nearly 300 gallons of water flow through the average U.S. household every day, reusing gray water can significantly lessen the drain (pun intended) on resources.

Usually, gray water goes down the drain and heads for a septic tank or water-treatment plant. When you reuse that water, your "waste" water is no longer wasted. If you use it on your lawn, for example, the soil acts as a natural filtration system, removing impurities (like dead skin cells and bits of food) from the water before it reaches the groundwater below. In fact, those impurities provide nutrients for the grass. Your gray water system can be as simple as dumping your dishpan's contents on your rose bushes, or as complex (and pricey) as installing a whole-house reclamation and filtering setup that feeds into your lawn irrigation system.

Before you start reusing gray water, check whether gray water recycling is legal in your area. For years, reusing waste water—gray or black—was illegal in most of the U.S. But recent water shortages have led many areas to reconsider gray water for specific uses. So make sure you understand and comply with local laws.

For a list of gray water basics, head to this book's Missing CD page at *www.missing-manuals.com*. To learn more about installing a gray-water system, contact one of these companies, whose products range from do-it-yourself plans and kits to fully installed systems:

- Clivus Multrum (*http://clivusmultrum.com*)
- Envirosink (*http://envirosink.com*)
- NutriCycle Systems (*http://nutricyclesystems.com*)
- Oasis Design (*www.oasisdesign.net*)
- ReWater Systems (*http://rewater.com*)

Mowing Tips

It's probably no surprise to learn that gas-powered lawn mowers create lots of pollution. For small lawns, consider an old-fashioned push mower (also called a reel mower)—you'll get a workout *and* a great-looking lawn. Electric mowers are another option; there are cordless models if you're worried about mowing over the cord.

Set your mower blades as high as they'll go. Like other green plants, grass converts light into food through its leaves, so if you cut the grass too short, you're basically starving it because it can't absorb as much sunlight. To help your grass grow upright, don't always start mowing in the same spot and go the same direction. For example, if you mow from east to west one week, try going from north to south the next time.

There's no need to collect the clippings after you mow (unless it's been so long since you last mowed that they cover the grass in big clumps). Let them decompose and enrich the soil—they add nitrogen and other nutrients, which means you won't need as much fertilizer. A mulching mower can help with this process. If you need to remove clippings from your lawn—either because it's been ages since you last mowed or the grass was wet so it clumped—don't bag the clippings. Toss them on your compost pile (page 191) instead.

Tip Most of the time, lawn mowers sit unused in sheds or garages. Use yours more efficiently by sharing it. Get together with some neighbors, pool your money to purchase a mower, and then take turns using it. (Assign days to avoid confusion.)

2 Save Energy, Money, and the Earth

With utility costs rising and global warming taking its toll, we have more reason than ever to reassess how we use resources. The Alliance to Save Energy estimates that the average U.S. household sends twice as much carbon dioxide into the atmosphere as the average car, so it's important for everyone to cut back their energy use. (Technically, power plants are the ones who spew the CO_2, but they do it while producing power for us.) As you learned in the last chapter, you can start fighting pollution right in your own home. Same goes for water and electricity: You can do your part to conserve both by making simple changes around the house.

The first step toward conserving electricity—*and* lowering your utility bills—is to examine how you use energy. This chapter shows you how to give your home a checkup to find out. After that, you'll learn all kinds of ways to increase your home's efficiency, including a whole section about heating and cooling systems, which (in an average home) eat up more than half of the energy you pay for each year. Then you'll get info about how much power your appliances use and, if you're shopping for new ones, how to find the most efficient models. You'll learn other great tips for cutting your electricity bill, saving water, and lighting your home, too. Making even a few of the changes suggested in this chapter will put you well on your way to using less energy and helping the planet.

How Efficient Is Your Home?

Most people use more energy at home than anywhere else. That's probably no big surprise: Your utility bills likely tell you as much each month. If you want those bills to tell a different story—like "Wow, look how much money you're saving!"—start by checking your home's energy efficiency. With an efficient home, you'll use less energy—and spend less money—to heat and cool it, light up rooms, and power appliances and gadgets. Being energy efficient is good for the earth, and good for your wallet.

Making your home more efficient is good for your wallet *and* the planet. The U.S EPA estimates that 17 percent of total greenhouse-gas emissions in the United States come from home energy use, which works out to four metric tons of carbon dioxide sent into the atmosphere every year for each person in America. (A metric ton is 2,200 pounds, about the weight of a small car.) That's one giant-sized carbon footprint!

> **Note** A *greenhouse gas* is any gas that contributes to the greenhouse effect, which traps heat inside the earth's atmosphere, absorbing infrared radiation. These gases include water vapor, carbon dioxide, methane, nitrous oxide, halogenated fluorocarbons, ozone, perfluorinated carbons, and hydrofluorocarbons.

How do you use all that energy? Figure 2-1 shows a typical home's energy use. (This info comes from the U.S. Department of Energy's 2008 *Buildings Energy Data Book;* some numbers are rounded up.) As you can see, more than half the cost goes to heating and cooling. Water heaters and appliances are also big energy hogs.

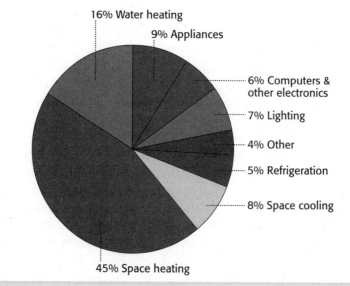

16% Water heating
9% Appliances
6% Computers & other electronics
7% Lighting
4% Other
5% Refrigeration
8% Space cooling
45% Space heating

Evaluating Your Home's Energy Use

Before you can use all the tips and tricks for making your house more energy smart that you'll learn later in this chapter, you need to get a sense of where you're starting from—how efficient (or inefficient) the home is right now. To find out, perform an energy audit yourself or hire a professional to do one. The audit will reveal some stuff you can fix yourself, and other issues you'll need help with. But checking your home for common problems is a good start in making your home more efficient—and cozier, too.

Do-it-yourself audit

You already know which rooms feel drafty or are always hotter or colder than others. Those rooms are good places to start your audit, but you should give your whole house a once-over to figure out how to make it more efficient and reduce your energy costs.

Here are the steps in a do-it-yourself home energy audit:

- **Look at your bills.** Pull out your old utility bills, going back a few years if you have them (if you don't, call the energy company for a summary of your account). Spread the bills out and look for patterns. Is there a particular season or month when they spike? What's different about your energy use then that causes the spike? For example, if you live in the snow belt, you know heating costs are a lot higher in January than in April. So you'll want to focus on improvements that can bring down those winter heating costs, such as beefing up your insulation or getting a high-efficiency furnace.

Tip The Energy Star program, sponsored jointly by the U.S. EPA and the U.S. Department of Energy, can help you interpret your energy bills. Bills in hand, go to *www.energystar.gov*. On the home page, click Home Improvement, and then (from the left-hand menu) select Home Energy Yardstick. This opens a calculator where you fill in facts about your home, the type of energy you use for heat (such as fuel oil or natural gas), and info from past utility bills. The yardstick compares how your home's energy use measures up to others across the country and recommends ways to improve efficiency.

- **Find and fix air leaks.** As much as 30% of the money you spend to heat and cool your home could be going right out the window—or through the mail slot or cracks in the wall. Air leaks aren't the same as ventilation because you can *control* ventilation; air leaks are *always* open and undermine your attempts to control the temperature. Here are some places you're likely to find leaks:

  — Window and door frames

  — Mail slots

  — Dryer vents

  — Spots where phone and cable lines enter the house

  — Around the chimney

  — Recessed ceiling lights

  — External water faucets

  — Electrical outlets and switches on external walls

  — Corners

  — Places where your home's foundation meets the walls and where the walls meet the roof

  — Places where floors and ceilings meet exterior walls

  — Mortar between stones or bricks (look for cracks)

  — Fireplace dampers (make sure they're closed when you're not using the fireplace)

  Here's how to check for leaks in those places:

  — **Feel for drafts.** If it's cold outside, pass your hand along the spot you're checking, such as a window frame. Cold air coming in against your hand means air is leaking there.

  — **Use a stick of incense.** Light the incense and hold it next to a place where you suspect a leak. (Watch out for anything that can catch fire, like drapes.) If the incense smoke goes straight up into the air, the spot is airtight. If the smoke streams into or out of the room, bingo—you've found a leak.

  — **Shine a light on leaks.** When it's dark out, grab a flashlight and send a friend outside. Turn out the lights in the room you're checking, and then shine the flashlight at potential leak sites. The other person will see light coming through any large holes. (This method doesn't work well for small cracks.)

- **Check the attic.** If you have an attic, make sure it's insulated enough to keep your house warm in the winter and cool in the summer. You can eyeball your insulation to see whether there's enough by looking across the attic: If the insulation between the joists is higher than the joists, you're probably okay; if it's lower than or level with the joists, it'd be good to add more. And make sure there's plenty of insulation on the exterior walls, too—they're notorious for air leaks.

> **Tip** Here's another way to check attic insulation: After a snowfall, go outside and compare your roof to your neighbors' roofs. If theirs are still snowy but yours is mostly bare, you probably need more insulation.

- **Get your heating system checked.** Even the most energy-efficient, top-of-the-line furnace won't save money and energy if it's connected to leaky ductwork. A thorough assessment of your home's climate-control system is best left to the pros, so if you haven't had it inspected in the past year, make an appointment.

> **Note** A professional heating inspection not only improves efficiency, but also confirms that your system is safe—making sure, for example, no carbon monoxide is getting into your home. Be sure to have one at least once a year.

In addition to getting a professional inspection done, here are some things to keep an eye out for when you check your heating system during your audit:

— **Dirty filters.** Dust on filters restricts air flow and makes the system less efficient. If your furnace or air conditioner's filter looks dirty, it is—swap it for a clean one. You may need to do this as often as once a month during the heating season.

> **Tip** Break the cycle of throwing out disposable filters and replacing them with new ones by buying a permanent *electrostatic filter* instead. These filters are highly efficient (they trap about 95% of dust and airborne particles) and last for the life of your heating/cooling system. Just wash them once a month or so. You can find 'em at any home improvement store.

- **Dusty AC coils.** If your air-conditioning unit's coils are dirty, vacuum them clean.

- **Leaky ducts.** One common problem is leaking ducts, which cause some of the warmed or cooled air to not get where it's going. Instead, it ends up in the attic, basement, crawl space, or garage, wasting energy and money (leaks can reduce your system's efficiency by 25–40%). To find leaks, look for disjointed sections, obvious holes, and dirty streaks on ducts.

> **Note** Believe it or not, duct tape *isn't* the best stuff for fixing leaky ducts. It won't last as long as a tape that's designed for hot surfaces, like foil tape. Look for Underwriters Laboratories–approved heat tape at your local hardware store.

- **Get more out of hot water.** Water heaters use lots of energy. If yours is due for replacement, get a high-efficiency or tankless one. Otherwise, make sure the tank and the pipes that carry water from it are well insulated (page 56).

- **Scope out your appliances.** As you saw on page 42, large appliances (including refrigerators) eat up nearly 15% of a home's energy budget. Just about any gadget you can plug in has a label that says how much power it uses. Table 2-1 (page 57) shows how many watts common appliances use. (The box on page 49 explains how utility companies use wattage to calculate your bills.) Another way to check energy use is with a power meter—page 47 tells you about 'em.

If you're replacing an older appliance that's a power hog, make sure the new model is Energy Star–rated. To learn about how they rate appliances, go to *www.energystar.gov* and click the Products tab. (You can find a list of all the websites mentioned in this book on the Missing CD page at *www.missingmanuals.com*.)

> **Note** Refrigerators are particularly big energy users. According to Energy Star, if everyone in the U.S. replaced their pre-1993 fridge with a newer, more efficient model, it'd save $1.7 billion in energy. Of course, no one wants of millions of abandoned fridges taking up space in landfills, so Energy Star has launched a refrigerator-recycling campaign. Go to *www.energystar.gov/recycle* for details.

- **Shed some lighting costs.** Another good-sized chunk of your monthly energy bill pays for lighting. As your old-style incandescent bulbs burn out, replace them with more efficient *compact fluorescent lamps* (CFLs); page 69 has more about them. In the meantime, try using lower-wattage bulbs. Are there places where you could replace a 100-watt bulb with a 75-watt one, or 60 instead of 75? And be sure to turn off lights when you leave a room, just like Mom taught you, or go high-tech with infrared sensors that turn lights on when someone enters the room and off when they leave. Dimmer switches, timers, and solar-powered lights can also reduce your power bill.

Professional energy audit

If you don't have the time or inclination to do an energy audit, consider hiring a professional to do it for you. They have the know-how, experience, and equipment to find problems you might not catch. For example, they can do a blower door test (which measures how airtight your home is) and take thermographic scans that show where heat is escaping.

To find an energy auditor, try calling your utility company. Many offer free or inexpensive audits. If you'd rather hire an independent auditor instead of using one who works for the utility company, the Energy Star site can help you find one. Go to *http://tinyurl.com/ocf24b*, select Home Energy Raters and your state, and then click Search to find auditors in your area.

Whichever kind of auditor you go with, the person will conduct a whole-house assessment and compile a list of suggestions for making your home more energy efficient. Common recommendations are things like increasing insulation, replacing old windows, sealing ductwork, and upgrading your appliances. The suggestions can range from quick-and-easy to disruptive-and-expensive. No one wants to spend $20,000 to save fifty bucks a month. If you discover it'll take *years* for energy savings to recoup the cost of the suggested renovations, consider downsizing (page 50) or implementing some of the other energy-saving strategies in this chapter.

Monitoring Energy Use with a Power Meter

Looking over past bills (page 43) is one way to learn about energy use and find trends. Or you can also use a *power meter* to get up-to-the-minute info about how much energy you're using *right now*—for a single appliance or your entire home. Once you know that, you can fine-tune your energy consumption and trim those monthly bills. The following sections explain your options.

Single-appliance power meters

If you want to know how much it's costing you to run that old air conditioner or new microwave, you can buy a power meter that'll tell you. Plug the meter into an outlet, and then plug the appliance into the meter and turn it on. The meter displays how much power the appliance is using and estimates how much it costs to run. Popular meters include Kill A Watt (*www.p3international.com*), Watt's Up? (*www.wattsupmeters.com*), and the EM100 (*www.upm-marketing.com*). They start at around $100, and can pay for themselves by helping you save money on electricity over the years.

> **Note** At this writing, the folks at Google are testing PowerMeter, a free service that will work with utility companies' *smart meters*, those digital doohickeys that collect info about your power use and report it to the utility company. Google PowerMeter will use that same info to display your household's electricity usage online. So if you're away on a business trip, for example, you'll know when to call home and pester the kids to turn off some lights. Your home's info will be secure, private, and presented in almost real time. To learn more about it, visit *www.google.org/powermeter*.

Whole-house power meter

To keep an eye on how much electricity your household is using, you can buy a *whole-house meter* (for most models, you'll need an electrician to install it). These gadgets tell you how much power you're using now and how much you've used so far this month, and give you a running total of your costs, based on local rates. So when you see that you're spending more than you planned for the month, you can do things like turn off lights and adjust the temperature by a few degrees.

Whole-house meters start at around $120. Models to try include The Energy Detective (T.E.D.) and The Meter Reader EM-2500. If you're in the U.K., take a look at efergy.com's (yes, that's *efergy*, not *energy*) wireless whole-house monitors, which you can install yourself.

Calculate power use for free

You don't *need* to buy a power meter to learn how much electricity you're using. The box on page 49 explains a simple formula for calculating how much an appliance is costing you. And once it's released, Google's Power-Meter (see the Note above) will provide a free and easy way to track your household's energy use.

It's Electric

Electrical terms can be confusing. Fortunately, you don't need a master's degree in electrical engineering to understand the basics. Once you know those, you can calculate how much power an appliance is using—and how much it's costing you.

Watts measure power, the rate at which energy gets used. (Energy is measured in *joules,* and a watt equals one joule of energy used per second.) An appliance's label usually tells you the wattage—that is, the power consumption—of the appliance.

You probably use *lots* of watts each month, which is why it's easier to talk about *kilowatts* (one kilowatt is 1,000 watts). A *kilowatt hour* (abbreviated kWh) is 1,000 watts used continuously for one hour. (A *megawatt hour* [MWh] is 1,000 kilowat-thours.) Your power company measures your energy use in kilowatt hours and charges a certain rate per kWh.

Here's how to find how much power an appliance uses:

(wattage × hours used each day) ÷ 1,000 = daily kWh consumption

For example, a typical vacuum cleaner uses 1,200 watts. If you're on a spring cleaning kick and run the vacuum continuously for two hours, 1,200 watts times 2 hours equals 2,400 watts used. To convert that to kilowatt hours, just divide by 1,000:

(1,200 watts × 2 hours) ÷ 1,000 = 2.4 kWh

So far, so good. Next, you want to figure out how much running the vacuum cleaner *costs*. To do that, you need to know what your power company charges per kilowatt hour—check your bill or give them a call to find out. For simplicity's sake, let's say the rate per kWh is 10 cents ($0.10). To figure out the cost, multiply the number of kilowatt hours by that amount. In this example that's 2.4 kWh × $0.10 = $0.24, which means your vacuum-cleaning session cost 24 cents.

Knowing appliances' wattages is a good way to comparison shop. Lower wattage items use less electricity and cost you less. For example, a 100-watt light bulb consumes 2.5 times more energy than a 40-watt bulb. For larger appliances, the Energy-Guide tag (page 58) tells you the item's wattage and compares it to similar models.

Tip Some devices' labels don't specify wattage, but they probably list numbers for volts and amps. To figure out wattage, simply multiply the number of volts by the number of amps. Easy, huh?

You can find lots of energy-cost calculators online. You enter info about your household and appliances and they estimate how much it costs you to run certain appliances, keep your house at a certain temperature, and so on. Here are some sites to try:

- **Consumers Power Online Usage Calculator** (*www.consumerspower. org/home_energy/billestimator.php*) is sponsored by Consumers Power Inc., a private nonprofit cooperative in Oregon. (It bases its estimates on average use for a family of four.)

- **EnergyGuide** (*http://energyguide.com/audit/HAintro.asp*) offers your choice of a fast-track analysis or a detailed analysis. The results include recommendations for saving energy and money. You can also check specific appliances to see whether it's time to replace them.

- **Generic Electrical Energy Cost Calculator** (*www.csgnetwork.com/ elecenergycalcs.html*) can give you cost estimates for categories like lighting, kitchen appliances, personal care, and so on.

- **Home Energy Saver** (*http://hes.lbl.gov*)—sponsored by the U.S. Department of Energy, the U.S. EPA, and other agencies—can tell you the energy costs of an average home and an energy-efficient home in your area. If you fill out a 19-item questionnaire, the site gives you more details about your power use and how to reduce it.

Should You Downsize?

Just after World War II, as GIs returned home and began to raise families, the average American house was 900 square feet. By 1970, bell bottoms were in and the average square footage was 1,300. In 2004, that figure had nearly doubled to 2,330. And homes built in the second quarter of 2008 averaged a whopping 2,629 square feet (it's decreased slightly since then thanks to, um, some recent economic problems). The parents of the largest generation in U.S. history raised their families in houses under 1,000 square feet, so why do we need nearly *three times* that much space today?

Bigger isn't always better. Large homes cost more to heat and cool (and, as page 42 shows, heating and cooling account for the majority of a household's energy use). More bathrooms mean more water use and water-heating costs. Some oversized houses have rooms that are rarely, if ever, used. Bigger homes also cost significantly more in mortgage, insurance, and property tax expenses. And neighborhoods with such homes tend to be far from workplaces, restaurants, and stores, so running errands means driving.

Lots of people are trading their so-called McMansions for smaller, more efficient homes. Not only are they saving money on energy, many also find that a smaller home makes them more aware of consumption (since there's no room for four TVs and three sofas). Downsizing can also bring the family together—replacing, for example, a separate den, media room, and living room with a multi-use family room. And smaller houses are often in walkable neighborhoods where you can get to know your neighbors and spend less time in the car.

Downsizing has a downside: As more people do it, demand for large houses may slack off, making it harder to sell a super-sized home. Selling your current home means you'll probably pay a realtor 6–7% of the sale price, and don't forget closing costs. In addition, moving is disruptive and never cheap, so be sure to take that upheaval and expense into account. Sit down with a calculator and figure out how long it'll take for the reduced costs of your new, smaller home to pay for the moving costs.

As you consider downsizing, think about these questions:

- How much do I currently pay for each of these expenses, and how much would I pay for them in a downsized home?:
    - Heat
    - Electricity
    - Insurance
    - Mortgage
    - Property and school taxes
    - Landscaping and maintenance
- Would downsizing lower (or get rid of) my homeowners' association fees?
- What's a realistic asking price for my current home?

Tip Consult a real estate agent or use *www.zillow.com* to get an idea of how much homes in your area are worth.

- Which rooms in my current home go unused or underused? (This helps you figure out how much square footage you could do without.)
- What stuff would I sell, donate, or recycle if I had 50% less space to store it?
- In the next 10 years, will my family grow or leave the nest?

- What are the schools like in the neighborhood I'm considering?
- Would my family use the car more, less, or the same amount in the new home?
- What renovations (if any) will the downsized home need, and how much will they cost? (If you're looking to lower energy use and heating costs, for example, don't downsize to a poorly insulated home.)
- How much will moving cost?
- What other one-time fees (mortgage application fee, assessment, closing costs, and so on) will I pay?

There's more to the downsizing decision than money, of course. If you love your current home or neighborhood, simply find other ways to reduce your carbon footprint and energy costs—the rest of this chapter has tons of suggestions for doing just that.

But the benefits of downsizing are worth considering. You can save money, live more efficiently, and reduce your greenhouse gas emissions, not to mention spending a lot less time on cleaning and yard work. In many neighborhoods of smaller homes, you can leave the minivan in the garage and walk to school, shops, and parks. And you might make friends with the new neighbors as you sit on your front porch.

Heating and Cooling Efficiently

According to the U.S. Department of Energy, keeping our homes and other buildings comfortable puts 150 million tons of carbon dioxide into the atmosphere each year, which contributes to global warming (page 263 explains how *that* nastiness happens). Heating and cooling also contributes to acid rain, which can change lakes' natural pH, making them more acidic, killing fish and other aquatic animals. Acid rain can also damage trees, statues and monuments, and even the paint on your car. And warming and cooling American buildings is responsible for 12% of the country's sulfur dioxide and 4% of its nitrogen oxides emissions.

When you hear numbers like that, it may seem like there's not much you can do to make a difference. But keep in mind that this eye-popping level of emissions didn't happen overnight: It built up one house at a time—and it can decrease the same way. More and more people are interested in lowering their energy costs, which also reduces harmful emissions and energy use. Whether your want to save the planet or some cash (or both), doing your share makes you part of a larger movement, one that *can* make a big difference.

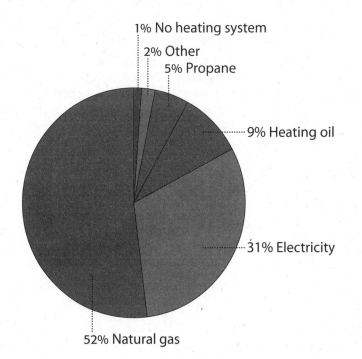

1% No heating system

2% Other

5% Propane

9% Heating oil

31% Electricity

52% Natural gas

According to the U.S. Census Bureau, more than half of Americans use natural gas to heat their homes. Natural gas is a good choice because it's more efficient and burns cleaner than other fossil fuels, producing virtually no ash particles and giving off fewer emissions of sulfur, carbon, and nitrogen than coal or oil. (As page 264 explains, burning *any* kind of fossil fuel has some impact on the environment.)

No matter how you heat your home, here are some easy, inexpensive steps you can take to use less fuel, reduce emissions, and save money:

- **Change the temperature.** Making your home a couple degrees cooler in winter and warmer in summer won't significantly affect your comfort, but it *will* lower your utility bills. Try keeping the thermostat 68° F (20° C) in the winter and 78° F (25° C) in the summer. If that's uncomfortable, change it one degree at a time until you find a temperature that works for you. And remember: Putting on a sweater is cheaper and better for the environment than cranking up the heat.

- **Get a programmable thermostat.** Your home doesn't need to be exactly 72° F (22° C) all the time. When you're at work, for example, it can be cooler (in winter) or warmer (in summer) than when you're at home.

When you're asleep under a down comforter, your body heat keeps you warm, so give the furnace a break. With a traditional, manual thermostat, it can be easy to forget to lower the heat when you're rushing out the door. A programmable thermostat, on the other hand, adjusts the temperature automatically on whatever schedule you want. You can even have one schedule for weekdays and a different one for weekends. Just set it and forget it—until the utility bill arrives and you see how much you've saved.

- **Get your heating system inspected each year.** As mentioned on page 45, this keeps the system in top working order and ensures that it's safe, too.

- **Check your furnace filters.** If they're dirty, clean or replace 'em. In the winter, it's good to do this once a month. Put it on your calendar so you don't forget.

- **Have ductwork cleaned.** You need to hire a professional for this job (have it done every 3 to 5 years), but for forced-air systems, it's worth the effort.

- **Check your heat-delivery system.** Make sure registers, radiators, and baseboard units are clean and clear (that is, not blocked by furniture or drapes) so they can do their jobs efficiently.

- **Bleed trapped air from radiators and baseboard heaters.** Some heating systems work by circulating hot water through radiators or baseboard units. But air can leak into the system, making it less efficient. Bleeding out this trapped air will make your home warmer and help you use less energy to heat it. Do this procedure twice each winter. If you don't know how, hire a professional who can show you how to do it safely.

- **Get an efficient air conditioner.** An AC's SEER rating (which stands for Seasonal Energy Efficiency Ratio) tells you how efficient it is—higher numbers are better. The rating, found on a sticker inside the unit, is assigned according to a standard developed by the Air Conditioning, Heating, and Refrigeration Institute. All residential ACs sold in the U.S. have a SEER rating of at least 13. To earn an Energy Star designation, they need to be rated 14 or higher, but the most efficient models are in the range of 16 to 23.

- **Put window air conditioners in north-facing windows.** These are the shadiest windows in your house (if you're in the northern hemisphere, that is), so ACs you place there won't have to fight the sun to cool the air.

Tip If your window air conditioner is too big for the space it's cooling, then it's wasting energy and cooling less effectively than it should. For help choosing the right-sized AC, head to *http://tinyurl.com/32w5h*.

- **Close off unused rooms.** Why spend money heating and cooling rooms that no one's using? Close the registers or baseboard units in such rooms, and then close the door, too.

- **Open (or close) the windows.** On a cool summer evening, a little cross-ventilation can go a long way in making your home more comfortable. Place a fan in the window (blowing outward) to draw cooler air into the house through other open windows. (A fan uses a lot less energy than an air conditioner.) When it's cold outside, make sure all windows are tightly shut to keep warm air in.

- **Put your window treatments to work.** Window treatments like drapes, blinds, and shutters can help lower your energy bills. Look for lined or thermal drapes that help keep heat from leaking out around your windows. In the winter, open the drapes of south-facing windows to let the sunshine in (close them at dusk for privacy and to keep out the cold). In the summer, keep windows covered during the day to help your house stay cooler.

- **Use ceiling fans.** These fans can keep your rooms cooler in summer and warmer in winter. In summer, they use less energy than ACs and the nice breeze they create means you can turn the thermostat up a few degrees. In winter, they circulate the warm air that's risen up to the ceiling, making the room feel warmer and helping your heating system do less work. Ceiling fans have switches that let you set the direction it spins. In the summer, set it to turn counter-clockwise; in the winter, switch it to clockwise and use the slowest rotation speed.

- **Install storm windows and doors.** These cut down on drafts by adding an extra barrier between your home and the air outside. Storm windows and doors are useful in older homes in cold climates. If your home has energy-efficient doors and windows, you don't need to worry about these.

- **Insulate windows with film.** This is an inexpensive do-it-yourself project that can keep heat from escaping through windows. You apply double-sided tape to the window frame, stick plastic film to the tape, and then tighten the film using a blow dryer. The film is clear and doesn't obscure the view, but you can't open the window while it's in place, so it's best for insulating against cold winters. Window film kits are available at home-improvement and discount stores like Target and Wal-Mart.

- **Be smart about exhaust fans.** Exhaust fans banish excess heat and humidity from your kitchen and bathroom. But in the winter, you don't want to send precious heat outside, so use these fans sparingly and for as short a time as possible—no more than 15 or 20 minutes after cooking or taking a shower.

- **Take showers instead of baths—and take shorter showers.** In general, showers use less hot water than baths, so they save water *and* energy used to heat the water. You win on both counts.

Tip Switching to a low-flow showerhead (page 66) is another way to save hot water.

- **Turn down your water heater.** For every 10 degrees you turn it down, you'll save 3–5% on your utility bill. If your dishwasher doesn't have its own water heater (meaning it draws hot water from your system), set the temperature to 140° F (60° C) to make sure your dishes are clean and sanitized. Otherwise, try a low/medium setting of 120° F (49° C).

- **Insulate your water heater**. This helps keep the water in the tank hot longer. If the pipes that carry hot water pass through unheated areas, insulate them, too. (You can buy insulation tape or foam pipe insulation at home-improvement stores.)

Getting More out of Your Appliances

There's no denying that appliances make people's lives easier—no one wants to go back to lugging clothes down to the river and beating them with a rock to get them clean. Today, though, we demand more from our appliances than mere convenience: We want them to be energy efficient, too. Otherwise, money and energy go down the drain along with the dirty laundry water. This section explains lots of ways you can save money and help the planet.

How Much Energy Does That Gadget Use?

As you learned in the box on page 49, if you know how many watts something uses, you can calculate how much power it consumes. If you don't know the wattage, Table 2-1 lists U.S. Department of Energy wattage estimates for common appliances.

Table 2-1. Wattage of Household Appliances

Appliance	Number of Watts
Ceiling fan	65–175
Clock radio	10
Coffee maker	900–1200
Clothes washer	300–500
Clothes dryer	1800–5000
Dehumidifier	785
Dishwasher	1200–2400
DVD player	20–25
Hair dryer	1200–1875
Iron	1000–1800
Microwave oven	750–1100
Personal computer: Desktop monitor and hard drive	60 (standby)–270
Personal computer: Laptop	50
Portable heater	750–1500
Refrigerator (frost-free, 16 cubic feet)	725
Television	65–170
Toaster oven	1225
Vacuum cleaner	1000–1440

When you're shopping for new appliances, look for Energy Star–qualified ones. Energy Star began in 1992 as a voluntary labeling program that let manufacturers identify energy-efficient models. The first Energy Star products were computers and monitors, but now the program includes office equipment, major appliances, lighting, home electronics, and even homes and other buildings (see page 119).

Many countries also label major appliances with an energy guide that rates the model's efficiency and estimates how much it costs to run. In the U.S., for example, the bright-yellow EnergyGuide tag has been rating energy efficiency since 1980. The EnergyGuide tag tells you three important things:

1. How much power the appliance uses (in kilowatt hours per year)

2. How the product's energy use compares to similar models

3. How much it costs to run the product each year, based on average prices for electricity

This figure shows an EnergyGuide tag for a dishwasher.

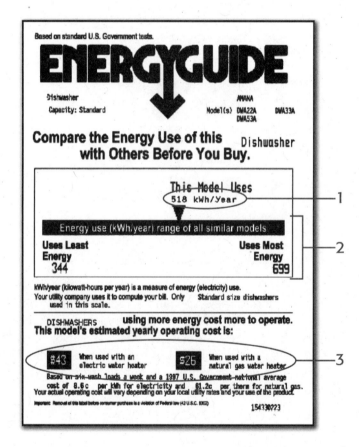

In Canada, look for the EnerGuide label, which has similar information. In the European Union, check out the EU energy label, which rates a model's energy efficiency from A (most efficient) to G (least efficient). And in Australia, you can compare appliances at *www.energyrating.gov.au*.

Tips for Using Appliances More Efficiently

No matter how efficient your appliances are, there are lots of simple things you can do around the house to consume less energy (and save money on your electric bill). Here are some easy-to-implement ideas:

- **Wait for full loads.** Don't run a half-empty washing machine or dishwasher. You'll get more bang for your energy buck by running them only when they're full.

- **Wash in cold water.** When possible, use cold water to wash clothes. It takes a lot of energy to heat water for a load of laundry—about 90% of the energy required to run the machine.

- **For small loads, try an electricity-free washer.** Wonder Wash is a portable washing machine that uses pressure to clean laundry loads up to five pounds—without electricity. (It requires a bit of elbow grease, though, because you have to turn the barrel with a crank.) Wonder Wash uses less water than hand-washing clothes in the sink and it's fast—your clothes get clean in two minutes or less. For more info, visit *www.laundry-alternative.com*.

- **Get a natural gas dryer.** If you have an electric dryer, consider replacing it with a natural-gas one, which costs about half as much to operate.

- **Clean the lint filter.** When your dryer's lint filter is clean, air circulates better and your laundry dries faster.

- **Skip the dryer.** When the weather allows, hang laundry outside to dry. If the weather's too wet or cold for that, use wooden clothing racks (they're cheap) to dry it inside.

- **Don't pre-rinse dishes.** Instead of rinsing dishes in the sink or using your dishwasher's pre-rinse cycle, scrape off any leftover food (which, incidentally, is great for compost—see page 193) before you load the dishwasher.

- **Air-dry dishes.** Your dishwasher's drying cycle uses heat to dry any water clinging to your dishes, and that takes a lot of energy. Instead, choose air dry or simply stop the dishwasher and open the door after the final rinse cycle.

- **Microwave smart.** Microwaves cook food around the perimeter of a plate faster than at the center. So arrange your meal in a circular pattern, pushing it away from the middle of the plate or bowl, to make it cook quicker. More surface area also means less cooking time; thin slices of potato, for example, cook faster than whole ones.

- **Thaw food in the fridge.** Put frozen food in the refrigerator overnight to thaw it, rather than using the microwave or hot water.

- **Cook with gas.** Gas stoves are about twice as energy efficient as electric ones, and they let you control burner temperatures more precisely.

> **Tip** Gas flames should burn blue. If they're yellow, you need to clean the gas ports. A pipe cleaner usually does the trick.

- **Use the right size pots and pans.** There's no reason to heat up more surface area than you need, so don't use a giant pan to fry up a single egg. (Flat-bottom pans make better contact with electric burners than those with rounded bottoms.) And don't use a burner that's bigger than your pan.

- **Don't open the oven to peek.** Each time you crack the oven door, as much as 25% of the hot air inside escapes, so look through the door's window instead.

- **Double up when baking.** Try to cook or bake more than one thing at a time, so you'll have the oven on for less time.

- **Clean your fridge's coils.** Dirty coils restrict airflow and make the compressor work harder (which uses more energy), so be sure to clean yours twice a year. Unplug the fridge, and then use your vacuum cleaner's long nozzle to suck up the dust.

- **Turn the fridge up a bit.** Your fridge may be working harder than it has to. Put a thermometer in the fridge to see how cold it is—somewhere in the range of 37°–40° F (3°–4.5° C) is ideal. If it's below 40°, try moving the temperature control to the next warmest setting. Check the temperature the next day, and repeat the process if necessary.

> **!** To keep food safe, make sure your fridge is set to 40° F (4.5° C) or slightly below (food spoils faster at temperatures above that).

- **Keep the fridge closed.** Don't stand in front of the fridge with the door wide open as you decide what you want for a snack. While you're making up your mind, your fridge is pouring out cold air—making the compressor turn on that much sooner.

- **Make sure your fridge is sealed.** If the seal on its door isn't tight, your refrigerator could be leaking cold air. Take a dollar bill and hold it against the seal, close the door, and then try to pull the dollar out. If it slips out easily, the seal probably isn't tight enough, so you should clean or replace it. If you have to tug on the dollar to pull it out, the seal is doing its job.

Minimizing Your Phantom Load

There's a phantom lurking in your house, a vampire that sucks energy and raises your utility bill. But you don't need an exorcist or wooden stake to banish this bogeyman. An appliance's *phantom load* is the power that it uses even when it's switched off. TVs, cable boxes, DVD and DVR players, video-game consoles, appliances with digital clocks, computers, power adapters, transformers, chargers, and anything with an instant-on function (meaning you can turn it on with a remote rather than pushing a button or flipping a switch) can all have phantom loads.

The load for a single appliance is usually in the range of 5–15 watts, which isn't a whole lot. But that small amount adds up fast when you consider all the devices in a typical home, and the number of homes across the country. Experts say that phantom loads accounts for as much as 5% of total U.S. electricity use—that's more than $3 billion annually! With those numbers, the phantom load starts looking more like a phantom menace.

The simplest and surest way to reduce your phantom load is to unplug things when you're not using them. The problem with this method, of course, is its sheer inconvenience, especially if you have to crawl around on the floor or reach behind furniture to get to the plug.

If unplugging isn't feasible, consider these load-reducing tips:

- **Replace rechargeables.** Instead of using power to constantly recharge the batteries of your cordless phone, electric shaver, vacuum, and so on, switch to the old-fashioned kind (you know, with a cord). Unplug the corded shaver when you're not using it, or go even more retro and use the kind of razor and toothbrush that don't need any electricity at all.

- **Go solar.** Use solar power to charge portable gadgets. You can buy solar-powered chargers to power up everything from MP3 players to cellphones to laptops. These can be pricey, though, depending on the device you want to charge. For example, you can pick up a solar charger for your cellphone or iPod for around $20; for a laptop, they start at around $150. (Of course, after you buy the device, the sunlight is free.) You can buy them from Solar Style (*http://solarstylemiami.com*) or Solio (*http://store.solio.com*), or go to *www.amazon.com* and search for *solar charger*.

> **Tip** If you use regular wall-socket chargers to juice up your cellphone, digital camera, iPod, and the like, be sure to unplug them when you're done.

- **Use a power strip with an on/off switch.** If you have several devices that you use together—like a computer and a printer or a TV and a video-game console—plug them into a single power strip or surge protector. When you're finished using them, turn off the strip. The main challenge with this method is remembering to switch off the strip.

> **Tip** If you have devices that you never use during a certain part of the day, such as overnight, plug the power strip into an inexpensive timer that turns off the strip automatically at night and back on in the morning.

- **Try a smart power strip.** If it's too much trouble to unplug devices or switch off their power strips, consider getting a "smart" power strip. When you plug a device into one of these gizmos, it can tell when you're not using the device and adjust the power accordingly. There are two kinds of smart power strips (some even come with a remote, which is handy when the strip is in a hard-to-reach area, like under your desk or behind the sofa):

  — **A master outlet controls the other outlets.** When this kind of strip senses a decrease in power use by whatever's plugged into the master outlet, it turns off the other outlets, too. This works well for office equipment: Plug your computer into the master outlet and your printer, desk lamp, fax machine, and so on into the other outlets, for example. When you shut down the computer, the strip also powers off everything else. To see this in action, check out BITS Limited's Smart Strip (*http://bitsltd.net*).

— **An occupancy sensor monitors activity.** These strips figure out whether each outlet is being used and turns them off or on accordingly. Watt Stopper's Isolé model uses this approach (*www.wattstopper.com*).

As you might guess, smart power strips create their own phantom load, but it's minimal. The BITS Smart Strip, for example, uses just 0.28 watts while in standby.

> **Tip** Here are the U.S. Department of Energy's guidelines for knowing when to turn off your computer to save energy: If you'll be away from the computer for more than 20 minutes, turn off the monitor; if you'll be away for more than 2 hours, turn off the computer, as well.

Water-Saving Strategies

Water is so basic to life that many people take it for granted, assuming it'll be there whenever they want to fill a glass, take a shower, or wash laundry. But the world is headed toward a water crisis—and getting there fast. A United Nations report estimates that two-thirds of the world's population will face shortages of clean water by 2025. In the U.S., many cities have outdated treatment plants and infrastructure (water mains, pipes, and so on) or are expanding quickly and the local water supply can't keep up. These problems could lead to serious water shortages throughout the country within the next 10 to 15 years. And it's not just people who need water, of course; a diminishing water supply also endangers animals, plants, and entire ecosystems.

It's clear that large-scale solutions are necessary to avert a crisis. But everyone can do their part. Currently, each person in the U.S. uses 75 to 100 gallons per day—that's *three times* more than the global average. People need to recognize water for the precious resource it is and use it wisely. Even if you live in an area where water is plentiful, conserving water is smart because it helps you:

- **Save energy.** Treating water and moving it into and out of your home takes energy, so using less water means using less energy, which reduces your carbon footprint and cuts back on greenhouse gas emissions. It also eases the burden on the water treatment plant that cleans the water you send down the drain; many of these plants are handling more water than they were designed for.

- **Be kind to the planet.** When you use less water, you leave more water for ecosystems (not to mention drinking water, recreation, growing crops, and myriad other uses).
- **Save money.** Less water means a smaller utility bill.

Most Americans use so much water that cutting back is probably far easier than you think. Read on to find out how.

How Much Water Do You Use?

The American average of 75 to 100 gallons of water per person per day sounds like a lot—and it is. But unless you take a *marathon* shower each morning, you don't use that amount all at once. Most people use a few gallons here and a few gallons there, which add up over the course of the day. To get a sense of how much water you're using, check out how much water these activities require:

- **Flushing toilets.** Older toilets (made before 1995) use about 5 gallons of water each flush. In 1994, Congress changed the maximum water use per flush to 1.6 gallons. So the age of your toilet determines how much water it consumes.

- **Taking showers and baths.** In the U.S., water comes out of taps, shower-heads, and the like at a rate of about 2.5 gallons per minute. So if it takes you 12 minutes to get clean and sing your repertoire of show tunes, your shower averages 30 gallons of water. If you prefer baths, you use even *more* water: 40 to 50 gallons, depending on how much you fill the tub.

- **Doing laundry.** The average top-loading washer uses 40 to 50 gallons per load—compare that with just 20–25 gallons per load for a front-loading model.

- **Washing dishes.** Energy Star dishwashers use about 4 gallons per load, and other models about 6 gallons per load. Pre-rinsing dishes before you load 'em into the dishwasher can use as much as 20 gallons, and hand-washing uses an average of just over 27 gallons of water.

- **Turning on faucets.** Americans average nearly 11 gallons of water a day for drinking water, cooking, washing hands, and so on.

- **Watering lawns.** The EPA reports that keeping lawns and landscapes green accounts for about 30% of residential water use in the U.S. Your specific usage depends on how big an area you're watering, how often you water, and the climate.

- **Leaks.** Here's a sobering statistic from the EPA: Each year, leaks waste more than 1 *trillion* gallons of water—and that's just in the U.S.! Many people don't know they have leaks, can't find the ones they have, or put off fixing small ones. Over the course of a year, one small, constant drip can waste thousands of gallons—water you're not using but still paying for.

> **Tip** To estimate how much water your household uses each year, try the Consumer Support Group's Water Consumption Calculator at *www.csgnetwork.com/waterusagecalc.html*.

Using Less Water

There are lots of changes you can make both inside and outside the house to send less water down the drain and keep more money in your wallet. The following sections have lots of recommendations, from the simple to the complex.

Bathroom

Flushing the toilet and bathing use the most water here. These strategies can help reduce the amount of water your family uses:

- **Install a new, efficient toilet** if your current one was manufactured before 1995 to save up to 3.5 gallons per flush. For a family of four, this could save over 20,000 gallons a year.

- **Consider a composting or incinerating toilet** and go virtually water-less. Page 131 tells you more about these technologies.

- **Make your existing toilet more efficient** by putting a *displacement device* in the tank—and save up to half a gallon per flush. To make one, get a tall, narrow half-gallon or two-liter plastic bottle, drop a few pebbles in the bottom, and then fill the bottle with water and screw the cap on tight. Carefully place the bottle in the toilet tank, making sure it won't interfere with the tank's flushing mechanism. Now, when the tank fills, the bottle takes up space that would otherwise be filled with water, so less water flushes into the bowl.

- **Check your toilets for leaks** by putting a few drops of food coloring in the tank and then waiting 30 minutes (don't flush during that time). If the color appears in the toilet bowl, you've got a leak—one that could be wasting hundreds of gallons each month. (Make sure you flush after you finish the test to avoid staining the porcelain.)

- **Reuse water to flush the toilet.** This can be as simple as using a bucket to catch water as the shower warms up, then pouring that water down the toilet to flush. Or it can be as involved as installing a gray-water system to reuse water from the bathroom sink for flushing the toilet, like WaterSaver Technologies AQUS system (*www.watersavertech.com*). For more about gray water, see the box on page 38.

- **Don't use the toilet as a trash can.** For example, don't blow your nose and then flush the used tissue—that wastes water and puts unnecessary strain on your septic or local water-treatment system.

- **Take showers instead of baths** to save 10 gallons or more each time.

- **Shorten your showers.** Remember that each minute in the shower averages 2.5 gallons of water, so shortening your scrubbing time by a mere two minutes can save a couple of thousand gallons a year. (You'll also save on the energy cost of heating the water.)

- **Install a low-flow showerhead;** they're cheap and easy to install. They can slow the flow rate to 1.5–2 gallons per minute, saving you 5–10 gallons or more for each 10-minute shower.

- **Don't leave the water running when you're not using it.** It's easy to leave the tap on while you brush your teeth, shave, or lather up to wash your hands or face, but you really only need it for part of that time. Turn the water off unless you're actively using it.

- **Install a faucet aerator.** This mixes air into the water, lessening the water flow. Aerators are also good for kitchen faucets.

- **If a leaky faucet drips, replace the washer.** Believe it or not, a faucet that drips once per second wastes 2,700 gallons of water in a year.

Kitchen

A few simple tweaks to how you use water in this room will save thousands of gallons a year. Here are some suggestions:

- When you're thirsty, **don't run the water until it's cold.** Instead, fill a pitcher and keep it in the fridge. You'll send less water down the drain and it'll be colder, too.

- If you're in the market for a new one, **get an Energy Star–rated dishwasher,** which saves a couple of gallons per load. Look for one that lets you adjust cycles and load size, so you can customize it to your needs.

- As page 59 noted, **run the dishwasher only when it's full** to save energy and water.

- If you wash dishes by hand, **don't leave the faucet running** to rinse them. Instead, fill up the second sink or a dishpan with water and use it to rinse. Or put soapy dishes in the drainer and clean them all at once using a sprayer.

- **Don't pre-rinse dishes** before you put 'em in the dishwasher.

- **Cut back on garbage disposal use,** which requires a lot of water. Start composting (page 191) instead.

- As in the bathroom, **check for leaky faucets** and replace washers if necessary.

Laundry room

Some of the energy-saving strategies on page 59—like waiting for a full load—also save water. In addition, consider these options:

- **Adjust the washer's water level** to match the size of the load. Don't fill the tub for a super-sized load when you're washing only a few things.

- **Use the shortest cycle.** The average permanent press cycle, for example, uses about five gallons more than the normal cycle.

- If you're in the market for a new washing machine, **look for Energy Star–rated models.** They use about half the water and energy of other models.

- **Consider a front-loading washer.** These use less water than top-loading models and, because they don't have agitators, there's room for bigger loads.

Outdoors

How much water you use outside depends on your living situation. Apartment dwellers with no car can skip this section, while suburbanites and people in rural areas can use these tips to conserve water. Watering lawns and gardens is one of the biggest household uses of water. Flip back to page 28 for tons of lawn-care tips. Here are some more suggestions for your lawn and beyond:

- **Check your watering system.** Make sure that sprinklers aren't aimed at the house or driveway. If you have an underground system, check it each spring to be sure winter frosts didn't damage it.

- **Water in the morning when it's cool;** you lose more water to evaporation during the heat of the day. Wind also ups the evaporation rate, so avoid watering on windy days.

- **Reduce the size of your lawn** by planting shrubs, groundcover, and native plants suited to your climate.

- If your lawn slopes so that water tends to run off it, **plant less-thirsty ground cover on the slope. Or water for shorter periods,** turning off the sprinklers every few minutes to give the ground a chance to absorb the water.

- If your area allows it, **consider installing a gray-water system** (page 38) to irrigate your lawn with recycled household water.

- **Collect rainwater** and use it on your lawn and garden. You can collect it in a simple rain barrel (which can have a spigot that lets you fill up a watering can, or a pump that routes water to your sprinkler system). More complex systems collect runoff from your roof and store it in an underground tank so you can water your lawn with it or it can get filtered or treated and pumped into your house for laundry and toilet-flushing. A good place to learn more about rainwater harvesting techniques and systems is *www.harvesth2o.com*.

Note Regulations about rainwater harvesting vary widely. Some state and local governments offer rebates when you purchase a rain barrel or cistern. In other places (notably Colorado and Utah), gathering rainwater is illegal at this writing.

- **Check garden hoses for leaks** and replace if necessary. Make sure hoses connect tightly at the spigot (there shouldn't be water running out at the connection); if they leak, use a wrench to tighten them, or patch them with waterproof tape. If your hose's nozzle drips, replace the washer.

- **Clean your sidewalk and driveway with a broom,** not a hose. If the dust makes you sneeze, wear a mask while you sweep.

- **Wash your car at a commercial car wash** rather than doing it yourself. You'll save up to 100 gallons per wash. (Many car washes also recycle the water they use, saving even more water.)

- If you wash your car at home, **turn off the hose except to rinse,** and use a spray nozzle to reduce water flow. Or try a waterless, environmentally friendly car-washing product such as EcoTouch (*www.ecotouch.net*), Freedom (*http://freedomwaterlesscarwash.com*), or DriWash (*www.driwashsolutions.com*).

- If you have one, **cover your swimming pool when no one's using it.** The average uncovered pool loses about an inch of water to evaporation each week. Also, **cool your pool** by a few degrees. Warmer water evaporates sooner, and you'll save electricity, too.

> **Tip** A solar pool cover uses the sun's energy to heat your pool when you're not using it. These covers minimize evaporation and keep the water at a comfortable temperature without running up your electric bill.

- **Don't overfill your pool.** Keep the water level about an inch below the bottom edge of the tile to minimize water lost through splashing.

- **Inspect your pool for leaks** and cracks and patch as necessary.

Let There Be (Compact Fluorescent) Light

Question: How many politicians does it take to change a lightbulb?

Answer: Both houses of Congress and a president to sign the bill into law.

By 2014, the whole U.S. will be changing its lightbulbs, thanks to a federal law passed in 2007 that phases out traditional incandescent bulbs in favor of *compact fluorescent lamps,* a.k.a. CFLs. Countries around the world are changing their lightbulbs, too: The European Union and Australia have already banned incandescent bulbs, and Canada, India, and other countries have made plans to replace all or some incandescents with CFLs.

Regular lightbulbs haven't changed a whole lot since Thomas Edison invented them in 1879; they're basically mini-heaters that give off light as a byproduct. They work by passing an electric current through a long, thin filament, which heats up and gives off light. The glass bulb is filled with an inert gas, such as argon, that keeps the filament from oxidizing (combining with oxygen and burning out).

CFLs are a bit different. They have two parts: a glass tube (coated on the inside with phosphor and filled with gas) and a ballast, which provides the lamp's starting voltage and regulates its current. When you turn on a CFL, electricity flows through the ballast into the gas, causing the gas to give off ultraviolet light. This light then excites the tube's phosphorous coating, which gives off visible light. Unlike standard fluorescent lights (the kind found in classrooms, offices, and stores), CFLs are small, come in a variety of shapes, and can fit in your existing light fixtures.

Tip Fluorescent lights have a reputation for giving off harsh, unflattering light. Some CFLs have diffusers to soften their light, making them less like the overhead lights at your office and more like the softer, warmer light of the bulbs at home. To get softer light, look for the *color temperature rating* on the package: bulbs with the "warmest" light (which is easier on the eyes) have ratings of less than 3,000 kelvins; bulbs with ratings above 5,000 kelvins give off much harsher light.

CFLs have several advantages over incandescent bulbs:

- **They're cooler,** producing about 90% less heat, so you're far less likely to burn yourself on a CFL.

- **They use about a quarter of the energy** to produce the same amount of light.

- **They last about 10 times longer**, so each CFL means 10 bulbs you don't have to replace.

As you've probably guessed from this list, CFLs save a lot of energy. Over its long lifetime, a single CFL will cost you $30 to $45 less in electricity than a succession of incandescent bulbs. And because CFLs use less energy, they reduce the amount of greenhouse gases spewed by power plants. Lighting accounts for 19% of the total electricity use in the U.S., and that means the benefits of CFLs add up fast: If Americans replaced all their incandescent bulbs with CFLs, it would prevent 158 million tons of carbon dioxide emissions over the next year—that's equivalent to taking about *30 million* cars off the road.

Buying CFLs

When you see the potential for reduced greenhouse gas emissions and sheer cost savings, it's no surprise that governments are eager to replace Thomas Edison's old invention with new-and-improved CFLs. What does that mean to you, the consumer? CFLs cost more than incandescent bulbs, but the long life and lower energy costs more than make up the difference. And you don't need to wait for incandescent bulbs to get outlawed before you make the switch—as your old lightbulbs burn out, replace 'em with CFLs.

Shopping for CFLs is a little different from buying regular lightbulbs. You're probably used to buying bulbs based on watts: a 100-watt bulb for bright light, a 40-watt bulb for softer light, and so on. But as the box on page 49 explains, watts measure power, not brightness. Because CFLs use less power, their wattage is much lower than what you're used to. So you can't replace a 40-watt incandescent bulb with a 40-watt CFL and get the same light—the CFL will be *much* brighter. Fortunately, most CFL packages tell you their incandescent-bulb equivalents.

When you want to know how much light a CFL will produce, think in terms of *lumens*, which measure light. Table 2-2 compares the number of watts used by incandescent bulbs and CFLs to produce the same number of lumens. For example, a 60-watt incandescent bulb and a 13- to 18-watt CFL both produce about 890 lumens.

Table 2-2. Incandescent and CFL Equivalents

Incandescent Wattage	CFL Wattage Range	Lumens
40	8–10	450
60	13–18	890
75	19–22	1210
100	23–28	1750
150	34–42	2780

You can buy CFLs in a variety of styles and shapes, from twisty tubes to round ones that resemble incandescent bulb. Some CFLs have multiple tubes (two, four, or six); others have spiral or circular tubes. The number and size of the tubes determine how bright the bulb is—more surface area means more light.

You can thread these bulbs in to any standard light fixture, but some CFLs don't work with dimmer switches or three-way fixtures, so if you're looking for a bulb that works at different brightness levels, check the package (dimmable CFLs can be a lot pricier). Also, most CFLs are designed for indoor use at warm temperatures, and they won't last as long if you use them outside. If you're looking for a CFL that you can use outdoors—especially if you live in a cold climate—check the temperature range listed on the box. Putting an outdoor-use CFL in an enclosed light fixture, like a lantern-style lamp, helps to protect the bulb from the elements—rain, snow, cold air, and so on.

Getting the Most out of CFLs

Now that you know how watts relate to lumens (Table 2-2) and what color temperature is (page 70), here are a few more tips to help you make the switch to CFLs:

- Unlike incandescent bulbs, **CFLs take time to reach their full brightness**—up to three minutes. This is normal—there's nothing wrong with the bulb—but it does take some getting used to.

- Turning a CFL on for only a short period shortens the bulb's life. To get the best performance, **leave CFLs on for at least 15 minutes at a time.** That means CFLs work best in rooms where you leave them on for a while, like a kitchen or family room. They're less suitable for closets or pantries, where you're likely to turn them on and off more frequently and for shorter periods; in these spots, consider LEDs instead (see the box on page 75).

- **CFLs don't work as spotlights**—try LEDs (page 75) when you need a narrow, focused beam of light—but they're great for area lighting, such as table lamps.

CFLs and Mercury

As you may have heard, CFLs contain mercury, a toxic metal that, at high doses, can make people sick and cause kidney, lung, and brain damage. An important part of green living is clearing toxins *out* of your home (see Chapter 1)—so you may be wondering if it's safe to replace your lightbulbs with CFLs.

There's no question that mercury is dangerous, especially for fetuses, infants, and children. And you probably already know to avoid or limit seafood that may contain mercury, like swordfish and tuna. So what kind of risk do CFLs pose? CFLs contain a small amount of mercury: about 4 or 5 mg, which is significantly less than in a typical watch battery, dental filling, or pre-1970 light switch. As long as a CFL's glass stays intact, there's no chance of the mercury leaking into your home. If the glass breaks a small amount of mercury vapor and powder containing mercury get released, and even a small amount can be hazardous. The next section tells you how to deal with that situation. Knowing how to dispose of CFLs safely—whether they're broken or no longer work—will keep mercury from contaminating your home and the local landfill.

> **Note** CFL companies including Philips ALTO, Feit EcoBulb Plus, Neolite, and Earthmate are starting to make low-mercury bulbs.

Cleaning up broken CFLs

Of course, the best way to protect yourself from the potential hazards of a broken CFL is to not break them in the first place. But accidents happen, and when they do these steps will help keep you and your family safe:

1. **Ventilate the room.** Get everyone—including pets—out of the room where the CFL broke (make sure no one walks through the broken glass). Open a window and leave the room, closing the door behind you.

> **Tip** If your heating and cooling system uses forced air, turn it off so it doesn't circulate mercury vapors.

2. **Let the room air out for at least 15 minutes.**

3. **While you wait, find and put on some protective gear: safety goggles, gloves, and a surgical mask.** This may be overkill, but you don't want to accidentally inhale or ingest even a little mercury.

4. **Clean up the glass fragments and any powder by scooping them up with two pieces of cardboard: one to push the CFL fragments and the other to collect them.** *Don't* use a broom, brush, or vacuum cleaner—those will just stir up the powder, plus you want to get the mercury out of your house completely, not leave some stuck to a broom or sitting inside the vacuum. Put the fragments and cardboard into a glass jar or plastic bag. If you use a plastic bag, double-bag the debris and make sure both bags are sealed.

5. **Use the sticky side of some wide tape, like masking tape or duct tape, to clean up any remaining pieces of glass and powder.** Put the tape into the glass jar or plastic bag.

6. **Wipe the area with a damp cloth or paper towel, and then put that in the jar or bag, too.**

7. **Seal the jar or bag tightly and put it in an outdoor trash can for collection.**

> **Note** Not all areas let you put broken CFLs in the regular trash; check with your city or town to find out if your area has special rules.

8. **Wash your hands thoroughly.**

If the CFL broke on a carpet, you'll probably want to vacuum the carpet after you've taken these clean-up steps. If you do, first make sure that you pick up all visible glass and residue. And afterward, remove the vacuum-cleaner bag and place it in a plastic bag. For bagless vacuums, empty the dust compartment into a plastic bag. In either case, seal the plastic bag and put it inside *another* plastic bag and seal that one, too. Then throw away the plastic bags and wash your hands again.

Disposing of CFLs

If a single broken CFL requires careful clean-up, what about the millions of CFLs that will eventually burn out? Will the mercury they contain hurt the environment?

Widespread CFL use will actually *reduce* the amount of mercury released into the environment. That's because CFLs use so much less energy than incandescent bulbs, and the biggest source of mercury pollution is burning coal. Over a five-year period, a coal-fired electric plant releases 10 mg of mercury for each incandescent bulb it powers. Because a CFL uses only about a quarter as much power, that same plant produces only about 2.5 mg of mercury to power a CFL over the same period. Even when you add to that the 4–5 mg of mercury in a typical CFL, that's *still* a 25% reduction in mercury released into the environment.

To minimize the environmental impact of mercury from CFLs even more, recycle used CFLs: The bulbs get separated into materials that can be used again, such as glass, aluminum, and mercury. The mercury is then sold to lighting companies to use in new fluorescent lamps and CFLs.

Home Depot and IKEA both have nationwide CFL recycling programs; you can drop off unbroken CFLs at any of their stores. If you don't live near one of those, go to *http://earth911.com and* find a recycling center in your area. The site lists both local results and mail-in programs.

Green Tech

LEDing the Way to New Choices in Lighting

The LED, which stands for *light-emitting diode*, is on its way to becoming the next big thing in lighting. LEDs are small, solid, highly efficient bulbs. You've probably seen them in flashlights, traffic lights, electronics, and holiday light displays, and they're starting to make their way into lamps and other light fixtures.

In an LED bulb, a cluster of LEDs provides light and a diffuser lens spreads that light to increase the lighted area. Recent advances in technology have made it cheaper to produce LEDs, so they're becoming more competitive with CFLs and traditional lightbulbs.

LEDs are cool to the touch and have some advantages over both incandescents and CFLs:

- **Energy efficiency.** A typical LED uses just 2 to 10 watts of electricity. A 3-watt LED gives off about as much light as a 45-watt incandescent bulb.
- **Lifetime.** LEDs last up to 10 times as long as CFLs. That's so long that you might even forget how to change a lightbulb!
- **No mercury.** LEDs are mercury-free, so you don't have to worry about safely disposing of them.
- **Durability.** Because they're solid, LEDs don't break easily—they can be jarred or shaken and keep on lighting up your world.
- **Short uses.** Unlike a CFL, it doesn't shorten an LED's lifespan if you turn it on and off frequently or leave it on for just a minute or two.

For standard household lighting, LED technology is still in its infancy. LEDs are expensive, and some consumers feel that the bulbs aren't yet bright or diffused enough to replace incandescent bulbs or CFLs. But given their efficiency, lifespan, and durability, LEDs are definitely a technology to watch.

3 Reduce, Reuse, Recycle

Your great-grandparents lived by the saying, "Waste not, want not," which means that if we don't squander what we have, we won't lack for it later. That's a far cry from today's throwaway mentality, isn't it? Whether it's clothes, a cellphone, or a DVD player, many people find it easier to replace something that's old, worn, or broken than to fix it. The amount of trash people in developed countries produce is staggering, as you'll see in this chapter. And it piles up fast—just how fast might surprise you. What happens to all that junk? And how can we scale back the literal mountains of trash that go into landfills?

Everyone has to do their part. You're no doubt familiar with the phrase, "reduce, reuse, recycle," which is an updated, eco-conscious version of the "waste not, want not" philosophy. By now, most people have heard these three Rs so much that they seem obvious—*of course* we should be doing all those things to ease the toll we take on the planet. But it's worth pondering whether you actually follow all three Rs as much as you could.

This chapter shows why wasteful living is a bad idea and teaches you tips to help minimize it. By taking a close look at each of the three Rs—how you currently implement them and how you might fine-tune your current practices—you'll minimize waste, conserve precious resources, and save energy that would otherwise be used to create and transport new goods. And you'll feel smug knowing you're doing your part for planet earth.

A Trashy Odyssey

Every week, you haul your trash to the curb, drop it down a chute, throw it into a dumpster, and then a truck comes by and takes it away. Have you ever thought about what happens after that?

Most people haven't. Yet the average American produces about 4.5 pounds of garbage *each day*—that adds up to over 1,600 pounds a year! Multiply that by 300 million Americans, and you may wonder why we're not wading through a layer of junk up to our knees. Just imagine—if you had no way to get rid of your trash, how long would it take to fill up your house or apartment?

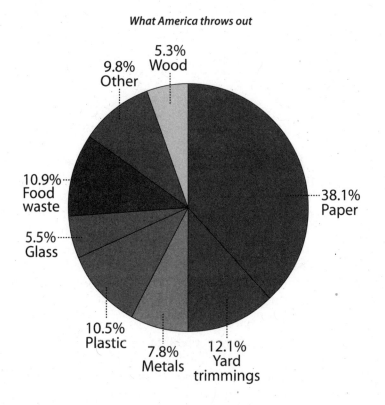

What America throws out

5.3% Wood

9.8% Other

10.9% Food waste

5.5% Glass

10.5% Plastic

7.8% Metals

12.1% Yard trimmings

38.1% Paper

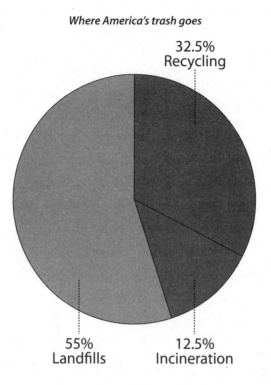

Where America's trash goes

32.5%
Recycling

55%
Landfills

12.5%
Incineration

After the garbage truck drives off, your trash is likely transferred to a barge or to other trucks, which might drive hundreds of miles before they dump it. There are two main places where trash ends up: buried in a landfill or burned in an incinerator.

Destination: Landfill

After your trash gets picked up, it probably gets taken to a landfill, which is where more than half of America's trash ends up. Today's *sanitary landfills* (what a name, huh?) aren't the hole-in-the-ground dumps where your grandparents tossed their trash. (The federal government banned open dumps in 1976.) Sanitary landfills isolate trash from the environment until the trash has degraded and doesn't pose health or environmental threats. That's the theory, anyway.

A *containment landfill*, a type of sanitary landfill, is a big pit that holds garbage from towns and cities. The pit has a waterproof liner, made of clay or plastic, along its sides and bottom to prevent contaminated liquids (known as *leachate*) from getting out of the trash-holding area and into the environment. A collection system drains the liquid from the pit and pumps it to a treatment system, where it's cleaned. Around the landfill, wells let workers collect groundwater so they can test it and make sure it's not polluted.

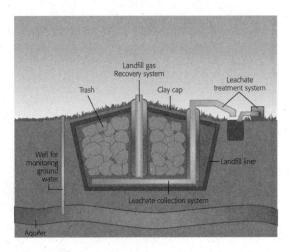

Note In containment landfills, even biodegradable stuff breaks down **very** slowly. Archeologists excavating old dumps have found 30-year-old grass clippings and still-legible newspapers. The trash in landfills stays with us for a long, long time.

As the garbage in the landfill degrades, it releases mostly methane and carbon dioxide, along with a few other gases. Usually, this gas gets burned off—if you've ever driven past a landfill and seen a flame at the top of a tall chimney, that's what it's for.

Note Methane is the main component of natural gas, and landfills are one of the top sources of man-made methane. Some landfills burn the methane they create to generate electricity.

Each day, workers bulldoze the trash and cover it with a layer of dirt or ash to help with the smell and to keep animals from using the dump as an all-you-can-eat buffet. Large landfills, which can cover hundreds of acres, have several pits, and only some of them get used at any given time, to minimize wind and rain exposure. When a pit is full, it gets covered with a clay cap to seal it, and then a layer of dirt and grass seed is put on top of that. The area then can get turned into a golf course, parking lot, or park. (It can take a long time for the ground to settle, so building on top of an old landfill is rarely an option.) Even after a dump has closed, scientists monitor the area's groundwater—for *30 years* or more.

Bioreactor landfills, another kind of sanitary landfill, are specially designed to help biodegradable trash decompose quickly. Air and water get circulated through the pit, speeding up the breakdown process. (You may have heard the word "bioreactor" before in different contexts. It's a broad term that can refer to any kind of setup that helps some biological or chemical process happen, from decomposition to making cells grow in a lab.) This kind of landfill produces more methane (which gets used to create electricity) and degrades organic garbage faster than the containment kind.

Modern landfills are much better than old-style dumps, which polluted groundwater and contaminated soil. But even with today's technologies, bulldozing trash into pits has its downside. Many areas are running out of space—often because locals don't want waste dumped in their area. (Would *you* want a garbage heap in your backyard?) Landfills also cause the following problems:

- **Increased traffic.** A parade of heavy trucks haul load after load of trash to the site. This increases traffic on local roads, which often weren't designed for such trucks.

- **Lower property values.** Although landfills provide jobs, they lower the value of homes and other real estate around them.

- **Rats, seagulls, and other scavengers.** Landfills attract critters looking for meals—and if it isn't well managed, these scroungers can overrun the area around it, too.

- **Greenhouse gas emissions.** As mentioned earlier, decomposing garbage produces methane, carbon dioxide, and other gases. Methane is a serious greenhouse gas—it stays in the atmosphere for 9–15 years and traps 20 times more heat than carbon dioxide. Burning the methane isn't a great option because that creates carbon dioxide and water, and CO_2 is bad for the atmosphere, too.

- **Leaky liners.** Landfills' liners sometimes leak and the leachate contaminates groundwater.

- **Hazardous materials.** Dumps that collect *municipal solid waste* (MSW)—that's the stuff regular people throw away—have different regulations than hazardous-waste landfills, which deal with pesticides, certain drugs, industrial wastes, and so on. Yet more scary stuff could be going into the local dump than you realize. Many MSW landfills accept soil contaminated by gas spills and certain kinds of hazardous waste from businesses. And some of the toxic household chemicals you learned about in Chapter 1 end up in landfills, too, mostly because people don't know how to dispose of them properly. All these nasty chemicals end up in the landfill's leachate.

- **Health issues.** Lots of problems have been reported among people living near MSW and hazardous-waste landfills alike, including low birth weights, birth defects, respiratory problems, dermatitis, neurological problems, and cancer.

Destination: Incinerator

Most cities areas have laws against burning trash in your backyard. That's because, aside from the risk of setting your house on fire, burning household trash sends a lot of pollutants—including cancer-causing dioxins—into the air. According to the EPA, backyard trash fires are the *number one* source of dioxin emissions in the U.S. (Dioxins, one of the most toxic substances on earth, build up in your body over time and have been linked to cancer, reproductive problems, thyroid disorders, central nervous system disorders, and immune system damage.) A single barrel of trash burned in the open may create as much air pollution as *tons* of garbage burned in a municipal waste incinerator serving tens of thousands of homes.

In many rural areas, it's legal to burn trash on farms. The dioxins that get released can settle on plants or wash into water, harming the critters that eat the plants or live in the water. And the chemicals move up the food chain: More than 95% of Americans' dioxin exposure comes through food—fish, red meat, poultry, dairy products, and eggs.

Municipal incinerators are a smarter way to burn trash. They deal with about 12% of the waste produced in the U.S. each year. (In other countries, like Japan and parts of Europe, the percentage of incinerated garbage is higher.) These facilities start with tons of trash, burn them at *really* hot temperatures, and end up with heat, gases, airborne particulates, and ash. They're safer than open burning and reduce the volume of solid waste by as much as 95%. The high temperatures destroy most germs, toxic chemicals, and other nasties, but the ash that's left over sometimes needs to be tested to make sure it's free of contaminants, depending on what was burned. Some of the ash gets used in paving materials and as daily cover for landfills.

Waste-to-energy (WTE) incinerators burn waste to generate power in the form of heat, steam, or electricity. There are currently 89 WTE plants in the U.S., generating enough juice each year to provide power to 2.3 million homes.

But there are problems with cremating trash. A big one is emissions: Incinerators spew out lots of carbon dioxide and some other seriously nasty gases like nitrogen oxide, sulfur dioxide, mercury, dioxins, and furans, although the EPA sets rules to minimize these. Even so, dioxins and furans are highly toxic—there's no "safe" exposure level.

Also, the teeny-tiny particles produced by burning that are too small be trapped can lodge in people's lungs, leading to respiratory problems and lung disease. And much of the ash created by incinerators isn't recycled and used for other purposes; it's dumped in single-use landfills called *monofills*. An ash monofill contains nothing but incinerator ash, and some environmentalists worry about toxic materials and heavy metals (such as lead, mercury, and arsenic) building up in these sites over time.

How Low Can You Go? Aiming for Zero Waste

Actually, all pollution is simply an unused resource. Garbage is the only raw material that we're too stupid to use. *–Arthur C. Clarke*

Dealing with ever-growing mountains of trash is a problem. People throw out too much stuff, including recyclables and perfectly good items that have plenty of useful life left in them. Instead of continuing down the same road and building more incinerators and landfills, why don't we reduce the amount of waste we produce in the first place? The following sections are chock-full of strategies that'll help you throw away less stuff.

If the current system of buying things, using them once or for a while, and then throwing them away creates too much waste, maybe the problem is the system. That's what people in the *zero-waste movement* argue. They take the concept of "reduce, reuse, recycle" to a whole new level. The idea is to cut waste as much as possible, preferably *all the way*—so "zero waste" isn't just an attention-getting name; the folks in this movement really mean it.

In nature, nothing goes to waste. In the fall, for example, it may look like leaves "litter" the forest floor, but those leaves turn into humus (page 30), which enriches the soil and helps plants grow. Zero-waste fans want to apply the same principle to garbage, which they like to call "potential resources" or "residual products" instead. They want to stamp out waste and come up with a whole new way of managing resources.

The old-school way of doing things, sometimes called the "cradle-to-grave" approach, starts with an item's production. That item gets sold, used, and then thrown away. Zero-waste advocates take a "cradle-to-cradle" approach, which means that every used product can become a new resource. Each stage in an item's lifecycle offers opportunities for increasing efficiency, reusing or recycling resources, and eliminating waste.

For example, think of a pickle jar. In the cradle-to-grave approach, a company makes silicon dioxide (that's the fancy name for sand) into glass and shapes the glass into a jar. Next, the jar gets filled with pickles and lands on your store's shelf. You buy the jar, eat the pickles, and toss the jar in the trash, and then the jar makes its final journey to a landfill (its "grave").

By contrast, here's the cradle-to-cradle approach: The jar begins life the same way, but after you eat the pickles, you rinse out the jar and use it as a vase for cut flowers from your garden. At the end of the growing season, put it in your recycling bin so it's no longer trash—it's a resource. It might get washed out and filled with a fresh batch of pickles, or smashed up and recycled into a jar, bottle, fiberglass, ceramic tile, concrete, or even sand to replenish an eroded beach. Reusing and recycling old jars means that fewer jars need to be made in the first place.

Note According to the National Recycling Coalition, glass is infinitely recyclable: It never wears out.

Zero waste aims to use energy and resources 100% efficiently. That goal applies to all the ways people use resources (both natural and manmade): manufacturers, retailers, transportation companies, consumers, communities, schools, and so on. Whether you're working to reduce piles of paper at work or the amount of stuff you throw out at home, any change you make helps nudge the world closer to zero waste.

Tip To learn more about zero waste or get involved, visit the Zero Waste Alliance's site at *www.zerowaste.org*.

Reducing: Doing More with Less

Whether your goal is zero waste or just sending less garbage to the landfill, a way to start is by reducing the amount of stuff in your life. Think about it: The less that comes into your house, the less gets thrown out. This section focuses decluttering, cutting back on packaging, and keeping out junk you don't want in the first place.

Clearing Out Clutter

An important first step in cutting down waste is changing your attitude toward stuff, which may be harder than you think. Most people in developed countries own far more things than they actually use, need, or even want. If old clothes, kitchenware, knickknacks, magazines, and other items are crammed into your closets or piled up in the basement, it's time to give yourself a little breathing room. If you're storing perfectly good items that you'll never use (or use again), you're cluttering up your life *and* keeping other people from having those things. Sell, donate, or recycle stuff you're not using to free up space and simplify your life.

The best way to attack clutter is one area at a time, so you don't feel over-whelmed. Cleaning out one closet or one junk drawer will give you one more decluttered space—and a sense of accomplishment. To get started, grab four boxes (three if you aren't planning on selling any of your cast-offs), and label them:

- **Give away.** This box is for items you'll donate to charity, give to friends or relatives, or simply hand to the first person who wants them. (Page 99 has suggestions of where to donate stuff.)

- **Recycle.** Put recyclable stuff in here, and sort it later using the guide-lines on page 105.

- **Sell.** Things you want to sell through a consignment shop or yard sale go here. Be sure to drop them off at the shop or hold the yard sale *soon*. You want to turn clutter into money—not just move it into a box that becomes clutter itself.

- **Throw away.** You'll undoubtedly find items you can't sell, recycle, or give away, like old cosmetics, expired medications, cleaning products you've replaced with green alternatives (page 15), and so on.

> **Note** If you're getting rid of household chemicals, old paint, fluorescent bulbs, or similar items, *don't* just toss them in the trash—they're hazardous waste. Check with your city to find out how to dispose of them properly. Or go to *http://earth911.com* and type in the kind of thing you're throwing out and your Zip to learn where to discard the item in your area.

As you look around your house, some clutter is obvious; start with that to make a difference everyone can see. You'll enjoy the new, streamlined look of your spiffed-up room. Then start tackling other areas. Here are some places where clutter tends to accumulate:

- **Closets.** Many people have clothes they haven't worn in years pushed to the back of closets, shelves, and dresser drawers. Anything that doesn't fit anymore or that you haven't worn in a year is a candidate for weeding out. That doesn't mean you have to toss your wedding dress or high-school varsity jacket—sentimental value counts for something. But so does making extra space for clothes you wear now.

- **Under beds.** All kinds of things can make their way under beds and other furniture. Pull out whatever's hiding among the dust bunnies, and then decide whether to keep it or get rid of it.

- **Kitchen cupboards.** Do you have expired food; pots, pans, or utensils you never use; or maybe a crock pot or toaster that you forgot about taking up space? Take a look at what's in your cupboards—going *all* the way to the back.

- **Bathroom cabinets.** Here, you're likely to find expired medications and cosmetics, past-their-prime sponges and cleaning products, and ratty old towels that would be more useful as cleaning rags.

Tip Decluttering is a perfect excuse to organize. For example, refill the medicine cabinet only with those items you use every day and need within easy reach.

- **Basement, attic, and/or garage.** It's not uncommon for these areas to hold stacks of boxes that you never unpacked the last time you moved. If that's the case, think about whether you'll ever to use what's in those boxes. Clear out any unused furniture, boxes of old kids' clothes or toys, half-empty cans of paint, and chemicals like insect spray, varnish, and cleaning products (and replace them with healthy, natural alternatives—see page 16).

- **Junk drawers.** They're called "junk drawers" for a reason: They accumulate years' worth of stuff—a lot of it useless. But you may find some useful stuff in there, along with things to throw out or donate.

Tip After you go through a junk drawer, organize it so it doesn't get jumbled again. An easy way to do that is to cut up old cereal boxes and other cardboard and create in-drawer storage containers from them.

- **Home office.** More than a third of the trash people throw out is paper (see page 78), so it's likely your office is getting buried under an avalanche of the stuff, much of which is recyclable. Shred anything with sensitive info that you wouldn't want in the wrong hands, like old credit card bills.

As you sort through your stuff, ask yourself:

- Have I used this in the past year?
- Realistically, will I use this again? (Don't say "could I," say "will I"!)
- If I think I might need this again, what would I use it for? (Be specific.)
- Do I love this?
- What's would be the worst consequence if I never saw this item again?

Keep this list of questions at hand as you work, so you won't forget them. Answering them honestly will help you decide which things truly help you or enrich your life and which are just taking up space.

> **Tip** If you've got lots of clutter, clearing out even one small area may feel too big to handle. In that case, try setting a timer for 15 minutes, and then do as much as you can in that time. When the timer goes off, you'll have made progress, and you may even be inspired to keep going.

Decreasing Consumption

One sure-fire way to reduce the amount of waste your household produces is to consume less stuff. That doesn't mean taking a vow of poverty or depriving yourself of things you enjoy, just being mindful of what you consume. For example, instead of buying four new shirts just because they're on sale and then dumping them in the closet and forgetting they're there, think about what you're buying and why. That'll help you buy only the things you actually need or want, which means less clutter and less waste.

Consider these numbers:

- Americans make up less than 5% of the world's population but consume about 25% of the world's oil, 23% of its coal, 33% of its paper, 27% of its aluminum, and 19% of its copper.
- Together, North America and western Europe account for about 12% of the global population but consume 60% of the world's goods and resources. At the other end of the spectrum, about 33% of the planet's people live in South Asia and sub-Saharan Africa, yet they consume little more than 3% of the worldwide total.

- Americans throw away about 200,000 *tons* of perfectly good food each day.

- In the U.S., the amount of money each household spends on goods and services has quadrupled since 1960.

- Back in the 1960s, Americans saw about 560 commercial messages every day; today we're barraged by about 1,500 ads each day.

- Excessive consumption can make you sick: A 2000 study found that people with a high ratio of credit card debt to income were in worse physical health than people with less debt.

Clearly, people in developed countries like the U.S. and most of Europe use far more than their fair share of resources and produce more than their fair share of waste. So when you cut back on consumption, you help the planet in two ways: conserving resources and reducing waste. And it might even help lower stress level and improve your health.

One easy way to consume less is simply to think before you buy. Many people buy stuff just because it's on sale or catches their eye at the checkout. Before you pull out your credit card or plunk down some cash, ask yourself, "Do I really need this?" and "What would I use it for?" These questions may help you put things you don't really need back on the shelf.

> **Tip** Keeping your hands off the merchandise can help, too. A study published in 2009 found that people were much more likely to buy something if they held the item for as little as 30 seconds.

Here are some other ways to buy less:

- **Set up a budget.** Figure out how much essentials like food, housing, utilities, transportation, and so on cost you each month. Set a monthly savings goal and budget in fun items, too. Sticking to a budget makes you more aware of where your money goes and calls attention to extra spending.

- **Pay with cash.** When you use a credit card, it's easy to lose track of how much you spend. Paying *only* with cash can help you stay within your budget and make fewer impulse purchases. So leave the credit cards at home—or cut them up.

- **Keep a spending journal.** For a month, write down *everything* you buy: the item, where you bought it and when, and how much it cost. At the month's end, review the list to learn about how you shop. For example, do you indulge in "retail therapy" when you have a bad day? Try meditating, doing yoga, taking a walk instead—anything that doesn't cost money. Or maybe you're an impulse buyer who goes into a store for one item and comes out with a bag full of stuff. If so, try writing down what you need before you leave the house, and then stick to that list when you're in the store.

- **Go for quality over quantity.** Disposable cultures emphasize buying lots of cheap stuff—and then tossing it when you no longer need it. Sustainable cultures, on the other hand, emphasize well made goods that last. Insist on durability and reliability. This applies when you're shopping for things like cars, clothing, electronics, or furniture. As page 91 notes, there are other times when it makes sense to buy in bulk.

Tip To move toward zero waste, get smaller trash cans. Having less space to hold trash makes you more aware of what you're throwing out.

Rejecting Wasteful Packaging

Sometimes it seems like what we buy is more packaging than product. Whether the item is hidden inside a box or sealed in a plastic clamshell, boxes and wrappings that look good on the shelf often end up in landfills. Reduce waste from unnecessary packaging by:

- **Voting with your wallet.** When you're choosing between two products, go for the one with less packaging. For example, when you're shopping for cereal, buy the kind that comes in a bag rather than a bag-inside-a-box. If you're buying a teddy bear or doll, pick one with a simple tag over one strapped inside a cardboard or plastic container.

- **Choosing earth-friendly packaging.** Recycled and recyclable wrapping is better than the kind you have to throw out. Sustainable packaging, such as that made from *bioplastics,* is also catching on. Bioplastics aren't made from petrochemicals but from renewable, natural materials like corn, potatoes, and sugarcane—and they're compostable, too.

When you're buying food plastic containers, make sure the plastic is coded 1, 2, 4, or 5, which are easy to recycle. (The table on page 107 explains these codes.) Many recycling centers don't accept plastics coded 3 or 6—which means they end up in landfills. Code 7 is a miscellaneous category; avoid it *unless* the container is labeled as a bioplastic.

- **Buying in bulk.** For foods you use a lot of, visit the bulk section of your grocery store. If the kids eat a lot of cereal, for example, buy one giant-sized box rather than two or three normal boxes. Same goes for economy sizes of everything from toilet paper to laundry detergent to condiments—you get more product with less packaging (and save money, too). Just don't buy more than you'll use, or you'll end up throwing away some of the product as well as what it came in.

Note Some retailers take advantage of consumers' desire to buy economy-sized products and actually *overcharge* for them. Check unit prices (which tells you how much the product costs by the pound or ounce) to make sure that economy-sized is the best buy.

- **Avoiding individually packaged items.** Frozen dinners, prepackaged kids' lunches, sliced cheese, snack cakes, chips—all these individually wrapped items have a lot of unnecessary, wasteful packaging.

- **Saying no to paper** *and* **plastic.** Instead of lugging purchases home in new bags each time you shop, take reusable bags with you to the store. The U.S. EPA says that Americans use more than 380 *billion* plastic bags, sacks, and wrappers each year—mostly single-use bags that end up in landfills.

Tip If you do use the store's bags, bring them back next time you shop for another go-round. Many stores also offer plastic bag–recycling programs; ask the folks at the service desk whether they do.

- **Using refillable cups.** Instead of buying a coffee and then throwing away the paper cup it came in, get a refillable coffee mug. Some coffee shops have clubs where you buy a mug and get discounts on refills.

- **Choosing sit-down restaurants over fast-food places**. Eateries that wash their dishes and silverware produce a lot less waste than ones that wrap everything in paper, plastic, or foam. When you do grab fast food, ask for it on a tray, and then pack it in your own reusable lunch bag. Also, skip the straw and use your own (washable) utensils. Cloth napkins are better than paper (keep one packed in your reusable bag), but if you're grabbing paper napkins, take just one or two, not a big handful.

- **Leaving doggy bags behind.** When you have leftovers, ask your server to wrap them in aluminum foil instead of a box. Then clean and recycle the foil.

> **Note** Some companies are working to curtail wasteful packaging. In a dozen European countries, for example, the Green Dot symbol indicates that the packager has contributed financially to the cost of recycling that container. In 2008, Wal-Mart launched a "packaging scorecard," with the goal of using more sustainable materials in and reducing packaging overall. And Amazon.com's Frustration-Free Packaging program replaces clamshells and other plastic containers with easy-to-open, recyclable alternatives. (For a list of the products in Amazon.com's program—currently toys and electronics—head to *http://tinyurl.com/59b7kn*.)

Ditching Junk Mail

More than 100 billion pieces of junk mail (called "direct marketing" by the companies who send it) get sent in the U.S. each year, for a total of just over 40 pounds of unwanted mail per adult. And these unwanted credit card offers, catalogs, and sales letters are more than just a nuisance:

- The paper used for junk mail causes the destruction of 100 million trees annually, including more than 74,000 acres of trees for catalogs alone.

- Creating, shipping, and disposing of junk mail produces more green-house gas emissions than 9 million cars.

- For each piece of personal mail your receive (letters, bills, magazines you subscribe to, and so on), you get about 18 pieces of junk mail.

- Nearly half of all junk mail gets thrown away unread. Even so, over the course of a lifetime, the average American spends 8 months to open-ing junk mail. Don't you have better things to do with your time?

- It takes about 28 billion gallons of water to produce a year's worth of junk mail.

When you get unsolicited mail, drop it in the recycling bin. (If it's a credit card offer or something similar, be sure to shred it first.) That deals with the stuff you received, but you help the environment even more by reducing the amount of junk mail you get in the first place. To do that, register with one of these services:

- **Catalog Choice** (*www.catalogchoice.org*). After you sign up for this free service, you submit the names of catalogs you don't want, along with info like your customer number. Participating companies promise to take you off their mailing lists within 12 weeks.

- **The Privacy Council** (*http://privacycouncil.org*). Sign up once and get your name off lists at the Direct Marketing Association (a trade group for the folks who send you junk mail), coupon outfits like Advo and ValPak, credit card companies, and more. This service costs $9.

- **41pounds.org** (*www.41pounds.org*). This nonprofit organization is named after the amount of unwanted mail each American adult gets every year. It charges $41 for a five-year membership and guarantees to reduce your junk mail by 80–95%.

- **Tonic MailStopper** (*http://mailstopper.tonic.com*). This service costs $20 a year and works with more than 6,500 direct marketers to reduce the junk mail you receive by up to 90%. MailStopper plants five trees for each person who joins.

- **DMAchoice** (*www.dmachoice.org*). The Direct Marketing Association (which runs this website) knows that marketing is most effective when it reaches people who are interested. When you register with the site, indicate what kinds of marketing you don't want: credit offers, catalogs, magazine offers, and other mail offers. DMAchoice keeps your preferences for three years and you can change 'em anytime. In 2008, this service stopped 930 million pieces of junk mail from getting sent.

Note: If you live in Canada, register for the Canadian Marketing Association's Do Not Contact list; visit *www.the-cma.org* and click the right-hand CMA Do Not Contact Service link. In the UK, register with the DMA's Mail Preference Service at *www.mpsonline.org.uk/mpsr*.

Or you can take a more do-it-yourself approach to reducing junk mail:

- **Contact customer service.** When you get a catalog you don't want, call the company and ask them to take you off their mailing list, or visit their website and ask to be removed (look in the Customer Service or Contact Us section of the site). Be sure to have the catalog handy; you'll need info from the mailing label.

- **Opt out of credit card and insurance offers.** Ever wonder how all those preapproved credit card offers flooding your mailbox know enough to approve you? They buy mailing lists of people who meet certain criteria from one of the credit reporting companies: Experian, Equifax, Innovis, or TransUnion. To keep your name off such lists, call 1-888-5-OPT-OUT (that's 1-888-567-8688) or register at *www.optoutprescreen.com;* either option takes care of all four credit bureaus.

- **Tell companies not to sell your name.** Every time you fill out a warranty card, enter a raffle, make a donation, or order something, tell the organization that it's *not* okay for them to give your name and address to other companies. Memorize these magic words: *Please do not rent, sell, or trade my name or address.* When you order by phone, say that phrase to the customer service agent and ask him to flag your account. When you fill out things like warranty cards magazine subscription cards, write those words on the form, even though there's no line for them.

> **Tip** Save yourself some typing by heading to this book's Missing CD page at *www. missingmanuals.com,* where you'll find links to all the websites listed above—and everywhere else in this book.

Reusing: Use It Again, Sam

New York City began collecting trash in 1905. In the hundred years that followed, the amount of trash people threw away increased by *13 times,* from 92 pounds per person each year to a whopping 1,242 pounds. Throughout the western hemisphere, the 20th century saw the growth of disposable societies, where consumerism and the ease of throwing things out combined to create literal mountains of trash. In such a society, people are taught that it's easier to throw things away than to fix them, use them again, or find a new use for them.

But much of what people throw out is still perfectly good. In the "reduce, reuse, recycle" mantra, *reuse* means not tossing out stuff that's still useful or fixable. Think about what people throw away: out-of-fashion clothes, electronics, food containers, toys, furniture, building materials. Next trash day, check out what people leave out on the curb—some of it might surprise you.

There are two main ways to reuse stuff:

- *Repurposing*—finding new uses for things you have.
- Finding people who want the stuff you don't.

The following pages suggest a zillion ways to do both (give or take a jillion).

Repurposing: New Uses for Old Stuff

Repurposing requires a little imagination. Instead of dropping something in the trash without a second thought, take a minute to figure out whether you could use it again. Here are some examples to get your creative juices flowing:

- Have a garden? Use **yogurt containers** or **egg cartons** to start seedlings. Or prick pinholes in the lid of a **cottage-cheese container** and then use the container to water the growing seeds.

- Use old **pantyhose** or strips of **socks** to tie plants to stakes. The stretchy material won't strangle the plants as they grow.

- The **foil pie plates** from frozen pot pies are just the right size for holding flowerpots (old plates also work well).

- Get organized with clean **glass jars**, which can hold everything from pens to spare change to beads. They also make fun shabby-chic vases.

- If last year's school **backpacks** are still in one piece, hang them on hooks to use as storage.

- The wide **rubber bands** that hold bunches of broccoli or other produce together make great, grippy jar openers.

- Reuse those little green **strawberry baskets** as storage containers or small gift baskets. Or put them to work in your garden: Turn 'em upside down over seeds or seedlings to protect them from birds and other hungry critters.

- Instead of throwing away **sandwich bags** and other **food-storage bags**, wash them with hot, soapy water, turn them inside out to dry, and then use them again. (*Don't* reuse bags that have held meat, raw or cooked.)

- Old **toothbrushes** are handy for cleaning grout, shining up jewelry, and getting the grime out of tight corners.

- Cut up old **t-shirts** and other clothing to reuse as cleaning cloths.

- Orphaned **socks** are good for all kinds of things: Fill them with potpourri (page 24) and use them to freshen drawers, slip them over golf clubs, knot several together for a dog toy, or use them as dusters.

- After **fabric softener sheets** have been through the dryer, use them to clean scorch marks off your iron. (When the iron is cool, of course!)

- Cut up an old **shower curtain liner** and use it to line drawers or shelves.

- Cardboard paper-towel or **toilet-paper tubes** can tame unruly electrical cords. Or fill them with lint from the dryer and use them to get a fire going in your wood stove.

- Sew the bottom of an old **tank-top shirt** shut to make a bag.

- Glue **wine corks** onto quarter-inch plywood to make a bulletin board.

- Reuse the **wire hangers** you get from the dry cleaner. If you have too many, return them on your next trip.

- When you buy a **plastic-net bag** of onions, put the bag to work as a scrubber for pots and pans.

- If you're the crafty type, *ReadyMade* magazine's project archive (*http://readymade.com/projects*) has tons of ideas for fun and funky repurposing, such as a lazy susan made from a bicycle wheel, a blanket made from old sweaters, and a candlestick made from shower knobs. And Etsy (*www.etsy.com*), a marketplace site for handmade items, has forums, blogs, and online classes packed with repurposing ideas and inspiration.

Tip If you've got a lot of empty plastic shopping bags lying around, fuse them together into a craft material you can use to make reusable shopping bags, placemats, waterproof liners for beach bags, and so on. Etsy has a good step-by-step tutorial at *http://tinyurl.com/2b6gpm*.

- Imagination Factory's Trash Matcher (*www.kid-at-art.com/htdoc/matchtmp.html*) has more craft ideas, with an emphasis on great projects for kids. Click a material you've got (such as brown grocery bags, crayon scraps, junk mail, and so on) to get detailed instructions for using it in a craft project.

- Empty **egg cartons** can store beads, sewing supplies, nuts and bolts, and other small items. Or use them as paint-mixing trays.

- Reuse **paper** that's got printing on one side for scrap paper, notes, and so on.

This list isn't even *close* to exhaustive; it's just to get you thinking about how to use old objects in new ways. Once you start thinking outside the box (or in this case, outside the trash can), you'll come up with all kinds of ways to give old stuff new life.

Tip Repurposeful is a blog devoted to "finding new uses for everyday things," and it has a ton of helpful suggestions. Check it out at *http://repurposeful.wordpress.com*.

Trash to Treasure: Sell It, Donate It, Give It Away

You never know what someone else will find useful. Even if you can't imagine anyone wanting the hideous bridesmaid's dress or less-than-tasteful neckties lurking in your closet, try to give them away before you throw them away. (Crafty types might make pillow cases from the dress or a skirt from the neckties.)

Whether you sell your surplus stuff, donate it to a good cause, or simply give it away, you're keeping perfectly good items out of landfills and cutting back on the amount spent on producing and transporting new goods.

Tip Reusing works both ways: The tips in this section for getting rid of things you don't want are also worth checking out when you're in the market to buy stuff.

Sell it

What could be better than doing your part to save the planet *and* putting a little cash in your pocket? Finding people who want to buy your used items is easy. Try one of these options:

- **Consignment shop.** Check the yellow pages for stores that sell used goods on consignment. These places sell everything from clothing and antiques to household goods (many specialize in a particular kind of stuff). When a consignment shop accepts your stuff, they do all the work for you—price the items, put them on display, staff the store, and make the sale. Then you get a percentage of each item's sale price.

- **Classified ad.** Call your local newspaper to check rates and run your ad. (If the cost of the ad would cut into your profit too much, see the next option.)

- **Craigslist.** You've probably heard of Craigslist; it's an online classified-ad site that lets you list most stuff for free. From the Craigslist home page (*www.craigslist.org*), find your city, state, or country to make sure your ad reaches local people. Choose a category, and then click the upper-right "post" link to create your ad.

Tip Be sure to include a photo of what you're selling in your Craigslist ad. People are more likely to respond if they know what the item looks like.

- **The Recycler's Exchange** (*www.recycle.net/exchange*). This site lists companies and people who buy, sell, or trade goods and materials. Its European site is *http://euro.recycle.net/exchange*.

- **eBay.** The world's largest online auction site makes it easy for you to reach of millions of potential buyers. For free tutorials on how to get started selling, go to *http://pages.ebay.com/education/selling.html*.

Tip eBay is international, with sites in more than two dozen countries. To see whether there's an eBay site for your country, go to *www.ebay.com* and scroll to the bottom of the page. If your country is listed, click its name to open the local site.

- **Yard or garage sale.** Here's a satisfying way to sell a lot of stuff at once. Or get several families to work together to hold a neighborhood yard sale. Yard-sale shoppers are looking for bargains, so don't price your items too high and be prepared to haggle. Lower prices as the day goes on, and be willing to give whatever's left away for free at the end of the sale. (Remember, your goal isn't to make a fortune; it's to get rid of this stuff without throwing it away.) If anything's left over, donate it to one of the groups described in the next section.

Donate it

Many nonprofits gladly take unwanted items off your hands and resell them in thrift stores. Some of these organizations also use your donations to provide training and employment to people in need. In most areas, there are lots of places that will accept donations. Ask around, check in the phone book under "Thrift Stores," or look into one of these options:

- **Goodwill Industries** (*www.goodwill.org*). Their main mission is to provide employment and training—and they do a good job of it, too, serving more than 1 million people through various programs. Goodwill has more than 2,200 stores across the U.S. and Canada, as well as online auctions (*www.shopgoodwill.com*). To find a store near you, visit *http://locator.goodwill.org*.

- **The Salvation Army** (*www.salvationarmy.org*). This Christian organization has programs in more than 100 countries. On their main webpage, use the "Select your Country" drop-down list to get to the site for your country and learn more about local programs and find a donation center or thrift store near you.

- **National Thrift Store Directory** (*www.thethriftshopper.com*). Type in your Zip code or city and state to find stores large and small in your area, and read other shoppers' store reviews or post your own.

- **Local religious organizations.** Many congregations raise money for programs in their communities by accepting and reselling clothes and household items.

> **Tip** In the U.S. and elsewhere, you can deduct the value of charitable donations from your taxes. When you donate, ask for a receipt and keep it with your tax records.

Give it away

If there's stuff cluttering up your life that you just want *gone* and you don't care about making money off it or getting a tax deduction, it's easy to give it away to someone who can use it. Regift new items, ask your friends if they could use any of the stuff you're giving away, or put items out on the curb with a sign that says FREE. (Some cities frown on this last practice, so make sure it's okay in your area before carrying items to the curb.)

If those options don't work, use one of these websites to match up your items with people who want them:

- **The Freecycle Network** (*www.freecycle.org*). This is a worldwide network of local groups where you can advertise items you want to give away. Membership is free, but you need a Yahoo account (also free) to join because Freecycle groups, which are moderated by local volunteers, are run through Yahoo Groups. Rules vary by group, but one general rule is that no money changes hands—everything on the Freecycle Network has to be really and truly free. It also has to be legal, suitable for all ages, and yours to give away. (Sorry, no trading your nephew for a stereo.)

- **FreeMesa** (*www.freemesa.org*). Similar to the Freecycle network, FreeMesa lets you advertise stuff you're giving away and things you'd like to get for free. It has over 18,000 participating local groups in more than 90 countries.

- **Craigslist** (*www.craigslist.org*). Find your local page by selecting a country, city, state, or region from the right side of the page. In the middle of the resulting page, the "for sale" category has a "free" subcategory. Click it to browse listings, or click the upper-right "post" link to list your giveaways.

- **Classified ad.** Your local newspaper probably has a Free section in its classifieds—and putting an ad in this section is usually free.

> **Tip** When you advertise what you're giving away, be specific. For example, don't just give your Craigslist ad a heading that says, "Random free stuff." Someone who's looking for a second-hand toaster oven may not click that heading to see what's on offer. But if your heading says, "Toaster oven, dishes, bath towels, other household items," you've got a much better chance of finding a recipient quickly.

Recycling: What Goes Around Comes Around

Recycling is a good idea that's been around for a while. Modern recycling was born in the environmental movement of the 1960s and '70s.

To coincide with the very first Earth Day—April 22, 1970—the Container Corporation of America, a major producer of recycled paperboard, sponsored a contest for art and design students to create a logo that symbolized the recycling process. UCLA student Gary Dean Anderson won with his triple-arrow design that has become one of the most recognized symbols on the planet.

In the 1970s, concern over rising energy costs led companies to consider recycling as a way to save money. Combined with a growing interest in protecting the environment and concerns over pollution and wasteful use of resources, the recycling movement gained momentum. Beginning in the early '70s, cities and towns passed recycling laws, arranged for curbside recycling pick-up, and set up recycling drop-off centers. States and countries banned certain kinds of recyclable materials from landfills and passed bottle-bill laws to encourage recycling of bottles and aluminum cans. Many companies and schools set up on-site recycling containers for paper, glass, and cans. The recycling movement has made it easy to recycle today—at work, at school, and at home.

Is Recycling Worth It?

Many people recycle without thinking twice about it. But have you ever wondered how much it costs to recycle stuff, how much it helps the environment, and whether it's really worth it? Well, you're about to find out.

Does recycling actually save energy?

It obviously takes energy to recycle. The process involves sorting, processing, and transporting materials. So does recycling save more energy than it uses? Consider these facts:

- It takes 95% less energy to get aluminum from recycled cans than it does to process aluminum from bauxite.

- Recycling plastic bottles uses about 70–75% less energy than creating new ones from scratch.

- It takes about 60% less energy to recycle steel than to mine iron ore and produce new steel.

- Recycling paper uses about 40–45% less energy than making new paper from trees (and each three-foot-high stack of newspaper you recycle saves one tree).

- Recycling glass uses about 21% less energy than producing new glass.

As these figures show, the answer is a resounding yes. Plus, recycling fosters a cradle-to-cradle approach to resources (page 84).

Does recycling really reduce greenhouse gas emissions?

Hand in hand with the issue of energy savings is the question of whether recycling keeps greenhouse gases out of the atmosphere and helps to reduce global warming. Again, the answer is yes: Materials produced from recycled steel, copper, glass, and paper have net carbon emissions *four to five times lower* than when those things are produced from virgin materials. For paper, we're talking 73% less and for aluminum, 95% less.

According the U.S. EPA, increasing America's recycling rate from its current rate of 32% to 35% would reduce greenhouse gas emissions by 5.2 million metric tons each year compared to what would be emitted if those recyclables were buried in landfills. That's the equivalent of taking more than 3.7 million cars off the road.

Does recycling save money?

Now we come to the bottom line: What's the economic impact of recycling? For manufacturers, recycling is good news, because it's cheaper and requires less energy to use recycled materials than to produce new ones from scratch. Industries that benefit from recycling include steel mills, companies that work with nonferrous metals (like aluminum), paper and paperboard mills, and plastic converters. Take aluminum cans as an example. Making one ton of aluminum requires nearly 9,000 pounds of bauxite and 1,020 pounds of petroleum coke as fuel. Recycling aluminum, on the other hand, requires 95% less raw material and 90% less energy.

Another benefit to companies is increased demand: When people like you buy recycled products, you support the manufacturers' recycled product line. That's a great example of voting with your wallet. Recycling is also good for the economy because it creates jobs: According to the National Recycling Coalition, in the U.S. alone, the $236-billion-a-year recycling industry employs 1.1 million workers at more than 56,000 recycling centers.

Now that you know more about recycling's benefits, it's time to focus on the nitty-gritty details of giving your old stuff new life by recycling.

Recycling Basics

There's a reason that recycling is the last leg of the "reduce, reuse, recycle" formula: If you reduce consumption, you'll have less used stuff to deal with. And if you get creative about reusing, you'll have still less to throw out or recycle. So follow those priorities: reduce first, reuse what you have, and *then* recycle what you don't need and can't think of a use for. This section covers recycling basics to help you set up or fine-tune your recycling system.

Know what to recycle

According to the National Institute of Environmental Health Sciences, you should always recycle (or reuse, when appropriate), these items:

- Acid batteries
- Aluminum cans
- Aluminum foil
- Appliances
- Building materials
- Cardboard
- Chemicals
- Compact fluorescent lamps (CFLs)
- Electronic equipment
- Glass (especially jars and bottles)
- Lead
- Metal
- Oil
- Paint

- Paper (magazines, newspapers, writing/copy paper)
- Plastic bags and bottles
- Steel cans
- Tires
- Wood
- Yard waste

Some of those things—like batteries, chemicals, paint, and oil—require special handling, so don't just leave them at the curb with your other recyclables. Call your city's recycling company or go to Earth911.com (*http://earth911.com*) to find out which materials need special treatment and where to take them.

Set up your system

The key to succeeding at recycling is to make it easy. If you're lucky enough to live in an area that offers ***single-stream recycling***, you don't need to do any sorting at all. More waste-disposal companies are starting to offer this option, but in many places you still have to separate your recyclables by material. If you need to sort, create a series of different bins for the various materials to build sorting right in to your system. Put the bins where you have easy access to them but they're not underfoot. If space is at a premium, stash them under the kitchen sink or set them on an under-the-counter cupboard that pulls out.

Tip Label your recycling bins so there's no confusion about what goes where.

Some areas make you use certain kinds of bins (usually blue or green ones) for recyclables. If you live in such a place, check with your town's waste department to find out where to get them. Other places let you use your own containers: plastic bins, wastebaskets—whatever. When picking a container, keep these tips in mind:

- Plastic bins last longer than cardboard boxes, and you can wash 'em. On the other hand, reusing empty cardboard boxes is a step toward zero waste, and when a cardboard bin wears out, you can recycle it.

- For newspapers and other paper products, choose a bin that's big enough for the newspapers to lie flat so it's easy to bundle them.

- When deciding how big a bin to get, think about how often you recycle. If you recycle frequently, a big container may take up space that you could use for something else.

- If you compost food scraps (page 193), choose a bin with a secure lid that will minimize odors and keep out insects and mice.

Sort smart

Different areas have different rules about sorting, so check with your city for guidelines. (As mentioned earlier, some places don't require any sorting at all; if you live in one of those spots—you lucky dog, you—you can skip this section.) In general, waste companies can deal with the following kinds of recyclables, each sorted into its own bin:

- **Paper.** Most kinds of paper are recyclable, including newspapers, magazines, phone books, catalogs, office paper, folders, paper envelopes, and cardboard. Bundle newspapers and flatten cardboard boxes. Glossy paper used to be excluded from recycling, but now most places accept it. You probably can't recycle food wrappers, carbon paper, used tissues and paper towels, or adhesive labels.

Tip Most paper can go into your compost pile. Page 191 tells you how to get started composting.

- **Glass.** Glass can be recycled over and over. Some places make you separate glass by color—clear, green, or brown. Rinse bottles and jars before you recycle them. (You used to have to remove labels, too, but most recycling centers no longer require this.) Many recycling centers don't accept lightbulbs, Pyrex, and safety glass; go to Earth911.com (*www.earth911.com*) to find a place near you that does. Compact fluorescent lamps (CFLs) need special handling when you recycle them (see page 75).

Tip In some places, you don't need to rinse bottles and cans. Call your local recycling center to find out—you might be able to conserve water as you recycle. If you do need to rinse these items, use gray water from washing dishes rather than fresh tap water.

- **Cans.** Wash out empty steel or aluminum cans (dirty ones may get rejected). Flatten them so they take up less space. You may also have to remove labels, so check your local guidelines

Tip Clean aluminum foil and aluminum pans (such as disposable pie or roasting pans) are also recyclable.

- **Yard waste.** Add yard waste to your compost pile (page 193) or take it to most recycling centers. Many cities schedule special pick-ups for things like autumn leaves or old Christmas trees.

- **Plastic.** Some kinds of plastic are easy to recycle, others are more difficult, and a few can't be recycled at all. To help you figure out what kind you're dealing with, look for the Plastic Identification Code, a number, from 1 to 7, which identifies the plastic. Table 3-1 shows what these codes mean. Types 1, 2, 4, and 5 are the easiest to recycle—1 and 2 are almost universally accepted by recycling programs. If you're trying to recycle another kind, call your recycling center or go to *www.earth911. com* to find out where to take it.

Tip Because 7 is a miscellaneous category, it includes the new bioplastics, which can be composted. So before you throw out a type-7 plastic, check to see if its label says it's a bioplastic.

Table 3-1. Recycling Plastic by the Numbers

Code	Type of Plastic	Where You'll Find It	Can Be Recycled Into
1	PET or PETE (polyethylene terephthalate)	Bottles for soft drinks, water, sports drinks, and jars for things like peanut butter.	Fiber, rope, fleece clothing, carpeting, tote bags, luggage, new bottles.
2	HDPE (high-density polyethylene)	Bottles for water, juice, shampoo, detergents, motor oil; shopping and trash bags; bags inside cereal boxes.	New bottles, toys, buckets, recycling bins, flower pots, tiles, benches, fencing and garden edging, plastic lumber.
3	PVC (polyvinyl chloride)	Pipes and medical tubing, shower curtains, car dashboards.	Packaging, building materials (paneling, gutters, flooring), traffic cones, garden hoses, mud flaps, plastic lumber.
4	LDPE (low-density polyethylene)	Bags for bread, frozen foods, and dry cleaning; sandwich bags and film for wrapping food; squeezable bottles.	Bags, trash-can liners, floor tile, plastic film.
5	PP (polypropylene)	Yogurt and margarine tubs; reusable storage containers; medicine bottles.	Car battery cases and cables, other car parts, brushes and brooms, ice scrapers, bins, pallets.
6	PS (polystyrene)	Meat and produce trays; egg cartons; hot-beverage cups; plastic utensils; packing peanuts.	Foam insulation, light-switch plates, cafeteria trays, egg cartons, foam packing, plates, cups, utensils.
7	Other plastics	Large, refillable water jugs. (This category includes compostable bioplastics.)	Bottles, plastic lumber.

Note: Each town and city has its own rules for curbside pick-up and drop-off sites (what kinds of materials they accept, for example). So find out the guidelines for your area.

More Tips for Easy and Effective Recycling

To get the most out of recycling, keep these things in mind:

- Find out whether your city offers curb-side pickup or makes you take recyclables to a drop-off center.

- If you have to drop them off, make the trip to the recycling center part of your routine. Schedule a regular day and combine the drop-off with other errands.

- Wheeled containers or a dolly makes it easier to move recycling bins around.

- The kitchen is probably where the most recyclable items get used. So if you store your recycling bins in another room, keep another bin in the kitchen to collect recyclables you'll sort later.

- Buy stuff that's easy to recycle. For example, choose glass containers over plastic ones, and buy recycled goods.

Note If every U.S. household replaced a roll of regular paper towels with a roll made from 100% recycled fibers, it would save 544,000 trees.

- Go online to find a recycling center near you. In the U.S., go to *www.earth911.com*; in the U.K., go to *www.recycle-more.co.uk*, and then click Bank Locator.

So Hard to Say Goodbye: Special Problems in Recycling

If you think breaking up is hard to do in relationships, just wait till you try to get rid of some of the items covered in this section. All of them *can* be recycled, but issues like cost, difficulty, or bulk may make your local recycling center say, "Thanks but no thanks" when you try to drop them off. Don't despair: This section tells you how to do the right thing and recycle these hard-to-get-rid-of items.

Polystyrene Foam

Polystyrene foam (what you probably call Styrofoam, which is a trademark owned by the Dow Chemical Company) is all around us—from hot-beverage cups and meat trays to insulation and packaging materials. This foam is mostly air, so while it's not heavy, it's *really* bulky. And because it doesn't biodegrade, it takes up lots of space in landfills and will be there pretty much forever.

Many curbside recycling programs don't take polystyrene foam. So what should you do with it? Here are some ideas:

- **Reuse it.** When you receive a box full of foam packing peanuts, don't throw them out. Reuse them when you mail stuff that needs cushioning, or offer them to a local company or mailing center, which may take them off your hands. Or use 'em in craft projects or donate them to a school or scout troop that can use them for such projects.

Tip If you ship a lot of items, don't buy foam packing peanuts. Instead, try Puffy Stuff (*http://puffystufftn.com*), an all-natural, plant-based packaging material that's 100% biodegradable.

- **Find a recycling center that accepts it.** Go to *www.earth911.com* and type in *polystyrene* and your Zip code to get a list of nearby centers that'll take it off your hands.

- **Mail it away.** If you can't recycle it locally, visit the Alliance of Foam Packaging Recyclers website (*www.epspackaging.org*) and click the Recycling Info Resources link. This takes you to a page that lists both drop-off and mail-in locations for polystyrene recyclers.

Tires

Tires and landfills are a bad combination: Tires are large and heavy, and their donut shape makes them take up a lot of room. They can also damage landfill liners, letting contaminant-filled leachate (page 80) leak out. Burning tires isn't an option because that releases toxic chemicals (including benzene and lead). According to the EPA, nearly 300 million tires are discarded in the U.S. each year—that's just about one for every American.

So what should you do when your tires wear out? It's important to dispose of them properly. Many tire shops and mechanics will take old tires (usually for a small fee) and send them to be recycled. Or call your waste management agency to find out how to recycle old tires and whether they charge to accept them.

Rubber is resilient and lasts a long time, so recycled tires go to a variety of uses:

- Some tires can be retreaded and hit the road again. A good-quality car tire can be retreaded and reused about three times before it's too worn for more retreading.

- Rubberized asphalt concrete (made of shredded, ground-up tires mixed with asphalt) is used to pave roads.

- Rubber granules from old tires make a springy, spongy surface for playgrounds.

- Materials made from recycled tires show up in lots of building and home-decorating materials, including carpets, floor tiles, structural supports, and shingles.

> **Note** One common use for old tires that's not so environmentally friendly is *tire-derived fuel* (TDF). The EPA estimates that about 45% of recycled tires become TDF. Industries that use TDF burn shredded tires along with coal or other fuels, which raises concerns about air pollution and health risks near such facilities. The Energy Justice Network campaigns against incinerating tires; go to *www.energyjustice.net/tires* to learn more.

Cellphones

Cellphone companies are always trying to sell you on their newest, slickest, thinnest, most feature-packed model. When you get a new cellphone, don't just throw the old one away. For one thing, it contains toxic metals, including lead, mercury, cadmium, and arsenic. For another, it could be refurbished and used by someone else. Even if your old phone is beyond repair, its components—including gold, copper, and plastic—can be extracted and recycled.

> **Note** The EPA estimates that 100 million cellphones go out of use each year. Recycling them would save enough energy to power 18,500 U.S. households for a whole year.

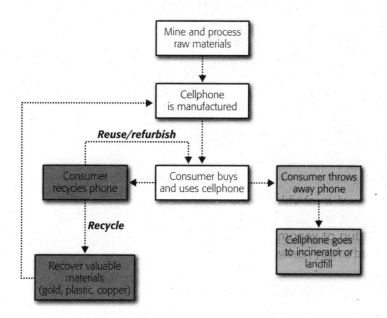

When it's time to hang up your old phone, you may be able to mail it back to the company that made it (check the manufacturer's website for instructions). Or consider one of these recycling options:

- Donate your phone to support a good cause:

  — **Cell Phones for Soldiers** (*www.cellphonesforsoldiers.com*) accepts donated phones and trades them to used-phone dealer Recellular for calling cards that U.S. soldiers stationed overseas can use to call home for free. There's also a Canadian version of this program: *www.cellphonesforsoldiers.ca*.

  — **HopeLine** (*http://tinyurl.com/9qu3wc*). Sponsored by Verizon, HopeLine collects cellphones and accessories and donates them to victims of domestic violence.

  — **Phones 4 Charity** (*www.phones4charity.org*) refurbishes phones and sends them to economically struggling areas in the U.S. and abroad.

  — **Recycling for Charities** (*www.recyclingforcharities.com*) lets you choose the charity you want to support with your donated phone, digital camera, or iPod.

- Raise money for a local cause or group. These organizations will help you organize a cellphone drive:

    — **Phoneraiser** (*www.phoneraiser.com*).

    — **Funding Factory** (*www.fundingfactory.com*).

    — **Ecophones** (*www.ecophones.com*).

    — **Shelter Alliance** (*www.shelteralliance.net*).

- If your phone still works and is a recent model, you may be able to put a few bucks in your pocket by selling it. These companies offer online quotes and live support:

    — **Gazelle** (*www.gazelle.com*).

    — **Pace Butler** (*www.pacebutler.com*).

    — **Cell for Cash** (*www.cellforcash.com*).

    — **Simply Sellular** (*www.simplysellular.com*).

> **Note** If you live in the U.K. and you want to recycle your phone, visit the Recycling Appeal's website at *www.recyclingappeal.com*.

E-Waste

It's called *e-waste*: computers, MP3 players, televisions, printers, cameras and the like that have stopped working or simply become obsolete, surrendering their place to newer, sleeker, more feature-rich models. The EPA estimates that such waste accounts for about 2% of municipal solid waste in the U.S. That may not sound like a whole lot until you consider that in 2007, all that e-waste added up to 2.5 million tons. And the amount of this kind of waste is steadily growing. In the United States alone, 130,000 computers get junked *every day*. It's no wonder that many charities limit or refuse donations of used computers and other e-waste.

Discarded electronics contain hazardous materials including lead, arsenic, cadmium, mercury, polyvinyl chlorides (PVCs), and brominated flame retardants (BFRs), which are suspected of causing a whole range of health problems, including brain damage and cancer. So when it's time to upgrade your computer or replace a TV that no longer works, you want to make sure those chemicals don't get into the environment.

With more and more electronics getting tossed out, it's becoming increasingly important to make sure they're reused or recycled properly. Here are some tips for making them into e-cyclables, not e-waste:

- **Choose your recycler with care.** Any company that accepts e-waste should reuse or recycle what they can and manage waste responsibly. But that's not always the case. Some of the stuff you take to a recycling center may end up in landfills, or get shipped to places like China or Nigeria, where it's dismantled in an unsafe and environmentally irresponsible way. To find a recycler who'll make sure your e-waste doesn't poison disadvantaged people or the earth, look for companies who've earned the Basel Action Network's e-Steward certification. This third-party program makes sure that a recycler doesn't dump toxic e-waste in landfills or burn it in incinerators, doesn't send it to developing countries or prison labor operations, documents where the e-waste goes, and destroys any private data stored on the discarded electronics. To learn more about this international program and get a list of certified e-Stewards, visit *www.e-stewards.org*.

- **Check with the manufacturer.** Many computer companies—including Apple, Dell, Gateway, Hewlett-Packard, and Sony—have recycling programs for their products. Some charge a fee, others require you to buy a new product from them before they'll take away the old one.

- **Check with retailers.** Stores such as Best Buy, Staples, and Office Max accept used electronics for recycling. They may charge a fee, but sometimes they offer special rebates on new equipment when you recycle your old electronics.

- **Ask questions.** Before you hand over your e-waste, make sure you get satisfactory answers to these important questions:

  — How do you destroy data that's currently on the machine? (If any personal data is lingering on the hard drive, you don't want it to end up in the wrong hands.)

  — Do you export any e-waste to developing countries?

  — Do you send any e-waste to incinerators or landfills?

  — Have you applied for e-Steward certification?

  — Do you ship any e-waste to programs or companies that use prison labor?

  — Do you donate used or refurbished electronics? If so, to which organizations do you donate?

- **Donate to Free Geek or a similar organization.** Free Geek, based in Portland, Oregon, is a nonprofit group that refurbishes donated computers and related technology and gives them to schools and other charitable organizations or sells them in its thrift shop. Anything Free Geek can't refurbish or sell for parts gets recycled responsibly. To find Free Geek programs in other states and Canada, visit *www.freegeek. org*; the site's Links page lists similar organizations around the world.

Appliances

Most appliances can be recycled for scrap metal. Here's how it works: The appliance gets torn to pieces by a giant shredder, magnets pull out iron-based metal, and then other metals such as aluminum get separated out from the detritus. Many appliances contain some materials, such the plastic liner in a dishwasher, that can't be recycled, but the process significantly reduces what gets thrown out.

Note Appliances containing Freon—including refrigerators, freezers, and air conditioners—require special handling. To find out where to recycle yours, check out Energy Star's Recycle page at *www.energystar.gov/recycle*.

Your garbage company may be set up to dispose of appliances, so give them a call to find out and see what special requirements they, if any. Some cities and utility companies offer rebates for recycling old appliances and replacing them with new, efficient, Energy Star models, so check for such programs in your area.

When you buy an appliance, the retailer may offer to take away your old one (possibly for a fee) when they deliver the new one. Ask what happens to appliances they collect, and find out whether they're a member of the U.S. EPA's Responsible Appliance Disposal (RAD) program. RAD is a voluntary partnership between utility companies, cities, retailers, manufacturers, and others to ensure that old appliances get scrapped responsibly. RAD partners agree to:

- Recover refrigerant, and then reuse or destroy it.

- Recover and destroy foam.

- Recycle metals, plastic, and glass.

- Recover and safely dispose of *polychlorinated biphenyls* (PCBs, chemicals linked to cancer, liver disease, and other ailments), mercury, and used oil.

Note According to the Steel Recycling Institute, back in 1988 only about 20% of appliances in the U.S. were recycled. By 2007, that number had soared to 90%.

Cars

When buying a new car, many people trade in their old one to get some credit toward the new one. The dealer then cleans up the old car and resells it. Everybody wins: You save money on your new car, the dealer makes a profit, and the person who buys the used car gets a road-worthy vehicle for less, and one less car goes to the junkyard.

If your car still has some life in it but won't get you much as a trade-in, consider donating it. Many charities accept cars and sell them to raise money. It's a great system: You support a good cause, get rid of a car you don't need, and get a tax deduction. If you're thinking of donating a car, keep these points in mind:

- The best way to donate your car is to find a charity you support and contact it directly to see whether it accepts cars.

- Watch out for middlemen who advertise on TV, in print, or online. Many of these companies take a big chunk—50% or more—of the profits from your donation.

- Be meticulous in your paperwork: Get a receipt, and if you plan to deduct more than $500 from your taxes, the IRS may want to see evidence showing how much the charity made from selling the car.

Finally, if your car is too old or broken down to donate, scrap it. Sell or give the old clunker to an auto wrecker, who will strip it of any parts that can be reused, then shred what's left and separate the pieces into:

- Ferrous metals like iron and steel.

- Nonferrous metals, such as zinc and aluminum.

- "Fluff," which includes remnants of the car's dashboard, carpet, seat cushions, carpeting, plastics, and so on.

The wrecker then sells the metals to companies that melt them down and reuse them. The fluff, considered unusable, goes to a landfill.

4 Building and Remodeling

Your dream house can be green, and we're not talkin' paint color here. Advances in construction technologies and materials can help you build the home of the future right now—one that's safe for your family, sips energy instead of gulping it, and is gentle on the earth. Green building standards can help you be sure that your contractor uses sustainable materials, pays extra attention to energy efficiency, and minimizes waste. If you already own a home, there are all kinds of remodeling projects that can help make it greener.

This chapter explains what makes a construction or remodeling project green. You'll also find out how to maximize energy efficiency and find a builder whose attitude toward the environment lines up with yours. Because green building can cost more up front than traditional construction—though you'll recoup some of the costs over time through energy savings—the chapter also explores special funding options for efficient and earth-friendly building projects.

Building green doesn't have to cost more if you're smart about planning. First, set a budget. Then, work with your architect and builder to determine your needs and set your priorities. For example, many people think they need more space than they actually use. Less square footage means lower building costs—and that you'll save money on heating, cooling, and lighting your home. Keep in mind, too, that some green features—like solar panels, a gray-water system, and composting toilets—can be installed later if they'd break your budget now. (And not everyone wants such extreme green solutions in their home.)

LEEDing the Way to Green Buildings

If you're in the market for a new house, the U.S. Green Building Council (USGBC, *www.usgbc.org*) has a rating system that can help you find a green one. This organization was founded in 1993 to promote energy efficiency and sustainability in the design, construction, and operation of homes and other buildings. Today, the USGBC has nearly 20,000 member organizations, including builders and contractors, architects, financial institutions, and just about anyone else involved in the construction industry. In 1998, the USGBC developed the Leadership in Energy and Environmental Design (LEED) Green Building Rating System, a set of standards for determining how green new buildings are. These standards rate construction projects' greenness in relation to these goals:

- Decreasing operating costs.
- Reducing the amount of waste sent to landfills.
- Conserving energy.
- Conserving water.
- Ensuring the building is safe and healthy for those who occupy it.
- Reducing greenhouse gas emissions.

The USGBC has a version of the LEED system specifically for homes (as opposed to commercial buildings, schools, and so on). The LEED for Homes rating system, which applies only to newly constructed buildings, has four certification levels (shown in Table 4-1). A building's rating is determined by the number of points it earns in these categories:

- **Innovative design process.** Sustainability begins before a structure is even built. This category evaluates how a building's plans integrate green technologies and techniques.
- **Location and linkages.** Where a home is built has an impact on the community and the environment. For example, this category awards points for situating a home near existing buildings and infrastructure and away from environmentally sensitive areas.
- **Sustainable sites.** This category focuses on things like keeping invasive plants out of the landscaping, managing surface water, and building in nontoxic pest control.
- **Water efficiency.** Buildings get points for rainwater harvesting (page 68) gray-water systems (page 38), and high-efficiency plumbing and watering systems.

- **Energy and atmosphere.** The more points a home has in this category, the lower your energy bill. The goal is to maximize efficiency—rating a home's Energy Star (page 43) performance for heating (both air and water) and cooling—and minimize greenhouse gas emissions.

Note A home can earn extra points in this category for using renewable power sources, like wind generators (page 127) or solar panels (page 125).

- **Materials and resources.** This one's about using efficient and earth-friendly materials. For example, the builder has to use FCS-certified lumber (page 28) and limit wood waste to 10% or less. They get points for locally produced and recycled building materials, too.

- **Indoor environmental quality.** You want the air in your home to be free of pollutants and toxins, including mold. Homes get points for meeting the Energy Star Indoor Air Package specifications, which focus on moisture, radon (page 140), and pest control; ventilation; efficient heating and cooling; and minimizing VOCs (page 12).

- **Homeowner awareness and education.** It's not enough to build a green home; USGBC members also have to tell the owners how to get the most out of their LEED-certified house. A homeowner's manual is a must in this category, and there are also points for educating the community about green homes.

A building can earn up to 136 points. Table 4-1 shows how points translate into ratings, and how much energy you can save compared to an average home.

Table 4-1. LEED Certification Levels

LEED Rating Level	Number of Points	Energy Savings for Your Home
Certified	45–59	About 30%
Silver	60–74	About 30%
Gold	75–89	48%
Platinum	90–136	50–60%

Note Governments love green. Many LEED-certified buildings qualify for tax rebates, zoning allowances, and other incentives. See page 143 for more about green financing, and check with your city to see what benefits there are for building green in your area.

LEED is a great set of standards, but it's not the only one. Countries and regions around the globe are establishing their own guidelines, including these, to name just a few:

- **Canada.** In 2004, the province of British Columbia became the first non-American LEED licensee. Since then, the Canada Green Building Council has adapted the USGBC's LEED ratings for Canadian climates. Visit *www.canadagreenhomeguide.ca* to learn more.

- **Mexico.** The Mexico Green Building Council (*www.mexicogbc.org*) is developing standards to rate green buildings.

- **United Kingdom.** The Code for Sustainable Homes sets minimum standards for energy and water use and gives new homes a 1–6-star rating. (Find more info at *www.planningportal.gov.uk*.) In addition, the UK Green Building Council (*www.ukgbc.org*) provides information, education, and training materials about green building and energy efficiency.

- **Australia.** Green Star is the Green Building Council of Australia's rating and certification program. Read all about it at *www.gbca.org.au/green-star*.

- **South Africa.** The Green Building Council of South Africa (*www.gbcsa.org.za/home.php*), formed in 2007, has adapted Green Star guidelines into its own rating system, Green Star SA.

- **Hong Kong.** The HK-BEAM Society (*www.hk-beam.org.hk*) has created the Building Environmental Assessment Method (BEAM), which rates new buildings' sustainability, energy efficiency, and healthiness for use in Hong Kong and the Asia Pacific region.

> **Note** For a clickable list of these sites and all the other links in this book, head to the Missing CD page at *www.missingmanuals.com*.

Principles of Green Building Design

The LEED system gives you a sense of how to make your newly built or remodeled home healthy, easy on the earth, and efficient. This section explains some of the key pieces of the green building puzzle in more detail so you can design and build your earth-friendly home or redo your current place to make it greener.

Tip When designing a house, think small. Smaller homes cost less to heat and cool, and cozy, multi-use rooms may be preferable to large, rarely used ones. (Page 50 lists other advantages of downsizing.) Work with your architect to see where you can scale back.

Building In Energy Efficiency

To help plan your new home, scan the home energy audit checklist on page 43. Whether you're building from the ground up or renovating, that list can help you focus on ways to conserve energy and improve efficiency. And be sure to discuss these issues with your contractor:

- **Efficient ventilation, lighting, and appliances.** Insist on Energy Star–rated products whenever possible. And go for the most efficient equipment you can afford to save energy dollars down the road.

- **Insulation.** To keep your home snug, use a nontoxic insulation made from stuff like soybeans or cotton (see page 134). The kind you choose should have a high *R-factor*, which measures how well it keeps heat from getting transferred from inside your house to outdoors or vice versa.

- **Windows and doors.** Energy Star rates windows, skylights, and exterior doors. Efficient windows and skylights have multiple panes with a gas (such as argon) between them and a spacer to hold the panes in place, as well as special coatings to reflect infrared and ultraviolet light. Doors may have a foam core or some other type of insulation. Windows and external doors should seal tightly to keep air from leaking around them.

- **Renewable energy.** Consider going off the grid—at least partially—and getting your home's power from the sun, wind, or ground. The next section tells you how.

Alternative Energy

As you learned in the last section, the best first step in greening your building project is focusing on efficiency, which helps you reduce costs and your household's toll on the planet. And an energy-efficient home puts you in a good position if you decide to take things to the next level by getting some or all of your power from renewable sources. You might even get a grant or rebate to help pay for it (see page 144).

With renewable energy, there's no one-size-fits-all answer. Consider factors like your home's location and climate, the impact of a particular technology on the environment and neighborhood (you don't want neighbors picketing your home and filing lawsuits, now do you?), and your budget. Discuss these issues with your architect or contractor to figure out the best choices for your home. The following sections discuss some options.

> **Note** Chapter 10 looks at alternative and renewable energy technologies in detail. This section focuses on applying some of those technologies to homes.

Going solar

Solar energy has been around for as long as the Earth has circled the sun—and it's free. Take advantage of the sun's light and warmth by drawing back the curtains and opening the blinds. Letting the sunshine in to spread its warmth is called *passive solar energy*. When you're building a new home, consider these ways of making the most of such energy:

- **Choose your site carefully.** If you live in a cold climate, try to situate the house so it gets maximum exposure to the south or southwest (assuming you're in the northern hemisphere, that is). If you live in a hot climate, *minimize* southern and southwestern exposure instead.

- **Include a sunroom.** In cold areas, a sunroom or solar greenhouse on the southern side of your home can trap heat and warm the inside air. From there, a convection system can distribute the warm air throughout the house. If you want to use this room in the summer, install shades and close them to keep it from getting too hot.

- **Take advantage of windows.** To warm your house with sunlight, put large windows and glass doors along south- and southwest-facing walls (and smaller windows along the north-facing wall). Install thermal drapes (which you can buy just about anywhere) and open them during the day and close them at night. In hot climates, make the south-facing windows smaller and cover them during the day, and avoid putting skylights on south- and west-facing roofs.

- **Ventilate.** Throw open those windows to take advantage of breezes that circulate air throughout your home. Place windows in spots that maximize cross-ventilation.

- **Invest in awnings.** If windows make south-facing rooms too hot, install retractable awnings to shade them during the hottest part of the day and let light in when the sun isn't shining directly into them. If you don't like the look of awnings, design roof overhangs that protect windows from the summer sun and let in winter sun.

- **Pick the right materials.** Choose building materials that have a high *thermal mass*, or capacity to store heat, like brick, stone, concrete, and ceramic tile. In rooms where the sun shines directly on the floor, ceramic tiles will store and gradually release the heat they absorb.

Tip Choose dark colors to maximize heat absorption.

- **Consider a Trombe wall.** This kind of exterior wall, built from a heat-absorbing material—like stone, concrete, masonry, or adobe—faces south so it absorbs heat during the day, and then radiates it into your home. One-way vents help circulate air during the day and lessen the amount of heat that escapes at night. An overhanging roof shields the Trombe wall from the hot summer sun but lets the winter sun shine directly on it.

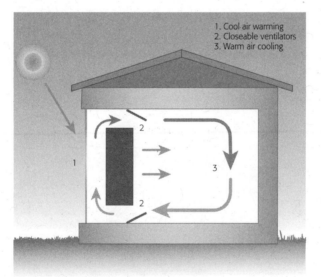

1. Cool air warming
2. Closeable ventilators
3. Warm air cooling

- **Create a buffer zone.** Opening and closing exterior doors lets inside air escape and brings outside air in, making your heating and cooling system work harder. So design entryways to minimize this problem. For back doors, putting a mudroom or utility room between the door and the rest of the house helps keep the main living area comfortable. For front doors, consider adding an anteroom or vestibule between the outside door and the door that leads into the house.

- **Choose the best ceiling height.** Heat rises, so lower ceilings keep cold-climate homes cozy, while higher ceilings make rooms more comfortable in hot climates.

> **Tip** Use ceiling fans (page 55) to circulate air and spread warm or cool air evenly throughout a room.

- **Landscape smart**. Plant deciduous trees (the kind that lose their leaves in the fall) to shade windows and doorways in summer and let the light through in winter.

Another option is to install *solar thermal panels* on the roof or in the yard and connect these to your heating system. The panels collect sunlight and convert it to heat, which is transferred via one of these:

- A **liquid-based system** pipes in heated water or an antifreeze mixture and stores the heat in a tank for warming water and for distributing it throughout the home.

- An **air-based system** uses air to circulate heat through your home.

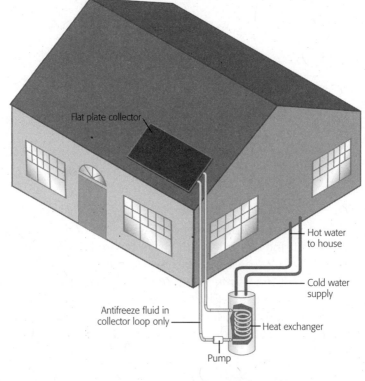

Flat plate collector

Hot water to house

Cold water supply

Antifreeze fluid in collector loop only

Heat exchanger

Pump

Solar water heater

The results you get with a solar-based system depend on factors including the number and size of the panels, the climate, how much sun your site gets, and so on. In hot, sunny climates, solar energy may meet all your heating and hot-water needs. In cooler climates that have lots of cloudy, snowy, or rainy days, this kind of system may work best as a supplement to a traditional heating system.

Green Tech

Powering Your Home with the Sun

Residential solar-electric systems have been around for quite some time, mostly in rural areas with no access to electricity through utility companies. You, too, can harness the sun's power to produce your energy using *photovoltaic (PV) cells*. The "photo" part means "produced by light," and "voltaic" means that electricity is created by a chemical reaction; more specifically, the photons in the sunlight excite electrons in the PV cells and generate power.

Today, PV systems are becoming increasingly popular in cities and suburbs for generating clean, sustainable electricity. Here's how it works: Series of PV cells are connected to form PV *modules*, which are wired together into PV *arrays*. You can mount these arrays on your roof or integrate them into the building's design.

If you're considering using PV cells to generate electricity, either as a supplement or to go off the grid entirely, keep these things in mind:

- Moisture corrodes metal contacts, so protect your PV array from rain and excessive moisture. In rainy areas, make sure the array is electrically insulated so that wires don't come into contact with water.

- Make sure that solar panels are placed at the *true angle*, the optimal angle to the sun. PVs work best at a prescribed angle (which depends on where you live) and on surfaces with full exposure to the daytime sky—so they soak up the most sun. The installation company will be able to find the true angle for your home.

- Wafer-based silicon PV cells (the most common kind) are brittle and can break.

The main thing that's been keeping PV cells from becoming more common is their cost. Another problem is that they work only during the day, which means you need backup batteries or a different energy source at night. But engineers are working to solve these problems. The cells are becoming less expensive, and infrared PV cells are showing promise—they're more efficient than standard cells and can produce energy even at night. These cells are definitely a green technology to watch.

Geothermal heating and cooling

The earth is made of thermal material, storing nearly half of the solar energy that reaches it. So why not tap into this *geothermal energy* to heat and cool your home?

Throughout the year, the earth stays at a relatively constant temperature just a few feet below the surface, no matter how hot or cold it feels above ground. Geothermal systems—also called geo-exchange, earth-loop, or ground-source heat pumps—use buried pipes to move heat from the ground into your home during the winter (or vice versa during the summer). Here's how they work:

- When the ground is warmer than the air, liquid circulates through pipes buried in your yard, absorbing heat. The liquid travels through a geothermal unit, which extracts heat from it and circulates that heat through the house. The cooled liquid then makes another trip through the buried pipes to bring in more heat.

- In the summer, the system's geothermal unit removes heat from your home's air by warming the liquid that circulates through the pipes and returning cooler liquid to the house. As this liquid travels through the buried pipes, the cooler earth pulls out the heat, and the liquid is ready for another go-round.

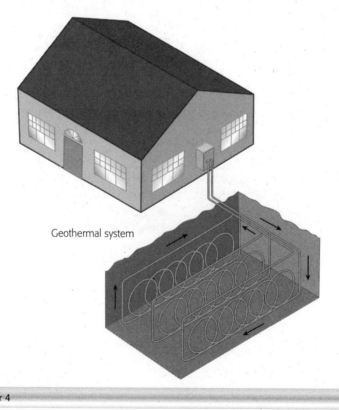

Geothermal system

Wind power

If you live on top of a windy hill, the answer to your quest for clean energy might be blowin' in the wind. A residential wind turbine can lower your electricity bill by 50–90%.

To harness wind power, a turbine sits on top of a tower that's tall enough to be well clear of buildings and trees—usually 80 to 120 feet high. When the wind blows hard enough—more than 7 to 10 miles per hour (about 6 to 9 knots)—the turbine turns, converting the wind's kinetic energy (*kinetic* means "related to motion") into electricity. When the air is still, your home gets its power from the standard electrical grid.

If you're considering wind-generated electricity, keep in mind that, in general, turbines aren't suitable for urban areas or suburban homes with lots smaller than one acre. Also, remember that no wind equals no power, so you don't want it to be your *only* energy source. Your site should have an average wind speed of at least 10 miles per hour (8.7 knots); the company that installs the turbine can use government-published wind resource data or use an *anemometer* (which measures wind speed) to determine how windy your spot is. For an average home, you'll want a turbine that's rated in the range of 5 to 15 kilowatts (page 49).

Be sure to do the following before you start building a turbine:

- **Check local regulations.** There may be set-back laws, for example, that restrict how close your turbine can be to your neighbors' properties.

- **Visit a residential turbine** in action before you commit. They aren't silent, and you may decide that they're too noisy for you.

- **Do a cost-benefit analysis.** Turbines are expensive; it can cost $10,000–$25,000 to get a small one installed. Make sure that the energy savings you anticipate are worth it. (If the turbine generates more power than you need, you may be able to sell the excess to the local utility company; call to find out.)

Note Hybrid electricity-generating systems combine solar and wind resources. This makes sense, because the peak operating times for wind and solar systems are at different times of the day and year—in winter, the sun is weaker and wind is typically stronger; in summer, the sun is brighter and the wind tends to be weaker. Wholesale Solar (*www.wholesalesolar.com*) sells this kind of system for homes.

Hydro power for homes

People have been harnessing the power of flowing water ever since they used waterwheels to operate mills. If a river or stream runs through your site, you may be able to use it to create electricity—called *microhydro power*—and it can generate enough for your whole home.

A microhydro-power system diverts running water and uses it to turn a turbine. The turbine spins a shaft, which can do things like power a pump or create electricity. After it turns the turbine, the water rejoins the river or stream it came from, so these setups have minimal impact on the environment.

Note In most situations, your home can be as far as a mile away from the turbine and still get electricity from it.

Microhydro-power system

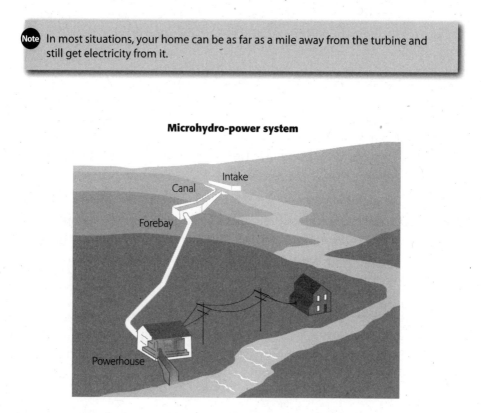

Using running water to create electricity has a couple of advantages over PV cells or wind turbines:

- The river keeps flowing—and generating power—day and night, whether it's sunny or cloudy, windy or calm.

- A relatively small amount of water flow (as little as two gallons per minute) or a vertical drop of just two feet between the intake (where the water gets diverted from the stream to power the turbine) and the exit (where the water rejoins the stream) is enough to generate electricity.

As with solar and wind power, before getting started with a microhydro setup, you need to make sure your site is suitable. Two factors determine how much power the system can produce:

- **Head.** This describes the vertical distance that the water travels between the intake and exit points.
- **Flow.** This is the volume of water.

To calculate how much electricity you can get from your site, use this formula:

$$\frac{\text{Head (in feet)} \times \text{Flow (in gallons per minute)}}{10} = \text{Output (in watts)}$$

As you can see, the greater the vertical drop and the faster the flow, the more energy gets generated.

> **Tip** Plan ahead for summer months, when reduced rainfall means less flow and therefore less power. Balance your stream's potential output with your energy needs during those months.

Burning biomass

Biomass is a fancy term for renewable fuel sources. It's applied to things that are grown for fuel and can be replenished with a new crop, like corn or wood pellets, even soybeans, nutshells, and dried cherry pits. Biomass burns more cleanly than regular firewood (but less so than natural gas), sending less ash and greenhouse gases into the air.

If you're interested in heating your home with biomass, you need an EPA-certified stove that limits the amount of particulates (ash) it emits. Look for a label that estimates the stove's smoke output, efficiency, and heat output, or go to *www.epa.gov/woodstoves* and download a list of certified stoves.

> **Note** Make sure you get the right stove for your home. A stove's *British thermal unit* (BTU) output indicates how much space the stove can heat; a higher maximum BTU heats a larger area. When buying a stove, ask how many BTUs you'll need to heat your home.

After you've installed a stove, you'll need biomass to burn in it, which you can get at hardware stores, stove companies, and farm supply stores. The fuel is rated by ash content—the lower it is, the cleaner it burns. That means fewer particulates released into the air and less time you'll spend cleaning the stove. A good pellet stove produces very little ash and you'll probably only need to clean it about once a week.

Tip Look for biomass fuel made from stuff that would otherwise be considered waste, like sawdust, sewage sludge, or dried manure.

Conserving Water

Water is an increasingly precious resource and everyone should do their part to use less. So build water conservation right into your new home or renovation project by doing things like installing a rainwater-harvesting system (page 68) and reusing gray water (page 38). And be sure to work with your contractor to:

- **Install efficient faucets.** The U.S. EPA puts the WaterSense label on highly efficient bathroom faucets, so insist on such fixtures.

- **Go with low-flow showerheads.** These can save tens of thousands of gallons of water from going down the drain each year. Look for ones with WaterSense labels or those with a flow rate of 2.5 gallons (or less) per minute.

- **Opt for less water pressure.** Nobody likes a wimpy shower, but you may not need the water going full-blast, either. Ask your plumber to install pressure-reducing valves to slow the flow. According to the EPA, changing the pressure from 100 pounds per square inch to 50 psi reduces water flow by about a third.

- **Put in low-flush toilets.** Since 1994, all toilets produced for homes in the U.S. can use no more than 1.6 gallons per flush, so any new toilet you install will be efficient. If you're outside of the U.S., look for models that use 1.6 gallons of water (or less) per flush.

- **Check out composting toilets.** A *composting toilet* uses little or no water and produces no waste. Its final product is compost you can use to enrich your lawn or garden. These toilets come in several different designs, but they generally work the same way, using heat and oxygen to break down waste. This process gets rid of germs and reduces the volume of the waste by as much as 90%. (And yes, you can dispose of toilet paper in a composting toilet.) With most models, you have to aerate the waste from time to time (usually by rotating a drum, which you can do by hand or use an electric motor) to make sure that oxygen is doing its job. After a few months, the compost is ready to use.

Note Local regulations about using toilet-produced compost vary, so check with your city and state before installing a composting toilet.

Will a composting toilet make your bathroom smell like an outhouse? Not if it's properly installed. Regular sewage smells bad due to *anaerobic* decomposition, which happens in low-oxygen environments, like when the waste is submerged in water. That produces methane and other smelly gases. But a composting toilet uses *aerobic* bacteria to break down the waste in the presence of lots of oxygen. The process gives off carbon dioxide, water, beneficial enzymes—and *no* nose-wrinkling smells.

Note Composting toilets are pricier than low-flush ones (they start at around $1,000), but they're less expensive than installing a septic tank.

Green Building Materials

Incorporating efficient systems into your new home or remodeling project is an important part of green construction, and so are the supplies you choose. From lumber to flooring, roof shingles to insulation, green materials come from sustainable sources and are made using responsible manufacturing processes. When choosing materials for building or remodeling, here are some questions to ask:

- **Does it come from a renewable resource?** Look for FSC-certified wood (page 28), cork, rubber, recycled and reclaimed materials, and so on. Keep reading for lots of suggestions.

- **Was it produced responsibly?** Try to support companies who strive to minimize energy consumption, greenhouse gas emissions, and waste.

- **Is it made of recycled materials?** Products with recycled content trump ones made from virgin materials.

- **Is it repurposed?** Whenever possible, use salvaged, reclaimed, or refurbished supplies. In one stroke, you keep stuff from being thrown away and cut back on the resources that would be used to make and transport brand-new goods.

- **Is it durable?** The material should last a long time, not require replacement in a few years.

- **Is it locally available?** Pick products made near your site over those shipped a long ways by pollution-producing trucks.

- **How much packaging does it have?** Do your part to reduce wasteful packaging (page 90) by selecting products that have little or none, or that use recycled packaging.

The next few sections have lots of suggestions for specific kinds of materials.

> **Tip** The Pharos Project (*www.pharoslens.net*) helps consumers evaluate and compare building supplies based on resource sustainability, health, and social justice. The Pharos Lens, a wheel-style graphic that rates products in these categories, appears on product labels and gives additional info about recycled content, durability, and country of origin. Look for the Lens when choosing your materials.

Lumber and framing

In the U.S. and elsewhere, wood is the material of choice for framing homes. It's a renewable resource, but you want to make sure the wood for your project was harvested from a well-managed forest that grows and harvests trees sustainably instead of plundering old-growth forests. Even with sustainable techniques, the sheer volume of wood used for construction has raised concerns about whether existing resources can support demand. And smaller forests lead to diminished air and water quality, contribute to global warming, and harm ecosystems and biodiversity.

Look for wood that's been certified by the Forest Stewardship Council (page 28). FSC-accredited certifiers give the FSC seal of approval to lumber from forests that are well managed, respecting indigenous peoples and the environment.

Salvaged or reclaimed wood is another option. It doesn't use a single new tree, and keeps old lumber from being thrown away. You can get reclaimed lumber from national dealers like Elmwood Reclaimed Timber (*www. elmwoodreclaimedtimber.com*) or Reclaimed Lumber Company (*www. reclaimed-lumber.com*). Make sure that the wood has been cleaned and is free of hidden nails (the company should use a metal detector to make sure). And the wood should be kiln-dried to get rid of any creepy-crawlies that might be living in it and prevent warping.

> **Tip** Tell your contractor you want to use efficient framing techniques to conserve materials. For example, if the contractor uses a 2 x 6 construction method for exterior walls, he may be able to space the studs apart by 24 inches on center (as opposed to the standard 16 inches on center). This method saves lumber and leaves more room for insulation.

And consider alternatives to wood: Plastic lumber, made from recycled or reclaimed plastic, may work for things like decks, walkways, and fencing. It doesn't rot and lasts pretty much forever. (There are also plastic-wood composites.) Plastic lumber comes from two main sources:

- Recycled high-density polyethylene, the kind of plastic used to make milk containers.
- Recycled polyvinyl chloride (PVC), the kind that's in shower curtains and car dashboards.

There are some downsides to plastic lumber. For one thing, it requires more energy to manufacture than regular wood products. And composites can't be recycled and may end up in landfills. Keep these issues in mind when you're thinking about incorporating plastic lumber into a project.

Insulation

Good insulation is essential to your home's energy efficiency, but what's the best kind to use? Traditionally, the most common materials are fiberglass and petrochemical-based products such as polyurethane and polystyrene. Fiberglass insulation often contains recycled material, but its fibers can get inhaled (similar to asbestos; see page 138), and it sometimes contains formaldehyde. Consider these alternatives when choosing insulation:

- **Cellulose.** Recycled newspapers can be turned into cellulose insulation, which is treated with chemicals to protect it from fire and insects. You can also find borate-treated cellulose, which is processed with a natural substance derived from the mineral boron.

- **Soy.** Instead of sprayed-in foam insulation made from polyurethane, check out soy-based foams.

- **Cotton.** The same fiber that's used to make warm sweaters can keep your house cozy, too. Cotton insulation is made from mill waste and low-grade and recycled cotton that's treated with a nontoxic fire retardant. It's available in batts—big rolled-up layers like the kind fiberglass insulation comes in—and as loose fill. There's no guarantee, though, that this kind of insulation comes from organic farms (nonorganic cotton farming uses lots of pesticides or genetically modified cotton; page 183 outlines some of the problems with genetically modified crops).

- **Cementitious foam.** This blow-in foam is made from magnesium oxide (which is derived from seawater) and blown through a membrane with air to create bubbles. The resulting insulation is nontoxic and nonflammable.

- **Perlite loose fill.** *Perlite* is a naturally occurring volcanic rock that expands when heated past 1600° F (871° C). It's often used as loose fill in masonry construction, filling the cavities, for example, in concrete blocks.

Walls

The drywall that forms the basis for your home's walls is mostly *gypsum* (a soft, inert mineral). To produce drywall, a layer of gypsum plaster is put between sheets of paper, the whole thing is pressed, and then dried in a kiln. This process takes a lot of energy—according to one estimate, it accounts for 1% of the total U.S. energy use. To minimize the carbon footprint of your building materials, look for drywall made from recycled or synthetic gypsum. Synthetic gypsum uses recycled and reused materials such as coal fly-ash, which comes from power-plant exhaust and would otherwise be waste. (More than 80% of the coal fly-ash sold in the United States goes into gypsum board.) Look for drywall made of at least 75% recycled content, including at least 10% post-consumer recycled content.

> **!** In 2008 and 2009, some homeowners complained that drywall imported from China gave off sulfur gases that caused health problems, including headaches and respiratory problems, and corroded copper pipes, coils, and wiring. Ask your contractor where your home's drywall comes from, and make sure it's a reputable source with a track record of safety.

Floors

When it comes to what's underfoot, you've got lots of green choices. If you're installing hardwood floors, be sure to buy FSC-certified (page 28) materials. Consider using reclaimed or salvaged wood, as well, and make sure that any finish applied to the wood is low in VOCs (page 12). Here are some other natural flooring options:

- **Bamboo.** Bamboo (which is technically a grass) grows quickly—growers can typically harvest it 4–6 years after planting it—so it's highly renewable. Some bamboo flooring, however, is made with adhesives that can off-gas formaldehyde, so ask about such emissions if you're considering this material.

- **Tile.** There are all kinds of tile to choose from, including ceramic and terracotta, stone (preferably reclaimed), and a wide variety made from recycled materials, like glass, ceramic, porcelain, and even aluminum. Be sure to use a low-VOC adhesive to install them.

- **Terrazzo.** This kind of flooring, which can be made from recycled glass, looks like marble.

- **Cork.** Most of the world's cork comes from Spain and Portugal, where it's harvested from cork oak trees that typically live for a couple of centuries, shedding their bark every decade or so. The bark gets made into flooring that comes in squares or sheets.

- **Carpeting.** The greenest options for carpeting are all-natural or re-cycled. Look for carpet made from things like organic wool or cotton, sisal (which comes from the agave plant), coir (made from coconuts), sea grass, and jute (made from plants native to Asia; it's what burlap is made of). Recycled carpet is made from old carpet, other textiles, or PET plastic (the kind soda bottles are made from).

> **Tip** Don't forget to buy recycled-content carpet *padding,* too, whose fibers come from old padding or reclaimed carpet.

- **Linoleum.** You may think of linoleum as the ugly flooring in your grandmother's kitchen. But take a look at today's designs before you dismiss this earth-friendly flooring. It's made from natural materials—linseed oil, pine resin, sawdust, cork dust, limestone, natural pigments, and a jute backing—and is long lasting and low maintenance. So Grandma was more of an environmentalist than you thought.

> **Note** Some people confuse linoleum with vinyl flooring, but they're different. Vinyl flooring is made from polyvinyl chloride (PVC). Both making and incinerating PVC produces dangerous dioxins, and the *phthalates* (chemicals added to PVC to soften it) in it may exacerbate allergies and asthma. Make sure you're getting real linoleum, not vinyl.

Kitchen and bathroom cabinets

These cabinets handy for storing things, but you don't want to have to hold your breath around them. Most of 'em are made from plywood, particle board, or fiberboard—all of which can off-gas formaldehyde. Better options are salvaged cabinets or ones made from regular wood, reclaimed wood, or metal.

Roofing

A good roof keeps the elements out, is relatively lightweight, and lasts a long time. Environmentally friendly materials include metal (look for lots of recycled content), fiber-cement composite (preferably made with fibers from recycled wood or paper), recycled shingles, and rubber tiles.

Paint

Low-VOC paint contains fewer *volatile organic compounds* than the regular kind. (Flip back to the box on page 12 to read all about VOCs.) For interior walls, use low- or no-VOC paint. Low-VOC means it can have no more than 250 grams per liter (g/L) of VOCs if it's latex based, or 380 g/L if it's oil based. And even if the label says "no VOCs," the paint can still have VOCs up to 5 g/L of the smelly chemicals. No matter what kind you choose, when you're painting inside, be sure to open the windows and have fans going for good ventilation.

Siding

Because of environmental problems caused by the manufacture of PVC (page 136), avoid vinyl siding. Instead, consider using siding made of recycled steel or aluminum, fibers and cement, or wood or other cellulose fibers bonded together (this last kind is called *reconstituted* siding).

Special Problems in Remodeling

When you build a new house, you start with a blank slate, limited only by stuff like the site, zoning, and budget. But remodeling is a whole different story. You have to work with what's already there, and that may include special problems found in older homes. This section looks at some of those issues—what they are and what to do about them—so you can make your remodeled home greener and safer for your family.

Asbestos

Asbestos is a naturally occurring mineral whose crystals form long, thin fibers. Its pliability and heat-resistance made it a popular insulation and fireproofing material. But the same fibers that make it a good insulator also make it deadly: Inhaling these fibers, especially over a long period of time, damages the lungs and causes lung cancer.

Here are some places where you might find asbestos, especially if your home was built before the late 1980s:

- **Boilers, pipes, and furnace ducts.** These parts of your heating system may have an asbestos blanket or asbestos paper tape for insulation. If the material is deteriorating or damaged (cut or scraped, for example), asbestos fibers can get into the air.

- **Furnaces and wood stoves.** The gasket that seals the furnace or stove door may contain asbestos and release fibers if it wears out.

- **Insulation.** If your house was built between 1930 and 1950, it may have asbestos insulation.

- **Textured paints, spray-on decorative materials, and soundproofing.** Sanding, scraping, or drilling into these materials will send fibers into the air. Old, crumbling material also releases asbestos.

- **Patching and joint compounds.** These things also release asbestos if you sand, scrape, or drill them.

- **Flooring.** Certain kinds of floor tiles (such as vinyl asbestos, asphalt, and rubber), the backing on vinyl sheet flooring, and adhesives used to install floor tiles can all contain asbestos. Removing, sanding, or scraping these materials may send fibers into the air.

- **Shingles, siding, and some roofing materials.** These probably won't release fibers unless you cut or drill into them.

If you have any of these materials in your home and they're in good condition—that is, they're not cut, scraped, crumbling, or damaged in any way—the asbestos they contain will probably stay where it is. But when you're renovating, disturbing or tearing out asbestos-containing materials is dangerous business. Even if you're a do-it-yourselfer, call a professional to remove the asbestos safely before you work with or around any of these materials. To find a company qualified for the job, check your local Yellow Pages under "Asbestos Abatement and Removal Service."

If you suspect that an asbestos-containing product is releasing fibers into your home (if basement pipe insulation is torn, cut, scraped, or water-damaged, say), keep people and pets out of the area, and call a professional who can remove or repair the asbestos safely. Here's what each option involves:

- **Removal** is more expensive, but it gets the asbestos out of your home. Renovating is a good time to remove asbestos and replace it with safer materials.

- **Repairing** involves either sealing the asbestos or enclosing it in a protective wrapper so that fibers can't escape.

Lead Paint

It's important to get the lead out—of your home, that is. Lead is super toxic to people (especially children) and pets, causing a slew of serious health problems including brain damage; nervous-system disorders; headaches; and behavior, learning, growth, and hearing problems in children. Lead can be ingested (as when kids or pets eat paint chips or get lead-laden dust in their mouths) or inhaled, a particular danger during renovations. Also, lead from flaking exterior paint can get into the soil around a home so that kids playing outside may be breathing lead dust and tracking it into the house.

Note The older your home, the more likely it is to contain lead-based paint. The U.S. banned lead paint in 1978, so if your home was built before then, have it tested for lead. To find someone in your area who's EPA-certified to test for and get rid of lead, visit *www.epa.gov/lead* and, in the left-hand menu, click Lead Professionals.

If you suspect anyone in your household has been exposed to lead, especially kids younger than 6, ask your doctor for a blood test. And hire a lead abatement professional, who can get rid of lead and clean up afterwards.

Mold

Mold is made up of microscopic fungi that thrive in moist areas and reproduce through spores. It's ugly, it smells musty, and it's bad for you. It can cause respiratory problems like allergic reactions and episodes of asthma. It may also contribute to sick building syndrome (see page 141).

The key to preventing mold is controlling moisture. First and foremost, make sure water doesn't penetrate your home from outside, getting into walls and other unventilated areas. The home's exterior, from foundation to roof (what builders call the "envelope"), needs to keep water out *and* let interior moisture escape. To keep water from seeping in, you need vapor barriers on the warm sides of the walls and roof, flashing around chimneys, and 6 mm polyethylene sheeting over dirt floors or crawlspaces. Also, the ground around your home should slope slightly away from the foundation to drain rainwater away.

During renovations, find and seal any leaks and make sure there's good ventilation throughout the house. Add insulation to prevent condensation on cold surfaces, like pipes, exterior walls, and floors. If certain windows always have condensation on them, replace them with Energy Star models. Dehumidifiers and air conditioners can also help. Finally, don't install carpet in damp areas where mold is a problem—or likely to become one.

Radon

You could have radon in your home and not even know it—you can't see, smell, or taste it, but it can have serious consequences. After cigarettes, this naturally occurring, radioactive gas is the *second* leading cause of lung cancer deaths in the U.S. and U.K. (If you smoke *and* are exposed to radon, your chance of developing lung cancer increases astronomically.)

Radon exists naturally in air, water, and soil, and enters buildings through cracks and gaps—in flooring, walls, joints, and where pipes enter the house. You can buy a do-it-yourself radon testing kit or hire a professional to do the test for you (find one in your state at *www.epa.gov/iaq/whereyoulive.html*).

According to the EPA, 1 in 15 U.S. homes may have elevated radon levels. Radon is very localized: One house may have a problem while the next-door neighbors don't. If a test finds radon in your home, take steps to get rid of it ASAP. There are several ways to reduce radon:

- **Sealing cracks and gaps.** Renovating is a good time to close up any openings in your home's foundations, walls, and so on.

- **Soil suction.** This method involves installing a vent pipe system and fan, which pulls radon from the soil beneath the house and vents it outside, where it dissipates in the air rather than getting into your home.

- **Sump-hole suction.** If your basement has a sump pump to keep water out, have the sump capped so it can also serve as the spot for a radon-suction pipe.

- **Pressurization.** With this approach, a fan blows air into the affected area from upstairs or outside the house. That raises the air pressure in the area it's blowing into, keeping radon from sneaking in. For this method to be effective, the windows in the affected area (for example, the basement) have to stay closed.

Sick Building Syndrome

If you've got health problems, it may not be *you* that's sick—it may be the building you live or work in. *Sick building syndrome* (SBS) causes a host of symptoms, including watery eyes, coughing, headaches, throat irritation, dizziness, nausea, and fatigue. If you have these symptoms when you're inside and they go away soon after you exit, SBS may be the cause.

One of the most common factors in SBS is indoor air pollution, which comes largely from tobacco smoke and VOCs (page 12). Mold, bacteria, and dust mites also contribute. If you suspect your home is sick, consider these measures when you renovate:

- Increase ventilation.
- Install air purifiers.
- Clean your heating and cooling system and replace filters.
- Install fabric air-duct diffusers.
- Control moisture (see page 140).
- Replace water-stained carpet and repair water-stained ceilings.
- Use low-VOC paints and finishes.
- Give construction materials adequate time to off-gas (check with your contractor to find out how long) before you re-inhabit a room.

Finding a Builder

You want a new or renovated home that's safe, healthy, efficient, and built from sustainable materials. So you need to find a contractor who can make your vision a reality. Because "green" is a buzzword, lots of people in construction and related trades lay claim to it—but how can you know if they're as good as their word?

A place to start is with your country's Green Building Council. For example, the USGBC has a searchable directory of members on its website (go to *www.usgbc.org* and click the upper-right Directories link). Or check out the Sustainable Sources' Green Building Professionals Directory at *http://directory.greenbuilder.com*, where you can search by category (such as General Contractors or Builders, Residential) and then narrow the search to your area.

When you've come up with a few possibilities, take time to interview those builders to make sure your values and priorities coincide. Use this list to judge just how green the builder is:

- Describe the philosophy and practices that make your company green.
- How long have you been building green homes?
- What are local examples of homes you've built?
- How many of those homes are LEED certified (page 118), and what level of certification did they earn?
- How do you ensure indoor air quality in the homes you build?
- What kind of insulation do you use and why?
- What percentage of recycled or reclaimed materials do you use?
- What are your strategies for making homes energy efficient?
- Do the homes you build ever use alternative or renewable energy?
- How do you reduce waste and mitigate environmental impacts on job sites?

Tip It's also a good idea to ask for some of the builder's previous clients so you can talk to others who've worked with this company to find out how it went and whether they're happy with the results.

Financing Green Construction

Few people have enough cash on hand to pay for a green building project without help. There are two ways of financing green construction, as this section explains in detail:

- Taking out a mortgage that gives you credit for energy efficiency.
- Finding tax credits, grants, and rebates to help with some of the cost.

Green Mortgage Options

An *energy efficient mortgage* (EEM) helps you qualify for a larger loan, because the money you'll save on energy costs gets taken into account right in the mortgage. That means you have more money to put toward a greener, more efficient home. EEMs are an option when you're buying a new home that's LEED- or Energy Star–certified.

If, on the other hand, you're looking to borrow money to make renovations that will improve the efficiency of your current home or one you want to buy, you can apply for an *energy improvement mortgage* (EIM).

To qualify for an EEM or EIM, you'll need to get a HERS report. No, that's not your wife's or best friend's opinion of the house; it stands for Home Energy Rating Systems. This report, which costs a few hundred bucks (but you may be able to get the seller to pay for it—no harm in asking), weighs factors such as utility rates, insulation, appliances, windows, and the local climate, and rates the house in the following categories:

- An Overall Rating Index of the house's current energy efficiency.
- A recommendation of cost-effective energy upgrades (that is, upgrades that'll save more money than they cost to install).
- Estimates of how much recommended upgrades will cost, how much money they'll save each year, and how long they're likely to last.
- An Improved Rating Index, which estimates how efficient the house will be after the recommended upgrades.
- Estimated total annual energy costs for the home before and after the upgrades.

Table 4-2 shows an example, taken from the U.S. Department of Housing and Urban Development's website (*www.hud.gov*), of how an EEM can increase your buying power. The figures in the table assume a 30-year term, a mortgage rate of 7.5%, and a down payment of 10%. (The table *doesn't* include the money you'll need to spend on taxes and insurance.)

Table 4-2. Afford More Home with an EEM

	For a Standard Home Without Energy Improvements	For an Energy-Efficient Home
Buyer's total monthly income	$5,000	$5,000
Maximum allowable monthly payment (28% debt-to-income ratio)	$1,400	$1,500
Maximum mortgage at 90% of appraised home value	$221,500	$237,300
Extra Borrowing Power of an Energy Efficient Mortgage		**$15,800**

Grants, Rebates, and Tax Credits

There are lots of national, state, and local programs out there to help homeowners who want to go green. The U.S. Internal Revenue Service, for example, gives tax credits for certain improvements that boost a home's efficiency, such as insulation, exterior doors and windows, solar panels, and so on. For the latest on federal energy tax credits for homeowners, visit *www.irs.gov*.

Tip Homeowners whose income is below a certain threshold may qualify for free home weatherization through the U.S. Department of Energy–sponsored Weatherization Assistance Program. You can get details at *www.eere.energy.gov/weatherization*.

State and local governments also offer tax credits for energy improvements. Because there are so many different programs, it's impossible to list them all here. Start with the website of your state's department of revenue or taxation and search for energy credits. You can also call your city or town hall and ask about any local credits, rebates, or programs related to improving your home's energy efficiency.

Many utility companies offer free energy audits (page 47) and give rebates or other incentives for upgrades such as replacing old, energy-hogging appliances with Energy Star–rated ones. Call your utility company or check their website to see what they offer.

Tip Check out the U.S. EPA's online guide to programs that fund green building projects: *http://tinyurl.com/l8xcrl*.

5 Raising a Green Family

People who care about the environment care about the future. When you start thinking in terms of family—your children, your grandchildren, their children, and so on—you begin to realize that the earth isn't yours to use and exploit. It doesn't belong to you, not even the patch of ground you live on—no matter what the property deed says. Your job is to care for and then pass on a robust, thriving, sustainable planet.

One of your duties as caretaker for your kids and the earth is to teach your children that they, too, have a responsibility to the planet and those who'll come after them. This chapter suggests lots of ways to do that. It also has tons of info about caring for you kiddo in environmentally friendly ways before she's old enough to be green herself. And pets are part of your family, as well, so there's a section on them, too.

Babies

When you welcome the newest member of your family, you want to be sure that baby's environment is safe, healthy, and natural. It's hard enough for new parents to get a good night's sleep without worrying about their babies getting exposed to harmful chemicals. This section explains the most important stuff to watch out for, and offers tips to help protect the newest member of your family—and the planet.

Furnishing the Nursery

There's more to getting the nursery ready choosing a pink or blue color scheme. Just like furniture for grown-ups, new baby furniture can give off icky vapors (page 13) like formaldehyde, which can irritate the eyes, nose, and throat and may cause coughing or wheezing and allergic reactions such as hives. In the late '80s, the U.S. EPA classified formaldehyde as a probable carcinogen when people are exposed to large amounts or for a long time. That's more exposure than your baby is likely to get in the nursery, but why take chances?

Where does formaldehyde lurk? Mostly in pressed-wood products made with adhesives that contain *urea-formaldehyde* (UF) resins. That includes particle board, plywood, or fiberboard; plywood paneling; and medium-density fiberboard, which often gets used for cabinets and drawer fronts.

Another group of chemicals you want to avoid are the fire retardants *PBDEs* (polybrominated diphenyl ethers). They're added to many foam and plastic items, and when such products are made, the PBDEs don't bind chemically with the plastic, so they leach out into the environment. According to U.S. Public Interest Research Group, an environmental and consumer advocacy organization, exposure to the specific PBDE *Deca-BDE* can have all kinds of nasty effects including brain and liver damage, problems with reproductive-system development, and impaired thyroid function.

That's scary stuff, so of course you want to avoid exposing your kiddo to PBDEs. They might be in common items like mattresses, textiles, and carpets. But even if you keep the nursery PBDE-free, you're not totally out of the woods. That's because PBDEs are stored in the body's fat and accumulate in breast milk, so if Mom gets exposed to these dangerous chemicals, she could unwittingly pass them on to her baby at feeding time. Outside the nursery, you might find them in things like computer and TV casings.

In 2008, the Environmental Working Group published a study that found the average American toddler's blood contains three times as much Deca-BDE than his mother's. That's not good. Fortunately, the European Union and several U.S. states have banned certain kinds of PBDEs, and a number of companies—including Dell, Hewlett Packard, Sony, Panasonic, and Phillips—have stopped using them. But many products still contain these chemicals, including Deca-BDE, which has been specifically excluded from some bans.

As if that wasn't enough to worry about, you should take steps to prevent every parent's worst nightmare: SIDS (sudden infant death syndrome).

While scientists don't know exactly what causes it, some studies have found a possible link between SIDS and the toxic fumes released by mattresses. One theory is that fungi, which occur naturally in the mattress, react with chemicals used to treat the mattress and produce toxic gases. To protect your baby, wrap the mattress in polyethylene sheeting (see the following list for details) to create a barrier and seal the gases inside. Although these studies remain controversial, it's important to know that foam mattresses may pose a danger to your baby.

When you're decorating the nursery, use this list to choose safe, healthy products, so you and baby can both sleep soundly:

- **Buy used furniture.** Furniture that's not brand-new has already done most of its off-gassing of any formaldehyde and other VOCs (page 12) used in its manufacture. Cribs and cradles, high chairs, playpens—most baby furniture is a good candidate for a secondhand purchase or hand-me-down.

> ❗ *Don't* buy a used mattress for your baby's bed or reuse an old mattress for a new baby. A study conducted in Scotland between 1996 and 2000 found that "Routine use of an infant mattress previously used by another child was significantly associated with an increased risk of sudden infant death syndrome."

- **Go organic.** Look for a crib mattress made from organic cotton, without toxic flame retardants or other chemicals. Same goes for pillows, sheets, and blankets—choose organic over synthetic and nonorganic fibers, and insist on no toxic chemicals.

> **Tip** The nonprofit Greenguard Environmental Institute certifies products that don't off-gas harmful chemicals—including bedding. You can find Greenguard-certified mattresses and mattress pads (as well as lots of other stuff) by going to *www.greenguard.org* and clicking the Find Products link.

- **Wrap baby's mattress.** To be extra-sure that your baby isn't inhaling toxic fumes from her mattress, wrap the mattress with a sheet of polyethylene that's at least 5 mm thick, which you can buy at hardware and garden centers. Be sure you get polyethylene, *not* vinyl (which gives off fumes of its own), and choose clear sheeting, not the colored kind. Wrap the mattress and seal it on the bottom with duct tape. Make the top and sides airtight, but not the bottom (the gas needs to escape, but you want it to do so away from your baby). This also makes the mattress waterproof, inhibiting the growth of mold and fungus.

- **Ventilate.** The nursery should have good ventilation. A constant supply of fresh air keeps VOCs from building up.

- **Use low-VOC paints**. For nursery walls and baby furniture, choose low- or no-odor paints (page 137) that give off as few VOCs as possible (page 12).

- **Select natural flooring.** Make sure that the pitter-patter of little feet happens on floors made from natural materials (page 135). And choose organic wool or cotton rugs and carpets.

- **Don't smoke.** Okay, so this tip applies everywhere, not just in the nursery. As you're no doubt aware, cigarette smoke is full of bad stuff: nicotine, formaldehyde, carbon monoxide, phenol, tar, and about 4,000 other chemicals. So don't let anyone smoke in the nursery—or anywhere around your baby's growing lungs.

The Diaper Dilemma

After choosing a name for your baby, perhaps the biggest question prospective parents face is what kind of diapers to use. Changing diapers is a dirty job—and one that you'll do roughly 6,000 times before your newborn is toilet trained. Disposable and cloth diapers both have an impact on the environment, but there's a cool (relatively) new option: biodegradable diapers. To help you decide which kind to use, the following sections explain the impacts of each.

Disposable diapers

When it comes to convenience, disposables are the clear winner. For a frazzled parent, anything that lets you cross an item off your to-do list is a good thing. And changing diapers is yucky enough—many people would rather throw dirty diapers away and forget them than rinse, soak, and wash used cloth diapers.

But disposables don't just disappear when you toss 'em. Those 6,000 diapers the average baby uses mean a lot of waste headed for the landfill. Each year, Americans throw out 18 *billion* disposable diapers, which will take at least a couple of *centuries* to decompose—if they're exposed to air and sunlight. In a containment landfill (page 80), they'll be around pretty much forever. And soiled diapers can contaminate the landfill's leachate (page 80), which may leak and pollute the area.

Manufacturing disposables takes a toll on the environment, too. The disposable diapers used in just one year in the U.S. require 82,000 pounds of plastic and more than 250,000 trees. Diaper companies don't give detailed info about what their products are made of, but they typically include bleached paper pulp, polypropylene plastic, petrolatum, tributyl-tin, stearyl alcohol, cellulose tissue, sodium polyacrylate elastic, glues, dyes, and perfumes. Here are some of the problems with those ingredients:

- **Dioxin,** a carcinogen, is a byproduct created when paper is bleached, and traces of it have been found in disposables.

- **Sodium polyacrylate** powder makes diapers absorbent—it can soak up 100 times its own weight in water. This chemical was banned from tampons in the U.S. in 1985 because of its link to toxic shock syndrome, a rare but often fatal illness. But it's still used in disposable diapers and the crystals that form when this powder absorbs water can stick to your baby's skin and irritate it.

- **Tributyl-tin** can cause hormonal problems in humans and animals.

- The **dyes** in some diapers can damage the kidneys, liver, and central nervous system.

- **Perfumes** can irritate skin and cause allergic reactions.

- Nobody likes a leaky diaper, but **leakproof disposable diapers** may increase the chances of diaper rash and make existing cases worse by keeping air away from babies' skin.

> **Note** Two studies published years apart in the *Journal of Pediatrics* noted cases of diaper rash in babies. The first, from 1959 (before disposable diapers), found diaper rash in only 7.1% of babies. A study from 1982, after disposable diapers had been around for a couple of decades, found that *63%* of babies had diaper rash at least once over an eight-week period.

Your kid will spend around 20,000–25,000 hours in diapers. So if you're concerned about the chemicals in disposables, choose cloth or biodegradable diapers instead.

A final factor to consider is cost: Buying 6,000 disposable diapers at 20 cents apiece adds up to of $1,200. That's a lot of money to spend on landfill filler!

Biodegradable diapers

These diapers offer the convenience of disposables without cramming land-fills full of waste. Made from bioplastics (which are made from plant material, not petroleum—see page 90), biodegradable diapers are compostable.

If you've got a composting toilet or vermicomposting system (page 195), it can break these diapers down in a matter of days, rather than years. Some cities, like Toronto, have door-to-door composting programs that accept soiled diapers. If your city has a composting program, check to see whether they take biodegradable diapers. Whatever you do, don't throw them in the trash: In a containment landfill, they'll take just as long to decompose as disposables.

> **Tip** The Irish company Ecobaby has instructions for building your own worm composter for biodegradable diapers at *www.ecobaby.ie* (in the left-hand menu, click DIY Worm Composter).

Brands to try include Tushies (*www.tushies.com*), Nature Babycare (*www.naty.com*), and Nature Boy & Girl (*www.natureboyandgirl.net*). gDiapers (*www.gdiapers.com*) makes a cloth-biodegradable hybrid, which combines a washable cotton outer pant with a fluffed-wood and rayon insert made from Sustainable Forestry Initiative–certified trees (*www.sfiprogram.org*). You can flush the insert.

> **Note** Some biodegradable diapers are made with sodium polyacrylate (page 149) or *AGM*, a super-absorbent gel linked to increased childhood asthma and reproductive problems in boys. Make sure any diapers you buy are gel-free.

Cloth diapers

There's no question that these diapers are less convenient than disposables. They're messy, stinky, and cleaning them takes work. But even when you factor in the water and energy it takes to wash them, cloth diapers are more earth-friendly than the throwaway kind. And maybe knowing you're doing right by the planet can help you ignore the smell.

> **Note** If you're nervous about using diaper pins around your baby, don't worry: Today's fitted cloth diapers have snaps or Velcro closures.

Before the stork arrives, buy 2–3 dozen cloth diapers and put them through the wash several times to soften 'em and remove any chemicals that might be in them. (Better yet, opt for unbleached diapers made from organic cotton, hemp, or bamboo.) Then get a diaper pail with a lid. When you change diapers, dunk the soiled one in the toilet bowl a few times to rinse it, and then put it in the pail. There are two approaches to using diaper pails:

- **Wet.** Fill the pail about halfway with cold water. Pour in a quarter cup of vinegar (this should minimize odor, but add a drop of essential oil if you like). After you rinse soiled diapers, drop them into the pail to soak. When it's time to do laundry, dump everything in the pail (including the water) into the washer. (Don't try this with a front-loading washer—things could get ugly. Go with a dry pail instead.) Run a spin cycle to drain off the excess water, and then wash as usual.

> **Note** Wet diaper pails have two disadvantages: The water makes them heavy to lug around, and they're a potential drowning hazard for young children. If you use this method, get a pail with a *locking* lid.

- **Dry.** Simply drop in rinsed, soiled diapers until you're ready to wash them. Sprinkle some baking soda on top of each new diaper to absorb odors, or spray a mixture of vinegar and water onto them before you put them in the pail.

On laundry day, here's how to get cloth diapers clean:

1. **If you use the dry pail method, start with a prewash in cold water.** Then, fill the washer with cold water and add half a cup of baking soda *or* vinegar (not both) and let them soak for several hours or overnight. (You can skip this step if you use a wet diaper pail.)

2. **Wash in hot water.** Even if you usually go with cold water to save energy, use hot water to kill germs.

3. **Rinse in cold water.** Add half a cup of vinegar to the rinse cycle. Don't add fabric softener, which can reduce diapers' absorbency.

4. **Dry 'em** either outdoors or in your dryer.

You'll probably wash a load of diapers every two or three days. Don't stuff too many into the washer, though—limit loads to two dozen diapers, max—or they won't get as clean.

What about the environmental impact of all that laundry? Cloth diapers have a much smaller ecological footprint than the disposable kind. One study found that home-washing cloth diapers has 47% less of an impact than disposables. And using a diaper service has only half the impact of washing diapers at home.

Cloth diapers put natural fibers next to your baby's skin rather than bleached paper, plastic, and potentially hazardous chemicals. And as noted on page 149, they're less likely to cause diaper rash than disposables (make sure you change them frequently).

How much do they cost? Between $200 and $700 for the time your baby is in diapers (that includes washing and drying them). The exact figure depends on things like the kind you buy, local water and electricity rates, and whether you dry them outdoors or in a dryer. And unlike disposables, you can reuse cloth diapers when the next baby comes along or as cleaning rags.

Feeding Your Baby

When your child is an infant, breast-feeding provides the best nutrition. Breast milk is the food nature intended for babies, and it's healthy for both mother and child. It's easier to digest than baby formula and is full of antibodies that protect your little one from disease. According to the U.S. Department of Heath and Human Services, breast-fed babies are less likely to get ear and respiratory infections, stomach viruses and upsets, and atopic dermatitis (a type of eczema). They also have lower rates of childhood leukemia, asthma, diabetes, and obesity. And breastfeeding moms are at lower risk of type 2 diabetes, breast cancer, ovarian cancer, and postpartum depression.

But sometimes breastfeeding is impossible or impractical. Breast milk changes as a baby develops, and occasionally the child refuses to feed. Or the mom may not produce enough milk. In rare cases, a doctor may advise against breastfeeding, such as when the mother is taking antiretroviral medications or undergoing chemotherapy. Moms who can't breastfeed their babies have these options:

- **Formula.** Even the best formula can't duplicate breast milk exactly, but if you decide to go this route, choose an organic formula. You don't want pesticides, steroids, growth hormones, antibiotics, and other chemicals to make their way into your baby's food. Here are three brands to try:

    — Earth's Best (*www.earthsbest.com*).

    — Similac Organic (*www.similac.com*).

    — Baby's Only Organic (*www.naturesone.com*).

Frequently Asked Question

Baby Bottles and BPA

Are plastic baby bottles safe?

In 2008, researchers published a study that showed that a chemical called *bisphenol A* (BPA), used to make plastic baby bottles, can leach out of the plastic when heated. Another study published the same year found that exposing plastic bottles to boiling water speeds up the release of BPA—by a whopping 55 times.

BPA is an *environmental estrogen*, an artificial substance that mimics the effects of estrogen in the body. It can interfere with a child's development by altering the ratio of sex hormones. Researchers have also found possible links between BPA exposure and birth defects, diabetes, obesity, attention-deficit disorder, and cancer.

Scientists don't agree on how much of a hazard BPA poses. The European Union allows BPA and says its risks are negligible. Canada, on the other hand, has banned BPA from baby bottles, and several U.S. states are considering a similar ban.

Many parents feel that the *potential* risks of BPA are enough to avoid baby bottles that contain it—and that's 95% of plastic baby bottles available in the U.S. If you want to keep BPA away from your baby, use glass bottles or plastic ones labeled BPA free. Brands to look for include Born Free, Medela, ThinkBaby, and Green to Grow.

- **Human milk banks.** These organizations collect milk from healthy donors, test the milk to make sure it's safe, and dispense it through hospitals or by prescription. For more information (including how to become a donor or make a financial donation), visit one of these sites:

  — U.S. and Canada: Human Milk Banking Association of North America (*www.hmbana.org*).

  — U.K.: United Kingdom Association for Milk Banking (*www.ukamb.org*).

  — Australia: Mothers Milk Bank (*http://mothersmilkbank.com.au*).

When it's time to start your baby on solid foods, begin with very thin cereals and vegetables that have a high liquid content. You can buy organic baby food (Earth's Best is one brand to try), or you can easily make your own so you know exactly what's going into baby's mouth. Whipping up your own takes just a few steps:

1. **Buy fresh or frozen fruits and vegetables (or grow your own).** Buy organic when you can, to avoid pesticides and artificial fertilizers. Good fruits and veggies to start with include apples, apricots, asparagus, avocados, bananas, blueberries, peaches, pears, peas, plums, potatoes, prunes, and sweet potatoes.

> **Note** Babies need to grow and develop before they can deal with some foods, including corn, broccoli, and cauliflower. The American Academy of Pediatrics recommends that you wait until your child is 4 to 6 months old before starting him on solid food. And some veggies contain *nitrate*, a chemical found in water and soil that—at high levels—can cause anemia in babies. So don't feed kids younger than 6 months homemade baby food with beets, carrots, green beans, spinach, or squash in it. (Companies that make baby foods containing these veggies test them for nitrates, so it's okay to feed store-bought food with these ingredients to younger babies.) Nitrates can also show up in well water, so if you get your water from a well, have it tested for nitrates, which should be below 10 parts per million.

2. **Wash your hands, and then wash the fruits and veggies thoroughly.** Peel and remove seeds if they have any.

3. **Cook the food in a small amount of water—boil or steam it—until soft.** If you prefer, use breast milk or formula instead of water. Don't add any sugar, salt, or spices: Your baby will like the unseasoned taste just fine.

4. **Pour the food and liquid into a blender or food processor and puree.** For children just starting solid foods, add water or breast milk to thin the mixture. As your child adjusts to solids, you can use less liquid to get a paste-like consistency.

5. **Let the food cool to room temperature.** Put a little of it in a bowl and feed it to your child in small spoonfuls (if any is left over in the bowl, throw it away after the feeding). Freeze the rest of the batch in an ice cube tray. When it's frozen, place each ice cube–sized portion in a plastic bag. Seal and label it so you know what type of food it is and the date you prepared it. You can store baby food in the freezer for up to two months.

Note Don't thaw frozen baby food in the microwave—that can create hot spots in the food that may burn your baby's mouth. Instead, plan ahead and let the food thaw slowly, in the fridge. Or thaw it over low heat on the stove. Check the food's temperature before feeding time by tasting it (use the spoon just once then wash it) or by dabbing a little on your wrist—the food should feel neither hot nor cold.

Keeping Baby Clean and Protected

Even the sweetest little bundle of joy has a way of getting dirty. To keep your baby clean, skip the products that contain preservatives and other iffy chemicals, dyes, and fragrances (nothing smells better than a baby's clean skin, anyway). Instead, try these natural alternatives:

- **Baby wipes.** These help with cleanup during a diaper change or to quickly clean a messy face and hands. But many commercial wipes contain chemicals that can irritate a baby's tender skin, including propylene glycol, parabens (page 217), and perfumes. Look for baby wipes without these ingredients, or make your own: Combine a teaspoon each of aloe vera gel (which you can find at any drug store) and olive oil with a tablespoon of liquid castile soap (page 17) and a cup of water in a spray bottle. When you're ready to use it, spray the mixture on a cloth, clean your baby, and then drop the cloth in the diaper pail for washing.

- **Baby lotion.** Commercial lotions may contain the same chemicals as baby wipes (parabens, fragrances, and propylene glycol), so avoid products with those. The best natural lotion is olive oil: Simply massage a small amount into your baby's skin.

Tip If you don't dry out your baby's skin, he won't *need* lotion. Bathe your baby 2–3 times per week, and use just a little soap and shampoo.

- **Shampoos and soaps.** Just because a product says "gentle" on the label doesn't make it true. Many bath-time products marketed to parents of babies and small children contain chemicals like formaldehyde, phthalates, 1,4-dioxane, and sodium lauryl sulfate. Dyes, preservatives, and fragrances can also be irritating. Even products labeled "all natural" can contain some of these chemicals—as you'll learn on page 185, this label isn't the same as "organic." Get products that carry the USDA Organic seal and are free of fragrances and dyes. These websites help you find safe bath products for your children:

  — **The Campaign for Safe Cosmetics** (*www.safecosmetics.org*). On this site, click Companies, and then click "The Compact for Safe Cosmetics". From there, click "Search Compact signers" to search a database of companies that have pledged to make products that are free of chemicals known to cause—or strongly suspected of causing—cancer, mutations, or birth defects.

  — **Skin Deep Cosmetic Safety Database** (*http://cosmeticdatabase. com*). Sponsored by the Environmental Working Group, a public-health organization, this searchable database reports on the possible toxicity of thousands of products. Click Baby Care to find the area of the site devoted to products for babies and kids. For each product, a scorecard lists health problems associated with its ingredients and rates the product on a scale of 0 (few or no safety concerns) to 10 (serious concerns).

  — **Sunscreens.** The best way to protect your baby's skin from sunburn is, not surprisingly, to keep her out of direct sunlight. If you do go out in the sun, dress your child in long sleeves, pants, and a hat; use a sunshade on the stroller; and try to avoid sunny areas between 10 a.m. and 4 p.m., when the sun's rays are strongest. When those strategies won't work (at the beach, for example) choose a physical sunscreen—one with zinc oxide or titanium dioxide—over a chemical-based one, which may have ingredients like PABA and oxybenzone, chemicals that filter the sun's rays but can irritate the skin. Look for a sun protection factor (SPF) between 15 and 30.

    If your baby is less than 6 months old, avoiding direct sunlight is your best bet. But the American Academy of Pediatrics says it's okay to occasionally use small amounts of a physical sunscreen on children this young when protective clothing and shade aren't available. California Baby (*www.californiababy.com*) and W.S. Badger (*www.badgerbalm.com*) both make chemical-free sunscreens.

- **Bug repellent.** Insect bites sting, itch, and can spread illnesses such as West Nile virus or Lyme disease. The first line of defense against bug bites is your kid's clothes: long-sleeved shirts, pants legs tucked into socks. Sometimes, though, you may need to increase protection with an insect repellent. Many of these products contain DEET, and the American Association of Pediatrics says that up to 30% DEET is safe for kids. But be aware that DEET has been linked to health problems—including headaches, seizures, and convulsions—particularly if swallowed. If your repellent contains DEET, keep it out of kids' reach, avoid applying it near their eyes and mouths, wash kids' hands after applying it, and don't put it on over cuts and scrapes.

  If you'd rather avoid DEET, try natural alternatives. Most of these repellants use plant oils, like citronella, rosemary, or lemon eucalyptus. But just because an ingredient is natural doesn't mean it's nonirritating. So try a little on a small patch of skin a day or so before you plan to use the product to ward off bugs. Try California Baby Natural Bug Blend (*www.californiababy.com*), The Natural Newborn's Bug Stopper Spray (*http://thenaturalnewborn.com*), or Badger Organic Anti-Bug Balm (*www.badgerbalm.com*).

! Very young babies have skin that's more porous than adults', which means their bodies absorb more of whatever gets slathered on them. So don't use insect repellent on a baby under 2 months old.

Other Baby Supplies

New parents often feel overwhelmed by all the stuff that comes into their lives along with a baby: stroller, car seat, high chair, bibs, toys, and a whole lot more. You can buy many of these things used, or get them from a friend or family member who doesn't need 'em anymore—that's putting the principle of reuse into action. This section takes a quick look at green approaches to specific baby supplies.

Car seats

Be careful when choosing a car seat. This is one item you should probably buy new rather than used. Why? Two good reasons:

- Safety standards keep evolving, and used seats may not be as safe as newer ones. And even if it served the previous owner well, age and stress may weaken the seat.

- If you get a second-hand car seat, you have no way of knowing whether it's been damaged in an accident; you may not be able to tell just by looking at it.

If a friend or family member offers you a used a car seat, make sure it's no more than a couple of years old and that it's never been in a fender-bender. Otherwise, buy new.

Clothing

Babies grow fast: You buy an adorable outfit, she wears it twice, and in a month it's too small. Instead of spending big bucks on new clothes, take the green route and buy used or go with hand-me-downs from older siblings, cousins, or friends' kids. Because kids grow so darn quickly, second-hand clothes are often in great shape.

Tip Be sure to wash used clothes before wearing them.

When shopping for new clothes for your kiddo, choose natural and organic fibers. Page 212 has green clothes shopping tips.

Toys

Babies and toddlers put everything in their mouths, so avoid toys with small parts, paint that can flake off, or harmful ingredients like lead, PVC, and chemical flame retardants. Look for stuffed animals made from organic materials, wooden blocks painted with lead-free paint, and plastic toys labeled phthalate-free. Planet Happy Kids (*www.planethappytoys.com*) is a good place to find nontoxic, eco-friendly toys.

It's also easy to find second-hand toys in good condition at thrift shops and yard sales. (Wash 'em before letting your kids play with them.) And encourage your tot to share toys with siblings and friends.

Diaper and baby bags

You can find eco-friendly baby bags made from organic cotton, hemp, or recycled plastic PET (page 107) bottles in various stores. Or try to get a second-hand bag that's in good condition.

Kids

Children love to explore the world around them, and you can explore right beside them. A child's wonder at nature is contagious—your own appreciation of the earth will increase while you teach good habits and respect for the planet.

Teaching Respect for the Earth

When children grow up in a household that respects the environment, they learn to respect it, too. Here are some ways to foster an appreciative, earth-friendly attitude in your child:

- **Set a good example.** Your kids watch you and learn from your actions. If you show them earth-friendly habits, they'll imitate you. Instead of littering, for example, use a trash can or recycling bin—*and* explain why. Rather than driving, walk, bike, or take the bus. Instead of carting home plastic shopping bags, take your own reusable bags to the store. You get the idea.

- **Get kids involved in recycling.** Don't present recycling as a chore— make it a game. Children like solving the "puzzle" of putting different materials into their bins. Crushing aluminum cans can be fun, too.

- **Teach reuse.** Show your kids that you don't need to throw things away after using them just once. Ask kids to come up with ideas for reusing things around the house. KinderArt has a page with all kinds of suggestions for craft projects like grocery-bag kites, a coffee-can drum, handmade recycled paper, and lots more; head to *www.kinderart.com/recycle*.

- **Praise earth-friendly actions.** When your child turns off the TV after watching it, closes the fridge after getting a snack, or turns off the water while brushing her teeth, notice and say, "Good job!" and explain why these small actions are important. This kind of praise will help your kids develop good habits.

- **Respect wildlife.** Whether you're pointing out robins building a nest in the backyard, a turtle sunning itself by a stream, or a deer in the woods, help your children admire animals while keeping their distance.

- **Visit a farm.** If your tot thinks food comes from the supermarket—and that's all there is to it—visit a local farm. Some places have "u-pick" crops like strawberries or blueberries that kids can harvest themselves. Others have tours that give a peek into life on a working farm.

- **Discourage consumerism.** Well-meaning family members and friends may shower your kid with unneeded, unwanted toys and clothes. You don't want your child to associate material things with love, so ask your family and friends to limit gifts. Then you can help your kid sort through their old or unused clothes and toys and donate them to charity.

> **Note** Another way to discourage consumerism is by limiting TV, which exposes kids to lots of advertising. According to the National Institute on Media and the Family, the average child sees about 40,000 commercials on television every year, and by age 3, can recognize logos and is developing brand loyalty. Kids that young can't distinguish between shows and commercials, so they don't realize that commercials are pitching products.

- **Play video games with an environmental slant.** Encourage your kids to play computer and video games that teach them to be green. NoteNiks Software (*www.noteniks2.com*) makes games that teach kids aged 5–10 about recycling, endangered animals, clean energy, and respecting the earth. And here are some websites that have games, activities, and info just for kids:

  — U.S. EPA Environmental Kids Club (*www.epa.gov/kids*).

  — EcoKids (*www.ecokids.ca*).

— Kids Planet (*www.kidsplanet.org*).

— TUNZA from the United Nations Environment Programme (*www. unep.org/Tunza*).

> **Tip** You can find these links and all the others in these pages on this book's Missing CD page at *www.missingmanuals.com*.

Go Play Outside!

Of course, the best way to help your kiddos appreciate and enjoy nature is to put them in it. But don't just shoo them out the door. Participate in green, outdoor activities with them so you can spend quality time as a family and teach them to value the big, wide world.

Outside fun also helps kids get and stay physically fit. According to the Centers for Disease Control and Prevention, 16% of U.S. children aged 6–19 are overweight or obese—that's *triple* the rate from 1980. Active kids also have higher self-esteem and get fewer chronic illnesses. Yet the average American child spends over three hours each day watching TV—that's 20% of the time they're awake! Playing outside with your kids is good for your health, too. Remember: The family that's green together gets lean together.

Here are some outdoor activities the whole family can enjoy:

- **Take a hike.** Or a walk. Or a bike ride. You'll get some fresh air and exercise while spending time together.

- **Have a picnic.** Let the kids help you make and pack the food. Use recyclable wrappings like aluminum foil and washable or biodegradable plates and utensils made from stuff like corn and sugar cane instead of petrochemical-based plastic.

> **Tip** Don't throw biodegradable things in the trash—they'll hang around for years in a landfill. Toss them in a compost pile (page 191) instead, where they'll get enough oxygen to decompose quickly.

- **Play games.** Think of the outdoor games you enjoyed playing as a kid, and teach them to your children, or ask them to show you their favorite games. Tag, kickball, hide-and-seek, softball, duck-duck-goose, hopscotch, badminton—there are endless backyard games to play with your kids.

- **Tend a garden.** Planting and taking care of plants with your children is fun and rewarding. Whether it's a flower garden that adds beauty to your home or a vegetable garden to teach them where food comes from, gardening puts taking care of the earth into action. Flip to page 191 for tips on organic gardening.

> **Tip** If you don't have space for a garden, grow plants in flowerpots and other containers. Kids love watching seeds turn into shoots and then blossom or bear fruit.

- **Watch birds.** Put up a birdfeeder and let the kids help keep it filled. Keep binoculars handy so kids can get a closer look without disturbing the birds.

- **Visit a nature center.** These places have staff (usually volunteers) who are trained to get kids interested in and teach them about nature and the environment. Look for special activities that appeal to your child.

- **Earn TV time through other activities.** To keep kids off the couch, limit the amount of TV they can watch each day. But you don't want them to think that turning off the tube is a punishment—if they do, they may resent whatever activity you have in mind to replace TV-watching. So try setting up a formula where they can earn their TV time: Each hour spent playing outside, reading, helping around the house, for example, earns half an hour of TV or video games. Your kids may even have so much fun playing outside that they forget all about TV.

Teens

When it comes to the environment, you might be able to learn a thing or two from your teenager. Today's teens are coming of age at a time when we understand more about the problem of diminishing resources, the effects of greenhouse gases, and the importance of taking care of the earth for future generations. They *are* a future generation, after all, and many of them worry about the planet they're inheriting.

School and community programs that teach about the environment give teens info about green issues and ways to get involved. Whether your kid is already environmentally savvy or cares more about playing video games than saving the earth, here are some ways to share your passion for green living with teens:

- **Have a conversation.** Ask your teen her thoughts on the state of the planet, and whether she has ideas for making your household greener.

- **Suggest community service projects.** Many high schools require some community service before kids can graduate, and college admission offices like to see meaningful volunteerism on applications. Encourage your teen to pick a project that helps the environment, like cleaning up a park or teaching younger kids about recycling. The EPA has suggestions for such projects at *www.epa.gov/highschool/community.htm*.

- **Encourage activism.** It's important for teens to know that they can make a difference. Getting involved—and seeing the fruits of their actions—is empowering. Several websites offer ideas, support, and communities for budding activists:

  - **Do Something** (*www.dosomething.org*) encourages teens to go offline and get involved in their communities, with suggestions for activism for the environment, animal welfare, health and fitness, and lots of other causes.

  - **Idealist.org** (*www.idealist.org*) suggests ways for folks of all ages to get involved. Kids and teens can find an area of the site that's just for them at *www.idealist.org/kt/index.html*.

  - **TeenActivist.Org** (*www.teenactivist.org*) describes itself as "a place for teens who volunteer, advocate, mobilize, [and] protest" about stuff they care about, from civil rights and peace to environmentalism and animal rights. Teens who register can submit journal entries describing their activism and participate in online discussions.

  - **YouthNoise** (*www.youthnoise.com*) fosters young leaders through support, mentoring, and giving teens a voice on issues they care about. International in scope, the site has ideas for action and encourages debate with forums and blogs.

- **Get creative about fundraising.** Sports teams, drama clubs, and other school groups are always looking for ways to raise money. Instead of (or in addition to) the usual bake sales, car washes, and raffles, consider a recycling drive (page 111 lists companies that recycle cellphones, for example) or raising money through one of these green fundraising companies:

  — **Equal Exchange** (*www.equalexchange.coop/fundraiser.php*) is a food cooperative that promotes fair-trade and sustainable farming practices. It lets organizations buy fair-trade products like coffees, teas, cocoa, nuts, and dried fruit, at wholesale prices and resell them at a 40% profit.

  — **Go Green Fundraising** (*www.go-green-fundraising.com*) offers flower bulbs, tree kits, natural foods, reusable shopping bags, and "smencils"—scented pencils made from recycled newspaper. The more items you sell, the higher the percentage of profits you keep, from 25 to 55%.

  — **Greenraising** (*www.greenraising.com*) stocks a wide range of earth-friendly products such as recycled wrapping paper, green cleaning supplies, fair-trade coffee and tea, and reusable bags. Fundraisers keep 25 to 40% of sales.

- **Teach green driving.** One of the major rites of passage of the teen years is getting a driver's license. Most parents encourage safe driving practices, but what about *green* driving? Page 263 explains how car emissions affect the environment. Talk about this with your teen and go over the tips listed on page 232. If your kid is saving up to buy a car (or if you're going to buy one or help out with the cost), do your research (page 235) and buy the most fuel-efficient car in his price range.

- **Find mall-ternatives.** Hanging out at the mall encourages consumerism and limits the time your teen spends doing more constructive or creative things. Help her find and participate in other activities: sports, music, dance, drama, photography, volunteering—whatever grabs her attention. Then, support her interests and hobbies: Go to games, recitals, and plays, or volunteer for the booster club.

- **Green the prom.** Challenge teens to come up with ways to make the prom (and other events) more environmentally friendly. Here are a few ways to do that:

  - **Decorations.** Instead of buying flowers flown in from thousands of miles away, go with local growers. (Same goes for corsages and boutonnières.) Green Party Goods (*www.greenpartygoods.com*) sells biodegradable crepe paper, garlands, and tableware.

  - **Tableware.** Go for reusable over throwaway: Choose cloth napkins, china, glasses, and silverware, which can be washed and reused. Or go with biodegradable plates and utensils, and make sure they get composted instead of thrown out.

  - **Favors.** Think about replacing party favors with a donation in the class's name to a good cause. At the prom, attendees can vote for the cause they want to support.

  - **Transportation.** Arriving by limo is one way to make a grand entrance; sharing the limo with several couples cuts down on greenhouse gases. Or be creative: Decorate the family car or rent a horse and carriage to get to the prom in style. If the dance is held at a site far from the school, arrange for a shuttle to run between the school and the venue so everyone arrives in the same ride.

  - **Attire.** When it comes to promwear, the guys already have it green—renting a tux is a great way to reuse instead of buying new. But most girls spend lots of money on prom dresses, wear them once, and then stuff them in the back of their closets. Greener options include buying vintage, renting a designer dress, trading with friends, or organizing a dress exchange, where girls donate their once-worn dresses so that others who can't afford new dresses can get a great one for free. For more information, go to *www.donatemydress.org*. If your daughter buys a new dress, ask her to consider donating it after the big day.

  - **Cleanup.** Encourage the prom committee to put recycling bins at the prom site. If the school has a composting program, arrange for food scraps to get composted instead of thrown out.

Pets

Ask anyone who has them—pets are part of the family. And they can go green, too. Pets rely on you to take care of them, so make sure you do that in a way that protects their health and treads lightly on the earth. Here are some suggestions for earth-loving pet owners:

- **Spay or neuter your pet.** According to the Humane Society of the United States (HSUS), between six and eight *million* cats and dogs go into American animal shelters each year. About half of those get adopted, but the other half—three to four million animals—are euthanized. Clearly, pet overpopulation is a problem, one that's unfair to the animals because there aren't enough homes to go around. HSUS estimates that a healthy, fertile cat can give birth to three litters (of four to six kittens each) per year and a dog can give have up to two litters (of six to 10 puppies each) every year. So help minimize pet overpopulation by getting yours spayed or neutered.

Tip Spaying or neutering your pet gets rid of the possibility of uterine, ovarian, and testicular cancer, and may also reduce the risk of illnesses like prostate disease.

- **Choose healthy pet food.** Just like people, pets need nutritious food for good health. But many commercial options are packed with preservatives, fillers, and low-quality ingredients like meat that isn't fit for human consumption. When you buy Fido's food, read labels and watch out for these ingredients:

  - **Animal byproducts.** This means that the food's protein comes from meat products that are unfit for people to eat, such as "4-D Meats." That label refers to animals rejected for human food because they're dead, diseased, dying, or disabled, and includes ones rejected due to drug residues from hormones, antibiotics, and pesticides.

  - **Fillers.** Many pet foods use too much grain as filler, which means your pet may not be getting enough protein. Vermont's Cold River Veterinary Center (*www.crvetcenter.com*) recommends that healthy adult cats get a diet of 50% protein, 25% vegetables, 10% carbohydrates, and 15% fats. For healthy adult dogs, it's 30% protein, 30% vegetables, 20% carbohydrates, and 20% fats. Try to find foods that match these proportions.

Tip If the first ingredient listed on a pet food's label is meat, followed by several byproducts and fillers, the food probably has too much filler and low-quality meat. Even though meat comes first in the list, the ingredients that follow add up.

— **Preservatives.** Watch out for chemicals like BHA, BHT, and ethoxyquin. Instead, choose food that's preserved with vitamins C and E; although less effective than chemical preservatives, they're much healthier for your pet.

Organic pet food can be pricey (just like the human variety), but you'll know Fluffy and Fido are getting healthy food that's free of artificial preservatives, pesticides, hormones, and antibiotics. Here are some brands to try:

— Canidae and Felidae All Natural Pet Foods (*www.canidae.com*)

— Flint River Ranch Super Premium (*www.flintriver.com*)

— Natura Pet Products (*www.naturapet.com*)

— PetGuard (*www.petguard.com*)

— Steve's Real Food for Pets (*www.stevesrealfood.com*)

— Wysong pet foods (*www.wysong.net*)

Tip The site Only Natural Pet Store (*www.onlynaturalpet.com*) helps you find just the right food for your pet. Search by type (dry, grain-free, organic, and so on), main protein source (such as beef or poultry), flavor, or brand.

One way to know what's in your pet's food is to make it yourself. For tips and instructions on do-it-yourself pet food, visit the Cold River Veterinary Center's Home Food page at *www.crvetcenter.com/homefood. htm*. Check with your vet to make sure that the treats you cook up are balanced.

- **Control fleas without poisons.** The pesticides used in flea collars, powders, and spot treatments have generated a lot of controversy. The U.S. EPA says that the chemicals—tetrachlorvinphos and propoxur—don't leave residues at high enough levels to pose health risks. Yet these chemicals can damage the central nervous system (in pets *and* humans) and cause cancer. Pets may lick the chemicals from their fur, and young children, whose developing bodies make them especially vulnerable, may also ingest them. *Poison on Pets II* (*www.nrdc.org/health/poisonsonpets*), a study by the Natural Resources Defense Council (NRDC), has found that residue can remain on a pet's fur at dangerously high levels for weeks after you've put a flea collar on your pet.

Tip To see a list of chemicals used in flea and tick products, and a rating of how hazardous each one may be to your pet's and family's health, visit the NRDC's Green Paws Guide at *www.greenpaws.org/products.php*.

If chemical flea and tick products aren't safe, how do you control these pests? Here are some nontoxic techniques (combine them to get the best results):

— **Use a flea comb.** These combs either trap fleas in the narrow spaces between its teeth or force them to jump off your pet. Brush your pet outside so the fleas won't jump off in the house, and have a container of soapy water ready (use a mild dishwashing liquid, like castile soap—see page 17). Between strokes, dip the comb into the water, leaving loose hairs in the water. In summer (or whenever fleas are active in your area), use the flea comb daily.

— **Bathe your pet frequently.** Use nontoxic shampoo (there's a recipe for a homemade one later in this list) and get your cat or dog good and soapy before rinsing. The fleas will hate it.

— **Wash pet bedding weekly.** Fleas and their eggs accumulate in the places pets sleep, so wash bedding at least once a week. Vacuum the bedding beforehand to suck up fleas, larvae, and eggs.

— **Vacuum regularly.** A University of California study found that this is one of the most effective flea-control techniques, capturing about 96% of adult fleas. Get in the habit of vacuuming all the areas of your house that your pet has access to—rugs, furniture, drapes, even bare floors. When fleas are bad, you may need to vacuum daily.

- **Pay attention to outdoor areas.** Fleas like to hide in long grass, so keep the grass short in your pet's outdoor areas. A biological weapon against fleas is nematodes, a kind of worm that feed on immature fleas. You can buy nematodes (you want the genus *Steinernema*) at garden supply stores. Apply 500 nematodes per square foot of outdoor area.

- **Use natural pesticides—with caution.** If the above methods aren't enough, you may want to try a natural pesticide with ingredients like lemongrass, cedarwood, peppermint, rosemary, or thyme oil. But just because a pesticide says "natural" doesn't mean it's safe. Some oils (including cinnamon, clove, lavender, and eucalyptus) may cause allergic reactions in pets. Avoid pennyroyal oil, which can cause severe reactions like seizures, comas, and even death. Before you use an all-natural pesticide, check the safety of its ingredients at the NRDC's Green Paws database: *www.greenpaws.org/products.php* (all types of oils are listed under *O*).

- **Keep your pet clean and healthy.** Page 218 has tips for finding healthy personal hygiene products that aren't irritating and won't make you sick. Do your pet the same favor with all-natural pet shampoo. Here's how to make one that's easy on your pet's skin—and your budget:

  - 1 quart liquid castile soap (page 17)

  - 4 ounces of glycerin (available at your local pharmacy)

  - 4 ounces of white vinegar

  Combine all the ingredients, and then add enough filtered tap water to make a gallon of shampoo.

- **Clean up responsibly.** It's a fact of life for pet owners: dealing with poop. To clean up after your pet, follow these suggestions:

  - **For cats.** Don't use clumping clay litter in the litter box. Sodium bentonite, which causes the clumping, can poison your kitty cat. When combined with liquid, it can swell up to 15–18 times its dry size, causing serious problems if ingested. And the dust from clay litter can harm your cat's lungs. Finally, mining minerals for use in litter isn't an environmentally friendly process.

    Instead, look for dust-free, mineral-free litters. A good choice is biodegradable litter made from plants. Many kinds can be flushed, and some clump naturally, without sodium bentonite. One brand to try is Feline Pine by Nature's Earth Products (*www.felinepine.com*).

— **For dogs.** Use biodegradable bags to clean up after your pooch, and then compost the bag and the waste. Unlike dumping pet waste in a landfill, where it will remain pretty much forever, composting turns dog poop into compost within a month or two.

If you compost dog waste, keep it separate from your other compost pile. Don't use dog-waste compost on a garden that produces food. For step-by-step instructions on building a composter for pooch poop, visit City Farmer's website at *http://tinyurl.com/ywf9bo*. Another option is Doggie Dooley, which works like a septic system for dog waste: Just shovel dog poop into the tank and, from time to time, add water and Digestive Powder (available from the company that makes the system). For more information, visit *www. doggiedooley.com*.

Tip If your pet wets the carpet, don't clean the spot with bleach. It's better for everyone if you use a mixture of half water and half white vinegar.

Melt ice safely. If you live in a cold climate, you probably use salt or some other product to melt ice on driveways, sidewalks, and walkways. If you read the fine print on these products, you'll probably see a warning about the dangers of salt to pets and children. It can get on a pet's paws or fur, where they may lick it off. Sodium chloride, calcium magnesium acetate, and calcium carbonate (common ingredients in ice-melting products) can cause a pet to suffer from loss of appetite, vomiting, diarrhea, increased thirst, excessive salivation, seizures—even death. To avoid that, try using sand or kitty litter to create a grippy surface. Or buy Safe Paw Ice Melter (*www.safepaw.com*), which is designed to be safe for pets, children, and the environment.

6 Eating Green: It's Not Just Spinach Anymore

"**E**at something green every day" is age-old motherly advice. Generations of kids have heard it as they scrunched up their faces and downed a forkful of spinach or broccoli.

Today, Mom's old advice has gotten an update: Eat *everything* green every day. You don't have to become a vegetarian (although, as page 182 notes, you'd reduce your carbon footprint if you did). Eating green means saying no to farming practices that harm the earth and treat animals as assembly-line products; choosing foods that aren't drenched with synthetic insecticides, weed-killers, and other potentially harmful chemicals; and, if possible, growing your own fruits and veggies to get the freshest, healthiest food possible.

This chapter looks at current farming practices—the good, the bad, and the unappetizing—and how they affect the food you eat so you can make informed choices. You'll also learn all kinds of tips for growing your own food—even if you're a city dweller.

What's in That Cheeseburger?

Some claim it's the pinnacle of American cuisine: a ground-beef patty with a slice of melted cheese served on a bun (pickles optional). In the U.S. alone, people eat more than 13 *billion* cheeseburgers each year, which works out to about one or two every week for the average American carnivore.

When you stop by your favorite fast-food place and order a nice, juicy cheeseburger, what are you really getting? Here's some info that might quell your appetite:

- **Bun.** The wheat used to make the buns was sprayed with pesticides and fungicides, and traces of these chemicals may remain. Butylated hydroxyanisole (BHA), often used as a preservative in baked goods, causes cancer in lab animals at large doses. And even though many fast-food restaurants have stopped using trans fats in their cooking, these fats—which increase your risk of heart disease and diabetes—are still found in many baked goods.

- **Cheese.** Diary products may contain growth hormones (the box on page 178 explains why that might be a problem) and antibiotics. And eating large amounts of alkaline sodium aluminum phosphate, used as an emulsifier in cheese, makes it harder for the body to absorb calcium and phosphorous, two important nutrients.

Bun: Pesticide residue, BHA, trans fats

Lettuce and Tomato: Pesticide residue

Cheese: Traces of hormones and antibiotics, sodium alumnimum phosphate

Beef: Antibiotics, hormones,

- **Beef.** The antibiotics and hormones used on cattle (page 177) can get into the meat you consume. According to the Center for Food Safety, several of these hormones likely have bad effects on people, including cancer and impacts on child development. The European Union has banned U.S. beef since 1985 because of concerns about hormones. The cattle may also be infected with antibiotic-resistant strains of food-borne bacteria, such *E. coli*.

- **Lettuce and tomato.** There could be pesticide residue on the veggies in your burger. These chemicals kill insects, mold, and other pests, so it's no surprise that they may pose dangers to humans, too. The Pesticide Action Network reports that chemicals commonly used on lettuce and tomato crops include diazinon, maneb, chlorothalonil, dimethoate, and methoxyfenozide—all of which can cause cancer, birth defects, infertility, and developmental problems.

Most of those 13 billion cheeseburgers get wolfed down without a thought. But the next time you're stomach's rumbling, think about what's in the food you're about to eat, and consider healthier alternatives (this chapter offers lots). Knowing where your food comes from is half the battle.

Factory Farming

When people think of a farm, many imagine animals grazing in green pastures, a big red barn, and a few chickens scratching around the barnyard. But that idyllic picture couldn't be more different from the realities of 21st-century farming. Small family farms are giving way to *factory farms*, huge operations that treat agriculture as an industry rather than a way of life. According to the U.S. Department of Agriculture (USDA), between 1974 and 2002, the number of corporate-owned U.S. farms increased by 46%, with the largest 1.6% of farms accounting for *half* of American agricultural production. That means big farms are getting bigger.

The food in your local grocery store likely came from a factory farm, a big, industrialized facility that produces large quantities of food. Animal farming lends itself to this practice more easily than grain farming, so the term "factory farm" usually refers to an agribusiness that raises large numbers of animals to slaughter weight in the shortest time possible.

The U.S. EPA calls these farms *concentrated animal feeding operations* (CAFOs). As that name suggests, these are crowded farms that are more concerned with keeping animals alive until it's time to butcher them than with giving them any decent quality of life. And as the EPA defines it, a CAFO is an agricultural operation that keeps animals confined. So instead of being sent out to graze in a pasture, animals get fed in their stalls, cages, or other enclosed area, and the animals are kept in this confinement for at least 45 days in any 12-month period. Table 6-1 shows how the EPA defines medium and large CAFOs for different kinds of livestock.

Table 6-1. How the U.S. EPA Defines Factory Farm Size

Type of Animal	Number of Animals	
	Medium CAFO	Large CAFO
Cattle or veal calves	300–999	1,000 or more
Dairy cows	200–699	700 or more
Swine (less than 55 pounds)	3,000–9,999	10,000 or more
Swine (over 55 pounds)	750–2,499	2,500 or more
Sheep and lambs	3,000–9,999	10,000 or more
Turkeys	16,500–54,999	55,000 or more
Laying hens or broilers (with a liquid manure handling system[1])	9,000–29,999	30,000 or more
Laying hens (with other manure handling system)	25,000–81,999	82,000 or more
Chickens other than laying hens (with other manure handling system)	37,500–124,999	125,000 or more

1. A *liquid manure handling system* uses water to flush chicken excrement into storage areas, which can be large, smelly, open lagoons. This creates a lot of pollution, so the EPA considers a poultry farm that uses this kind of system "large" based on a much smaller number of animals.

Why, you might wonder, is the EPA involved in farming? Because the waste produced by big farms can cause significant harm to the environment. Large and medium CAFOs have to comply with the Clean Water Act to minimize the pollution they cause. (For more on factory farms and the environment, flip ahead to page 182.)

Proponents of factory farms argue that they're more efficient than traditional farms—they produce more food faster and more cheaply. That means more affordable food, which helps address the hunger problem that prevails in many parts of the world.

Opponents question whether a corporate structure that values efficiency above all else is appropriate for farming. These voices call for smaller farms that use sustainable practices to produce fresh food that will be eaten locally, putting food production and environmental stewardship in the hands of local communities.

Note In the U.S., approximately 10 billion animals are slaughtered for food each year. That's about 33% more animals than the human population of the *entire planet*.

As factory farming has grown more widespread, environmentalists, ethicists, scientists, and others have raised concerns about its practices. The sections that follow give a brief overview of these issues.

Concern #1: Factory farms are too big.

The numbers in Table 6-1 are *minimum* thresholds. In practice, large CAFOs may be much, much bigger, cramming far too many animals together in far too small a space. For example, a cattle feedlot, where young cows are severely confined and fattened up before slaughter, may have tens of thousands of animals, while a large-scale egg farm may have a million chickens. The sheer size of such farms presents difficulties in caring adequately for the animals and managing their waste.

Concern #2: Factory farms are cruel.

Animals on factory farms live in appalling conditions. Crammed into narrow pens and cages, they have little or no freedom to move around. Laying chickens spend their lives in crates that are smaller than a cubic foot, giving them about as much floor space as a sheet of copy paper. And some animals are mutilated to make them easier to handle—for example, chickens and turkeys may have their beaks cut off so they won't peck each other in tightly packed cages. And pigs and cattle may be castrated, dehorned, or have their tails cut off—without anesthesia. Animals may be transported in overcrowded trucks for long distances without food, water, rest, or protection from the elements. In poultry-processing plants, chickens are sometimes scalded, skinned, and dismembered without first being killed or even stunned.

> **Note** Although all 50 U.S. states have animal-cruelty laws, most exempt working farms from these laws. So factory farms get away with treating animals in ways that ordinary citizens would get arrested for.

Many people question the ethics of treating animals as nothing more than products to be processed. Even animals destined for the slaughterhouse, they argue, deserve humane treatment while they're alive. Governments are responding to these concerns:

- In 1979, the British government created the Farm Animal Welfare Council, which acts on the principle that farm animals are entitled to five freedoms: freedom from hunger and thirst; freedom from discomfort; freedom from pain, injury, and disease; freedom to express normal behavior; and freedom from fear and distress.

- *Gestation crates*, which confine pregnant sows in a space so narrow they can't turn around or even lie down comfortably, are already banned or are being phased out in the European Union and several U.S. states.

- *Battery cages*, which confine egg-laying hens, and **veal crates** (two-foot-wide cages where calves are confined for their short lives) are also subject to bans and phase-outs in European countries and U.S. states.

> **Note** Maybe you buy "free-range" meat and eggs thinking this label means the animals are treated humanely. But the reality may not match your understanding of the term. The USDA defines "free-range" poultry as birds that have access to the outside, so a farmer could open the coop door for just a few minutes a day and call his products "free-range."

Note Farm Sanctuary, which has facilities in California and New York, educates people about how factory farms treat animals and offers refuge to farm animals. Its website (*http://farmsanctuary.org*) has tons of info about factory farming and stories of rescued animals that now live at Farm Sanctuary.

Concern #3: Factory farms misuse hormones and antibiotics.

Factory farms are in a hurry: The faster they can slaughter animals, the more money they make. So these farms use pharmaceuticals as a shortcut, giving animals hormones and antibiotics to make them grow faster. The box on page 178 has info about the hormones used in beef cattle and dairy cows and the threat that these may pose to people's health. The Union of Concerned Scientists estimates that 70% of all antibiotics produced in the U.S. are given to livestock—that's *eight times* the amount used to treat people. And the animals aren't even sick: The drugs prevent disease and accelerate growth.

Those drugs can make their way into the meat and milk people consume. Hormones, given to two-thirds of U.S.-raised cattle, may promote cancer: breast and reproductive-system cancers in women and prostate cancer in men. See the next section for more on the problems with giving nontherapeutic antibiotics to farm animals.

Hormones in Your Hamburger (and Other Foods, Too)

What hormones does the agriculture industry use on animals? What's the effect of these hormones on human health?

The USDA lets farmers give six different hormones to cattle to make them grow faster: three natural ones—estradiol, progesterone, and testosterone—and three synthetic ones—zeranol, trenbolone acetate, and melengestrol acetate. Typically, a pellet that releases hormones is inserted under the skin of an animal's ear (at slaughter, the ear is discarded).

The natural ones are sex hormones that occur naturally in animals. Because of that, the U.S. Food and Drug Administration (FDA) can't regulate them. The synthetic ones, which *are* monitored by the FDA through random testing, are used in cattle and sheep but are banned in poultry and pigs.

The USDA and the FDA claim that the hormone levels in beef are minimal and won't harm humans. But the European Union bans hormone-treated beef because of concerns that hormone residues in beef may cause hormone imbalances, early-onset puberty in girls, and cancer. There aren't any large-scale, long-term studies to settle the issue one way or the other. The EU has opted for caution, while the U.S. and Canada think that regulated use of these hormones is safe.

Another controversial hormone is *rBGH* (recombinant bovine growth hormone, also known as recombinant bovine somatotropin, or BST). This synthetic hormone is injected into dairy cows to make them produce more milk. The FDA says rBGH is safe to consume, doesn't affect milk's nutritional value, and doesn't have any biological effects in humans. (In other words, human cells don't recognize rGBH and don't respond to it.) But FDA approval came after examining just one unpublished study, conducted by the company that makes the hormone, which tested rBGH on 30 rats for 90 days.

Other countries—including Japan, Canada, Australia, and the European Union—have banned rBGH due to health concerns. The hormone can increase animals' risk of mastitis (inflammation of the udder), malnutrition (because cows lose more nutrients through the milk they produce than they get from their food), reduced fertility, and lameness. Extra milking also causes distress to cows' bodies, shortening their lives. In humans, the main concern comes from the chemical *IGF-1* (insulin-dependent growth factor-1). rBGH makes cows produce extra IGF-1, which can show up in their milk. IGF-1 is naturally present in humans, but increased levels of it have been linked to breast cancer.

In the U.S., you may not be able to tell whether milk comes from rBGH-treated cows, because many states have laws against labeling milk hormone-free. If you prefer hormone-free milk, check out Sustainable Table's rBGH dairy map (*www.sustainabletable.org/shop/dairymap*), which has a state-by-state listing of brands and dairy products that are rBGH-free.

Concern #4: Factory farms cause disease.

It's not a very appetizing thought, but a lot of food-borne illnesses come from animal feces contaminating food. The conditions in factory farms—where tightly penned animals sometimes stand in mounds of manure—and large slaughterhouses can cause the food they produce to get contaminated. Outbreaks of things like *E. coli* and salmonella have increased right along with the rapid growth of factory farming.

One of the main concerns about factory faming practices and disease is the way these farms use antibiotics, which may contribute to the development of so-called *superbugs,* antibiotic-resistant strains of bacteria. An example of a superbug is *methicillin-resistant Staphylococcus aureus* (MRSA), a potentially fatal staph infection that resists the broad-spectrum antibiotics typically used to treat such infections. These superbugs can be passed to people, and they're really hard to treat.

The Union of Concerned Scientists is lobbying to keep farms from putting seven kinds of antibiotics that are important to human medicine into animal feed: penicillins, tetracyclines, macrolides, lincosamides, streptogramins, aminoglycosides, and sulfonamides.

Note Thanks to recent globalization of food production and trade, the likelihood and scope of food contamination has increased. In the past, outbreaks of food-borne diseases were usually contained in a small area, but now they can happen on a national or international scale.

Concern #5: Factory-farmed food is less nutritious.

Some practices used by factory farms decrease the nutritional value of meat from the animals they raise For example, meat and milk from grass-fed cows have more conjugated linoleic acid (CLA)—an antioxidant that may fight cancer and help with weight loss—than feedlot cattle. Grass-fed beef also has more omega-3, a heart-healthy fatty acid that's essential for normal growth.

Similarly, meat from pasture-raised chickens (those that don't live in crowded pens) has less saturated fat and about a quarter fewer calories than meat from their factory-farmed counterparts. According to the group Sustainable Agriculture Research and Education, eggs from pasture-raised hens have 10% less fat, 40% more vitamin A, and **400%** more omega-3 fatty acids than eggs from factory farms.

So what do factory-farmed animals eat, anyway? You know the phrase, "You are what you eat"? The idea is that good nutrition equals good health. If you consume factory farm–raised meat, though, you're eating what those animals ate, which may include:

- **Other animals.** If you think cows eat grass, pigs eat table scraps, and chickens eat seeds and grubs, think again. On factory farms, animals can legally be given feed made from ground-up animal parts, including bones, blood, intestines, feathers, hair, skin, and hooves. (An exception is that cows can no longer eat feed made from certain parts of other cattle, in an effort to combat mad cow disease.) The feed may also contain parts of dead horses, roadkill, and euthanized cats and dogs.

- **Manure.** Believe it or not, manure from cattle, pigs, and poultry is a common ingredient in animal feed.

- **Plastic.** Yes, you read that right. Plastic has no nutritional value, but because animals on factory farms eat manufactured feed instead of the food their bodies are designed for, many don't get enough *roughage*, the dietary fiber they need to stimulate their intestines. So some factory farms use plastic pellets to make up for the lack of natural fiber in the animal's feed.

- **Grain.** Finally, something that's good for the animals, right? Not all of them. Cows, for example, aren't designed to eat the grain-rich diet that's used to fatten them up for slaughter, and such food can cause problems with their digestive systems and livers.

Concern #6: Factory farms drive family farms out of business.

The USDA estimates that between 2005 and 2006, the United States lost 8,900 farms—that's about a farm an hour. One major cause is the agribusiness industry. Large factory farms can take advantage of government subsidies that are out of reach for smaller operators. Just four industrial farming firms make up 60–80% of the important agriculture markets in the U.S., including beef, poultry, and pork processing. This near-monopoly prices smaller producers out of the market.

Some people think that family farms are the agricultural equivalent of eight-track tapes and typewriters: an outmoded way of doing things. Family farms, they argue, may be a nice, nostalgic idea, but if they can't produce food as efficiently and cheaply as large-scale corporate operations, perhaps their time has come and gone. This argument ignores several important aspects of family farms:

- **Most farming families live on the farms that they tend.** That means they have more respect for the land and care for it better because it's more than a means of income—it's their home. For this reason, family farms tend to be greener than corporate farms.

- **Family farms sustain local economies.** Small farms hire local help and buy supplies from local businesses. Factory farms, on the other hand, are designed to produce the maximum about of food with the minimum number of workers, and they usually buy supplies from outside the area and truck them in, adding to traffic and air pollution.

- **With local family farms, you know where your food came from.** You can talk to the farmers who produced it, and you know it's fresh because it came from right down the road. With corporate farms, the people in charge are often in offices far away from the land their company farms. Factory farms are less interested in feeding the local community than in transporting their products to wherever they can get the best prices.

If these benefits of family farms are important to you, seek out local, seasonal food to support them, rather than buying whatever's cheapest.

> **Tip** The Slow Food movement promotes local food that's sustainably grown, and the idea that food is "a cornerstone of pleasure, culture, and community." To become a slow foodie or just learn more about the movement, visit *www.slowfoodusa.org*.

Concern #7: Factory farms make bad neighbors.

When you think about the countryside, you probably imagine green fields and fresh air. That's not what it's like near a factory farm, though: They stink. People living near hog farms, for example, have higher-than-normal rates of respiratory problems, runny noses, sore throats, burning eyes, and headaches. A factory farm also causes increased traffic in the area (from trucks bringing in supplies and carrying animals to slaughter) and can lower property values.

Concern #8: Factory farms cause pollution.

The smell that comes from factory farms isn't the biggest problem for the surrounding area. These farms pose a serious threat to the environment. When you've got thousands of animals crowded together, all the manure they produce has to go somewhere. Unfortunately, much of it pollutes the air and water around the farm—and adds masses of greenhouse gases to the atmosphere. The next section has more info about the impact factory farms have on the environment.

Note Industrialized farming causes a lot of pollution by trucking food vast distances. If you live in the U.S., the average distance food travels before it reaches your table is between 4,000 and 5,000 miles—another reason to buy local food whenever possible.

The Meat Industry's Environmental Hoofprint

As you learned in the previous sections, industrialized farming raises concerns about health, humane treatment of animals, and farming communities. Another big concern for people who want to eat green is how the meat and dairy industries affect the environment. These farms pollute the air, water, and earth, and have a massive carbon footprint. Way back in 1997, a report by the U.S. Senate Agricultural Committee warned, "The threat of pollution from intensive livestock and poultry farms is a national problem."

There's no getting around the fact that lots of animals equals lots of manure. On many farms, that waste goes into huge, open-air, artificial lagoons. In fact, "huge" may be an understatement: On a big factory farm, a lagoon may span 5–7 acres and contain 20–45 *million* gallons of waste. Aside from the obvious stench, these lagoons also pollute the air with chemicals including ammonia, methane, and hydrogen sulfide.

In the U.S., it's the EPA's job to make sure that factory farms comply with the Clean Water Act. Still, pollution happens. In fact, the EPA estimates that hog, chicken, and cattle waste has polluted 35,000 miles of rivers in 22 states and contaminated groundwater in 17 states.

Some farms spray liquefied manure on crops as a fertilizer, which may contain bacteria and cause food-borne illness. The manure can also run off and contaminate streams, rivers, and lakes, pollute drinking water, kill fish, and disrupt ecosystems.

But in this era of rapid global warming (page 263), one of the biggest problems with the meat industry is the amount of greenhouse gases livestock produce. According to the U.S. EPA, worldwide livestock farming releases more methane—a potent greenhouse gas—than any other human activity. Globally, such farming sends about 80 million metric tons of methane into the atmosphere each year—much of that from animals' flatulence and burping—which is about 28% of all methane released by people's activities. Other greenhouse gases produced by livestock farming include nitrous oxide and carbon dioxide.

Different kinds of animals create different amounts of greenhouse gases. The U.K. Department for the Environment, Food and Rural Affairs says that beef and lamb have the biggest carbon footprint: Each ton of meat accounts for 16 tons of carbon dioxide. Pigs and poultry have a smaller (but still significant) carbon footprint: five tons of carbon dioxide per ton of pork and four tons for chicken.

So what can you do to reduce the greenhouse-gas emissions from farming? The best thing is to reduce demand by eating less meat. A Carnegie Mellon University study concluded that each person who shifts from a meat-based diet to a vegetable-based one reduces greenhouse-gas emissions by the equivalent of driving 8,000 fewer miles.

Note Journalist Jamais Cascio calculated the energy costs of producing a cheeseburger: the farming, production, transportation, cooking, and so on. He figured that each year, all the cheeseburgers eaten in the U.S. are responsible for between 65 million and 195 million metric tons of greenhouse gases. That's the same amount of gases emitted by 6.5–19 million SUVs in a year. To see how Cascio crunched the numbers, go to http://openthefuture.com/cheeseburger_CF.html.

Genetically Modified Foods

Opponents call them Frankenfoods. Proponents say they're hardier, more nutritious, and more resistant to pests and disease than regular crops. Many European consumers won't touch them, and many Americans don't realize they're already eating them. Although *genetically modified* (GM) foods have become increasingly widespread—particularly in the U.S.—they're still controversial.

A GM crop is engineered in a lab by adding a gene that's not normally a part of that plant. For example, the first GM crop to hit the market back in 1994 was a tomato, called the FlavrSavr, which had an added gene that made it more resistant to rot, giving it a longer shelf life.

Such crops are designed to improve upon nature, and they do offer lots of advantages. For example, some have been engineered to be resistant to pests, which means farmers can cut back on pesticides. Others resist diseases and herbicides (which farmers may use to kill weeds). Still others tolerate cold or drought better than regular crops, contain higher levels of vitamins and other nutrients, or deliver medicine.

So what about the Frankenfood claims? One of the biggest objections is that these crops have already made their way into the food chain and onto supermarket shelves without any long-term studies of their potential health effects. Introducing foreign genes into foods may have unexpected negative impacts on people who eat them. One study, for example, compared rats that ate GM potatoes with rats that ate regular potatoes and found adverse effects in the intestines of the GM-eating rats.

Another concern is that GM foods may cause or activate allergies. Some cotton workers in India, for instance, have allergic reactions to GM cotton—yet are unaffected by normal cotton. Or someone who's allergic to a certain food may unknowingly eat a supposedly "safe" food that's been modified with a gene from the allergen, triggering a reaction.

GM foods pose environmental risks, too. For example, such crops may cross-pollinate with regular plants, creating undesirable hybrids. They may also harm wildlife, such as a pest-resistant crop that kills butterflies or other beneficial insects. And, ironically, herbicide-resistant GM crops can lead to an *increase* in the use of weed-killers because farmers can spray their fields without worrying about damaging their crops.

Finally, there are ethical questions about GM foods. These crops are patented, and the companies that create them see them as an investment. Unlike traditional crops, whose seeds farmers can save and plant next year, GM seeds have to be licensed or bought new each year. This reduces farmers' sustainability and threatens to send seed prices sky-high. Similarly, GM crops grown near an organic farm can cross-pollinate that farm's plants. Because USDA regulations say organic crops can't be GM, the organic farmer ends up with produce he can't sell as organic.

In the U.S. (unlike in Europe), there aren't any laws that make companies label GM foods. So U.S. consumers have no way of knowing whether stuff they buy, particularly processed foods, have been genetically engineered. The most common GM crops in the U.S. are soybeans, corn, and canola (pressed for cooking oil). If you want to avoid GM foods, stay away from these foods or buy from local farmers who don't grow GM crops.

Go Organic

If you've read this far in the chapter without feeling a little queasy, you've got a strong stomach. But just because it's strong doesn't mean you want to fill it up with junk and synthetic chemicals. When your stomach starts rumbling, look for clean, healthy foods that'll feed your body, nourish your soul, and support sustainable agriculture. The following sections teach you how.

What Does "Organic" Really Mean?

In general, saying a food is organic means it was produced without any artificial substances, like chemical pesticides on crops or synthetic hormones in beef. That's the basic definition. But once governments get involved, things get more complicated. The official definition of organic depends on where you live.

In the U.S., the USDA is the agency that defines *organic*. It lets foods carry the "organic" label if they meet these requirements:

- Crops are grown without the use of most chemical pesticides and synthetic fertilizers (page 34). Fields have to be free of these substances for at least three years before crops grown there are considered organic.

- Farmers can't use sewage sludge to fertilize crops. They can use fresh manure, but there's a waiting period between when the fertilizer is applied and when the food can be harvested. (This waiting period doesn't apply to nonorganic crops.)

- Foods have to be free of genetically modified ingredients (see page 183).

- Producers can't use irradiation to kill bacteria.

- For eggs, meat, and dairy products, the animals have to be fed 100% organic feed. For ruminants (animals whose natural diet is grass), this includes letting them graze in pastures.

- Livestock farmers have to create and maintain living conditions that accommodate animals' natural behavior and good health, such as access to the outdoors, shade, shelter, fresh air, and sunlight.

- Livestock farmers have to manage manure so that is doesn't contaminate crops, soil, or water.

- Farmers can't use synthetic growth hormones or antibiotics to treat healthy animals.

Those are the main guidelines for raising organic food. On a label, though, "organic" doesn't always mean organic, so read carefully:

- **100% organic.** Foods with this label contain nothing but organically produced ingredients (excluding water and salt).

- **Organic.** This label means that the food has at least 95% organically produced ingredients.

- **Made with organic ingredients.** Some of the stuff in items with this label is organic—but not all of it. Processed foods marked this way have to contain at least 70% organic ingredients.

> **Tip** To learn how other countries define organic, visit Organic Europe (*www.organic-europe.net*), the Canadian Food Inspection Agency (*www.inspection.gc.ca*), Australian Certified Organic (*www.australianorganic.com.au*), or the New Zealand Ministry of Agriculture and Forestry (*www.maf.govt.nz*).

Why Organic Is Better for the Earth

Because of the constraints placed on organic farmers, the food they produce is less harmful to the planet than factory-farmed foods. Organic farming creates:

- **Less pollution.** Page 182 describes the huge toll factory farming takes on the environment. Nonorganic crop farming causes other environmental problems, as well, chiefly through the use of pesticides (page 29) and synthetic fertilizers (page 34), which can run off and pollute lakes, rivers, and groundwater.

- **Healthier soil.** A 21-year field trial conducted in Switzerland found that organic farming practices enhanced soil fertility and biodiversity—the soil had more mycorrhizae (fungi that attach to roots and help plants absorb nutrients), beneficial microbes, and earthworms than soil farmed using conventional methods. Other studies indicate that soil on organic farms holds water better, which means less watering and more water conservation.

- **Fewer greenhouse-gas emissions.** The main reason that organic farming produces fewer greenhouse gases is that it doesn't use synthetic fertilizers, which take a lot of energy to produce. For example, it takes 9.8 kWh to produce a single kilogram of nitrogen fertilizer.

Why Organic Is Better for You

Many people go organic because they figure food produced without a lot of synthetic chemicals and other iffy substances must be better for their health. As this section shows, the evidence is on their side.

There's plenty of data to suggest that organically produced food is more nutritious than its nonorganic counterpart. For example, a four-year study for the European Union, completed in 2007, found that organic fruits and vegetables contain up to 40% more antioxidants than nonorganic ones, and organic milk had 60% more antioxidants than the nonorganic kind.

A three-year Italian study published in the *Journal of Agricultural and Food Chemistry* in 2002 found higher levels of antioxidants in organic peaches and pears (and about 8% more vitamin C in organic peaches) than in nonorganic fruits. A 2003 study in the same journal found 52% more vitamin C in frozen organic corn than in conventional corn. And a Washington State University experiment found that people thought organically grown apples tasted better—firmer, sweeter, and less tart—than nonorganic ones.

But not everyone agrees that organic food is more nutritious. For example, researchers at the University of Copenhagen grew carrots, kale, peas, apples, and potatoes using three different farming methods:

- With animal manure as fertilizer and without pesticides.
- With animal manure as fertilizer and with legal amounts of pesticides.
- With mineral fertilizer and with legal amounts of pesticides.

After harvest, they analyzed the crops and, in 2008, published their results. They found no differences in the levels of major and trace nutrients in the fruit and vegetables, whichever farming method was used.

Grass-fed beef

Beef from cows that eat grass may be healthier for red-meat eaters than the factory-farmed kind. The Union of Concerned Scientists surveyed available studies, which suggest that grass-fed beef contains less fat per serving, and higher levels of omega-3 fatty acids (which are good for your heart) and CLAs (conjugated linoleic acids), which are thought to fight cancer, clogging of the arteries, and type-2 diabetes as well as strengthen the immune system.

Two kinds of beef can be labeled "grass-fed" in the U.S.:

- **Grass-finished.** The animal ate grass throughout its life.
- **Grain-finished.** The animal was fed grain, not grass, for up to six months before slaughter. This technique can dramatically diminish levels of omega-3 fatty acids and CLAs.

When you're buying beef, read the fine print to avoid grain-finished beef. If you're paying more for grass-fed beef, you want all the health benefits.

Pesticide-free foods

Given current farming practices, it's best to go organic when you buy certain fruits and vegetables because they may contain high levels of pesticide residue. Other foods don't get the same heavy doses of pesticides because pests don't particularly like the crop (such as asparagus) or the crop has a thick or tough skin (like kiwis and pineapples). Table 6-2 shows which foods to buy from the organic aisle and which ones aren't likely to have high levels of pesticides even if you buy non-organic.

Table 6-2. When to Buy Organic Produce vs. the Regular Kind

Buy Organic	Buy Regular Produce
Apples	Asparagus
Bell peppers	Avocado
Carrots	Bananas
Celery	Broccoli
Cherries	Cabbage
Citrus fruits (if you're using their peel for zest)	Cauliflower
Grapes (imported)	Corn
Kale	Grapefruit
Lettuce and other leafy greens	Eggplant
Nectarines	Kiwis
Peaches	Mangoes
Pears	Melons
Potatoes (if you plan to eat the skins)	Onions
Raspberries	Papayas
Spinach	Peas
Strawberries	Pineapples
	Sweet potatoes
	Watermelons

To minimize your exposure to pesticide residues in food, follow these common-sense tips:

- **Wash fruits and vegetables thoroughly before eating them.** Rub or scrub produce while rinsing them in tap water for 30 seconds to a minute. (You don't need to use soap!)

- **Get out the paring knife and peel.** This won't remove *all* pesticide residues because some get absorbed into the fruit or veggie, but it significantly reduces the amount of pesticide by getting rid of the part that got sprayed with the stuff. The downside: You may lose some nutritional value by taking off the skin.

- **Cook when possible.** Heating foods helps remove some of the pesticides that may linger after washing and peeling.

- **Vary your diet.** Variety is more than the spice of life; it's also a protection against pesticides building up in your body. Because different pesticides are used on different crops, eating a wide array of fruits and vegetables, instead of just a few favorites, helps ensure you're not getting too much of any one pesticide.

- **Trim the fat.** Carnivores take note: Pesticide residue doesn't just lurk in produce, it can also accumulate in animal fat. So be sure to trim the fat from that steak before you toss it on the grill. (This also reduces your intake of saturated fat—and as your doctor will tell you, that's good for your heart.)

Finding Organic Products

Whether you want to buy organic products for your health or the earth's (or both), there are lots of places to find them. The organic aisle of your grocery store is a good start—particularly if the produce there comes from local sources. Here are some other options:

- **Farmers markets** cut out the middle man; the growers sell organic foods directly to consumers. So the stuff you find here is fresher and often cheaper than at the grocery store. You can also ask farmers about how they grow their crops.

- **Food co-ops** (short for "cooperatives") are businesses that have members who buy shares and then get food at a discount. Most co-ops focus on local food, and usually stock lots of organic products. Some are open to the public; others are for members only. To find one near you, check out Cooperative Grocer's directory at *www.cooperativegrocer.coop/coops*.

- **Community-supported agriculture (CSA) programs** are one way that small farms have been able to compete with larger operations. The farms sell shares to people in the community, and use the money to run the farm. In return, shareholders get weekly shipments of food at harvest time.

- **Health-food stores** are a reliable source of organic food and worth checking out. These places can be pricey, though (they often charge more than the local grocery store), so keep an eye out for sales.

- **Online stores** are happy to sell you organic products and ship them right to your door. If you go to a search engine like Google, type in *organic*, and then click the Search button, you'll find a gazillion possibilities.

> **Tip** To find sources of organic foods near you, visit the Organic Consumers Association (*www.organicconsumers.org*), LocalHarvest (*www.localharvest.org*), and the Eat Well Guide (*www.eatwellguide.org*).

How Green Does Your Garden Grow?

One way to know exactly how your food was produced is to grow it yourself. Organic gardening isn't just for professional farmers and hippies on communes: All kinds of people grow their own food, from suburbanites with back-yard vegetable patches to city folk growing tomatoes on fire escapes. This section gets you up to speed on basic organic gardening techniques.

> **Tip** A great source of seeds for the organic gardener is Seeds of Change (*www.seedsofchange.com*), a company committed to preserving biodiversity and promoting sustainable, organic agriculture.

The Joy of Composting

Composting has two main benefits: It reduces the amount of biodegradable garbage you send to the landfill and creates **compost**, dark brown, crumbly, decomposed organic matter. Compost improves soil structure and health, helps beneficial microbes, attracts earthworms, and releases its nutrients slowly, so they're available to plants throughout the growing season. No wonder gardeners call compost black gold.

Compost gets created when different kinds of waste—often referred to as "green" (materials that are moist and rich in nitrogen, like grass clippings and kitchen scraps) and "brown" (materials that are dry and high in carbon, like dead leaves, shredded paper, and sawdust)—combine with air and water and decompose over about three or four weeks.

Getting started with compost

Compost is easy to make. You can just pile scraps in your back yard, but because kitchen garbage smells appetizing to hungry critters, it's best to use a compost bin, which you can buy or build your own. The bin can be square or round, and be made of wood, plastic, wire, even bricks or cinderblocks. **Compost tumblers** are bins that turn, making it easier for air to get at the compost inside.

> **Tip** One easy way to make your own compost bin is to buy a plastic trash can with a lid (about three feet tall). Drill 8–10 holes in the bottom of the bin and a few in its sides. That's all there is to it—you're ready to start making compost.

After you've chosen a bin (or decided to go with a simple pile), choose where you'll make compost. A sunny spot will speed up the process, as long as you don't let the compost dry out. Partial or full shade is okay, but it may take a bit longer.

When you're ready to get started, follow these steps to create compost for your garden:

1. **Layer waste in your bin.** Use a mixture of green and brown materials (Table 6-3 offers suggestions to get you started). On top of that, add a layer of existing compost, garden soil, bone meal, cow manure, or other compost starter. This introduces the beneficial bacteria that get compost going. The materials in your compost bin should be damp but not sopping wet; if they seem dry, sprinkle on some water.

2. **Keep adding green and brown materials,** with water and a compost starter between the layers, until you have a pile two to three feet high.

3. **Turn the pile regularly (at least once a week)** to keep the developing compost in contact with the air it needs. Use a pitchfork or shovel (or turn the handle if you have a compost tumbler). The more often you turn the pile, the quicker you'll have compost.

> **Tip** To make the turning process easier, keep two bins next to each other: one full and one empty. Simply shovel the contents of the full bin into the empty one.

4. **After several weeks, you should have some compost that's ready to use.** Finished compost smells earthy and is crumbly and black or dark brown; it looks like potting soil. Sift your compost through a screen and return any coarse stuff to the compost bin.

Mix compost with garden soil and use it in the garden or for potted plants. If you're planting a lawn, enrich the soil with compost first to make your grass grow lush and green. And remember to save a little compost to help start the next batch.

Table 6-3. Compost Ingredients

Green	Brown
Coffee grounds	Dead leaves (shred them to speed the process)
Used tea bags	Hay
Grass clippings	Straw
Weeds and other plants	Shredded paper (including newspapers, napkins, and paper bags)
Fruits and fruit scraps	Sawdust
Vegetables and vegetable scraps	Pine needles
Eggshells	Wood ash
Manure from grass-eating animals (horses, cows, sheep, rabbits, etc.)	Compostable packaging

Composting tips and tricks

Once you've got your compost started, nature takes its course. Aside from the steps in the previous section, there's not much you have to do. The following advice, however, can help make sure your composting is as fast and easy as possible:

- **Know what *not* to compost.** Some items don't belong in the pile, including:
    — Meat scraps.

    — Bones.

    — Fatty foods.

    — Dairy products.

    — Highly salted foods.

    — Coated or glossy paper.

    — Human waste.

    — Pet waste.

    — Diseased plants.

    — Materials that have come in contact with a sick person.

    — Plant matter treated with pesticides or weed killers.

- **Balance green and brown.** Traditional wisdom says your pile should be two parts brown materials to one part green. Some gardeners, however, say that there's no need to be strict about this ratio—even a 50–50 mix can create good compost.

- **What's that smell?** Properly developing compost doesn't smell bad. If your pile starts to smell sour, it's not getting enough air. Turn it more frequently, and the smell should go away. If the pile smells like ammonia, you've got too much green material; add some extra brown stuff to balance it out.

- **Time your composting.** You can make compost year round, but the process goes faster in warm weather. Some gardeners start new compost in the spring so it's ready in time for them to begin planting; others start in the fall, composting the leaves they rake up from the yard.

Natural Pest Control

If you grow your own food, you're not the only one who wants to eat it: Insects and other hungry pests want to snack on it, too. This section explains how to keep pests from spoiling your harvest, without resorting to toxic synthetic chemicals.

Vermicomposting

Vermicomposting supercharges regular compost by adding worms to the mix. These critters create high-quality compost by eating the wastes you throw on the pile and producing *worm castings* (that's the technical term for worm poop). These castings are full of nutrients plants love and contain microbes that break down nutrients in the soil into forms plants can use. Worm castings also contain mucous, which slows the release of nutrients.

Vermicomposting uses two kinds of worms: red wigglers (*Eisenia foetida*) and red earthworms (*Lumbricus rubellus*), which you can order online from sites like Uncle Jim's Worm Farm (*www.unclejimswormfarm.com*) or Kazarie Worm Farm (*www.kazarie.com*). The worms are hungry little guys; they can eat up to half their body weight each day.

A vermicomposting bin should be wide and shallow, with air holes in the bottom and a lid (worms don't like light). Line the bin with a bedding material like leaves or shredded paper. (It should be damp but not soggy.) Mound up the bedding to create air pockets, and then sprinkle in some dirt or compost. Next, add the worms and the materials you want to compost.

As with a regular compost bin, you can feed your worms fruit and vegetable scraps, paper, eggshells (it helps if you crush them)—pretty much any kind of green material (see Table 6-3). Acidic fruits and vegetables and salt can harm the worms' skin, so avoid these. And keep an eye on the temperature: Worms can freeze to death, so if you keep the bin outside, bring it in when the weather hits freezing. (If everything's working right, the bin shouldn't smell bad. If it does, you're probably giving the worms more scraps than they can eat.)

Birds do it, bees do it—and so do red wigglers. If all goes well, your worms will reproduce, probably pretty quickly. Use the extra worms to start a new bin or your own worm farm, or give them away to gardening friends.

Some people use vermicomposting to break down dog poop. For a good article on the topic, go to *www.wormmainea.com/Projects.html*. The Pet Poo Converter is a vermiculture compost bin specifically designed for pet waste that you can buy at many organic gardening suppliers. If you use this method, keep these three caveats in mind:

- Create a separate bin for dog waste—don't mix it with regular compost.
- Don't vermicompost waste from a dog that has recently been treated for worms.
- Don't use compost made from dog poop on a garden that'll produce food; it's fine for flower gardens and trees, though.

Neem oil

This oil is a natural pesticide that's popular with organic gardeners. It comes from the seeds of the neem tree, which is in the mahogany family and native to India and Myanmar. When insects munch on leaves sprayed with this stuff, it disrupts their hormonal balance and prevents them from maturing. Its smell repels many insects, and it kills mites and fungus. Even though bugs hate it, neem oil is nontoxic to humans (it's used in traditional Indian medicine).

Mix the oil with water according to the package directions and spray it on plants. Water washes it away, so reapply it after rains. Neem oil can take a while to work, but it's really effective because it kills developing insects.

Floral insecticides

These pesticides are natural substances extracted from flowers and other parts of plants. They have strong, distinctive odors that repel pests or attract them to a trap or poisonous substance. Some also keep cats and dogs away from your plants. These plant-derived products include rose, cinnamon, and clove oils. They're nontoxic to humans (some are even considered foods), but sometimes they're mixed with toxic stuff, as in bug traps, so be sure to read the label carefully.

Tip For a fact sheet that lists the floral attractants, repellants, and insecticides registered with the EPA, along with their properties and uses, visit *http://tinyurl. com/dxvgd6*.

Insecticidal soap

This soap is typically made from potassium salts combined with fatty acids and used as a spray. When it touches a bug, the soap penetrates the bug's cell membranes and makes the cells collapse, killing the insect. To work, the soap has to come into direct contact with a bug; it loses effectiveness after it's dried. This stuff works best on soft-bodied insects like aphids, whiteflies, mealybugs, thrips, and spider mites.

Insecticidal soap is nontoxic to humans and animals. In fact, you can use it on your veggies right up to the time you harvest them. It can be mildly irritating to eyes and skin, though, so wear gloves and be careful when you're spraying. It washes away cleanly, leaving no residue.

One word of caution: Insecticidal soap can burn plants, causing brown or yellow spots or scorching on leaves. The label should tell you which plants it may stress. Avoid using it too often, when it's really hot out, or in direct sunlight.

Pyrethrin powder

Pyrethrins come from the seed casings of the chrysanthemum plant and are available as powders to dust on plants. The powder attacks insects' nervous systems, killing them quickly. Pyrethrins can cause respiratory and skin irritation—so use them with care around pets and kids—and degrade within a day. Be aware, though, that pyrethrins will kill just about *any* insect, including ones you want in your garden, like butterflies and honeybees.

Sabadilla powder

This insecticide, a powder derived from the seeds of the Sabadilla lily, works as both a contact and a digestive-system poison, meaning it kills bugs that get powder sprinkled on them and those that eat it. It's highly toxic to insects (including honeybees) but nontoxic to people and animals. Be careful using it, though—it can irritate eyes and mucus membranes and cause sneezing fits.

Insect barriers and traps

Physical barriers keep insects away from your plants without any nasty substances. Here are three common ways to keep bugs off your plants:

- **Fabric covers.** These barriers (also called *row covers*) are made of lightweight, loosely woven fabric that lets sunlight and rain though but keeps bugs—and birds—out.

Note Remove covers when a plant flowers, so bees can pollinate the plants.

- **Traps.** These devices attract insects, and then trap them in something sticky.
- **Bug vacuums.** These cordless vacuums (some are rechargeable, others battery-operated) suck insects into traps, where the bugs die. (Some have built-in bug zappers to kill the insects.)

Manual removal

For small gardens, one of the most effective, chemical-free ways to get rid of bugs is to pick them off with your fingers (wear gloves to avoid stings and the general yuck factor). It's tedious, but it works. Look for caterpillars, egg masses, beetles, slugs, and so on. Drop your pickings into a bucket of soapy water to make sure they don't come back. You'll probably need to do this daily for the best results.

Bacillus thuringiensis

Bacillus thuringiensis (Bt) is a kind of bacteria; more than 80 types of it are used to control pests. When you sprinkle Bt powder on your plants, bugs eat it and the bacteria disrupt the bugs' digestive systems so the bugs stop eating and starve. (As you might guess, it takes a while time for this method to work.) The powder breaks down quickly in sunlight, so you have to reapply it frequently.

Bt strains are specific to particular hosts; they won't harm people, pets, honeybees, or birds, although Bt will kill butterfly larvae. Products labeled simply *Bt* will kill caterpillars and some worms, such as tomato horn worms. Other kinds of Bt get rid of pests like mosquitoes and potato beetles. Check the label to see which bugs a particular kind of Bt kills.

Insect predators

The bugs you're battling in your garden have many natural enemies, so make these predators your allies. Ladybugs, lacewings, spined soldier bugs, pirate bugs, nematodes, and other carnivorous bugs will make a meal out of your garden's pests. You can buy them at natural gardening stores.

> **Tip** Extremely Green Gardening Co. has an extensive list of pests and their predators at www.extremelygreen.com/pestcontrolguide.cfm.

For City Dwellers: Community Gardens and Other Ways to Grow Your Own Food

Just because you live in a city doesn't mean you can't have an organic garden. Even if your outdoor space is limited to a postage stamp–sized balcony, fire escape, or spot in front of a window, you can still supplement your diet with healthy organic food.

Tip A great resource for urban farmers is City Farmer, a Vancouver, Canada–based organization that educates people about composting and growing food in cities. The group's website (*www.cityfarmer.info*) has tons of great news, tips, and inspirational stories.

Container gardens

When you think of container gardens, you might think of flowers in terracotta pots artistically arranged on a deck, balcony, or patio. But you can grow veggies in containers, too. Start seedlings in seed trays or empty egg cartons while you find and ready your containers.

Any type of container will work as long as it has adequate drainage. Get creative and see what's around the house that you can reuse as a mini-garden: baskets, buckets, metal cans, and so on. For most crops, you'll probably want a five-gallon container. Drill or punch holes around the container (between 1/4 and 1/2 inch from the bottom), drop in about an inch of gravel, and then fill it with potting soil. That's it—just transplant your seedlings into it.

Here are some plants that do particularly well in containers:

— Avocados

— Cantaloupes

— Cucumbers

— Eggplants

— Green beans

— Lettuces

— Peppers

— Radishes

— Some fruit trees, like citrus and figs

— Squash

— Strawberries and other berries

— Tomatoes

Hungry yet?

Tip Herbs and seasonings—including basil, parsley, thyme, and green onions, to name just a few—are also good candidates. They thrive in smaller containers: pots 6–10 inches in diameter.

Here are some tips for making your containers bear fruit (or vegetables, as the case may be):

- For tomatoes, beans, cantaloupes, cucumbers, and other plants that need support as they grow, put a wire cage around the container or tie the plants to stakes. (Old pantyhose work great for tying plants to supports.)

- Make sure your container has proper drainage, or water will collect in the soil and kill the plants. In general, watering once per day is plenty.

- Avoid getting the leaves wet when you water.

- Mix soil with compost for nutrient-rich potting soil.

- If you use plant food that dissolves in water, rinse out the soil once a week with plain water so unused fertilizer won't build up and burn the roots.

Rooftop gardens

One often-overlooked piece of urban real estate is the roof. You can use any flat roof as a space for containers or a place to build raised beds (make sure they drain well).

Rooftop gardens are subject to some special considerations, so answer these questions before you begin:

- **Can you use the roof?** If you don't own the building, ask your landlord or condo/co-op board if it's okay to garden up there. You may also need to check with your city to make sure you're not violating any zoning laws.

- **How strong is it?** Soil, water, and plants can be heavy. Don't plan a bigger garden than your roof can support. (The edges of the roof can hold more weight than the center.)

- **How's the weather up there?** Rooftop gardens may be more exposed to sun and wind than their ground-level counterparts. Heat rising from the building combined with more sunlight means it can be 30–40° F (16–22° C) warmer on the roof than at ground level. You may have to shade your plants or shield them from the wind.

Tip Rainwater harvesting (page 68) is perfect for rooftop gardens. A simple rain barrel in the corner means you won't have to lug a full watering can upstairs.

Community gardens

Community gardening (called *allotment gardening* in the U.K.) gives city dwellers a chance to tend a plot in a shared garden. These gardens, owned by cities or nonprofits, are about as varied as can be: some are for flowers only, others grow vegetables. Some rent out plots and let the renters grow what they want and keep the results, while others share the harvest among growers, sell food to local restaurants or at farmers markets, or donate to local food banks.

When you apply for a plot in a community garden, ask about rules, expectations, and what you'll need: How much does it cost to apply for or rent a plot? What are the garden's hours? Are any plants prohibited? (Trees or tall plants, for example, may create too much shade on a neighboring plot.) Is there a shed where you can store tools? Do gardeners share tools or should you bring your own? Knowing what to expect will help you get the most of the experience.

To find a community garden near you, visit one of these sites:

- **American Community Gardening Association** (*http://community-garden.org*) lists gardens in the U.S. and Canada and has info on how to start a community garden in your city.

- **City Farmer** (*www.cityfarmer.info/category/community-gardens*) has news about and photos of community gardens to provide inspiration.

- **National Society of Allotment and Leisure Gardeners** (*www.nsalg.org.uk*) works to promote allotment gardening in the U.K.

- **Australian City Farms and Community Gardens Network** (*www.communitygarden.org.au*) has lots of info about community gardening and a directory of gardens in Australia and New Zealand.

Can I Ever Eat Out Again?

After reading this chapter, you may wonder whether it's safe to even set foot in a restaurant, thanks to factory farming and other questionable agricultural practices. But what fun would life be without the occasional candlelit dinner for two, family get-together, or meal with friends—where someone *else* prepares the food and cleans up afterward?

You don't have to give up dining out when you go organic, you just need to put a little more thought into it. Here are some tips:

- **Check the Yellow Pages.** Many phonebooks list "organic" as a restaurant category. Call and ask what percentage of the menu is made from organic foods, and for examples of organic dishes.

- **Look for restaurants that buy locally.** As you learned earlier, locally grown food is fresher and hasn't been flown, shipped, or trucked hundreds or thousands of miles to reach you. And small, local farms are more likely to use sustainable farming practices. Knowing this, many restaurants who buy from local farms advertise that fact. If you haven't seen any such ads, call a few restaurants and ask if they buy locally (especially from farms that use organic or sustainable techniques).

Tip LocalHarvest, a website that promotes local and organic food, has a search feature to help you find organic restaurants in the U.S. and Canada. Go to *www.localharvest.org* and, in the "What are you looking for?" section, turn on the Restaurants radio button. Enter a Zip or postal code, or a city and state or province, and then click Search. LocalHarvest can also help you find farms, farmers markets, and co-ops that sell organic food. You can also find organic restaurants with the Eat Well Guide (*www.eatwellguide.org*) and HappyCow's Vegetarian Guide (*www.happycow.net*).

- **Try vegan.** Even people who aren't committed vegetarians enjoy an occasional vegetarian or vegan meal. Many vegan restaurants focus on fresh, local, organic ingredients.

- **Meat-eaters can be organic, too.** If you're in the mood for a nice, juicy steak, look for a steakhouse that serves beef from grass-fed cattle. Ask to make sure it's grass-finished, not grain-finished (see page 188).

- **Make your preferences known.** If you have a favorite local restaurant but you're not sure where they get their food, talk to the chef. Ask which items on the menu are organic and which aren't—and let the chef know that you strongly prefer organic. Suggest that they put a couple of organic specials on the menu.

7 Responsible Shopping

I t'd be great if saving the planet were as easy as changing our shopping patterns: Just buy the right stuff and you've done your part. The reality isn't quite that simple. As any environmental expert—and Chapter 3—will tell you, reducing consumption is the first and most important step in living an earth-friendly lifestyle. But nobody said that going green means depriving yourself. Just think before you buy, and consider where your shopping dollars are going. Support merchants and manufacturers that respect the earth as much as you do.

This chapter discusses some of the things to keep in mind when you shop and suggests good places to find the things you need. And because environmentally responsible shopping can get expensive, this chapter also covers more affordable options like thrift stores and homemade health and beauty products.

Think Globally, Buy Locally

Globalization has made people realize that the world is smaller than it seems. We know that our actions can have a big impact on the planet as a whole, and many are treading more lightly to lessen their impact: buying green-living guides like this one, producing less waste, minimizing their carbon footprints.

One way to keep the whole world in mind when you shop is to support local businesses. What exactly is a local business? The American Independent Business Alliance (AMIBA) defines it as a company that's mainly owned by people who live in the area where it operates. (It can be owned privately, by its employees, by the community, or cooperatively.) The owners are responsible for making decisions (unlike a franchise, where corporate bosses can overrule local branch owners), and there aren't more than six outlets in a state or province. Your own definition may vary, but AMIBA's is a good starting point; it emphasizes the local, independent nature of companies that deserve your support.

Why shop locally? Because local businesses:

- **Contribute to the community.** Whether they make things, provide a service, or sell products, these companies create jobs in your area and pay taxes locally. They care about the quality of life in your city because they've invested time, money, and resources there. And the money you spend at such companies stays in your community rather than landing in the pockets of distant shareholders or corporate bosses.

Note According to the New Rules Project (*www.newrules.org*), for every $100 you spend at a local business, $44 of it stays in your community. When you shop at a franchise or national chain store, by contrast, only $14 of that $100 stays local.

- **Create diversity.** If you're sick of walking into chain stores that look exactly the same whether they're in Topeka, Toledo, or Tampa, visit independent stores and restaurants. Local businesses cater to local tastes and choose products based on what the community wants, not on some corporate office's national sales plan.

- **Encourage entrepreneurship.** Many people dream of owning a business, but that dream can't succeed without community support. And entrepreneurs aren't the only ones who benefit: According to the U.S. Small Business Administration, small companies—not corporate behemoths—are responsible for 75% of all new jobs.

- **Enliven town centers.** You'll often find local businesses in the heart of a town, rather than gigantic malls and big-box stores surrounded by acres of asphalt. When you shop downtown, you help to sustain vibrant, walkable town centers, and reduce sprawl, unnecessary driving, and loss of wildlife habitats.

- **Save you tax money.** Because they tend to be in downtown areas, local merchants require less public infrastructure (that means fewer dollars spent on roadwork) and make more efficient use of city services (such as police) than big-box stores and shopping centers on the outskirts of town.

Because supporting local companies makes good economic and environmental sense—and improves the quality of life in your town—a number of groups have sprung up to promote them:

- **The American Independent Business Alliance** (*www.amiba.net*) is a coalition of independent, locally owned businesses and people who support them. Visit its website to learn how to form an alliance or start a "buy local" campaign in your area. AMIBA also sponsors America Unchained and Canada Unchained, campaigns that encourage consumers to "unchain" their shopping for a day by patronizing local merchants instead of chain stores.

- **The Institute for Local Self-Reliance** (*www.ilsr.org*) has, for more than 30 years, supported community development that's good for the environment and equitable to all local citizens. Its New Rules Project calls for fresh approaches to politics and economics that put local communities first.

> **Tip** If you'd like to start a buy local campaign, ILSR can get you started. Go to its Big Box Tool Kit site (*www.bigboxtoolkit.com*), click "Build Alternatives to Big Boxes," and then download "How to Start a Buy Local Campaign."

- **The Organic Consumers Association** (*www.organicconsumers.org/btc.cfm*) has a Breaking the Chains campaign that encourages consumers to be a force for change by supporting "organic, Fair Made, and locally produced products, and businesses."

All these sites are listed on the Missing CD page for this book at *www.missing-manuals.com*.

Buy Recycled

Chapter 3 talks about how to get recyclable items out of the trash and turn them into raw materials for making new products. This section looks the other side of the equation—recycled products you can buy. Buying recycled closes the loop, bringing you closer to a zero-waste lifestyle (page 84).

For example, take one of the most common recycled products: paper. According to the U.S. EPA, buying recycled paper instead of paper made from virgin materials helps the environment by:

- Reducing greenhouse gas emissions from the manufacturing process.
- Using less energy and water.
- Keeping paper from ending up in landfills.

When companies cut down trees to make paper, carbon dioxide (a greenhouse gas) gets released into the atmosphere by the chainsaws, the trucks that transport the lumber—and even the trees themselves, which release some of the CO_2 they've absorbed. And since trees take in carbon dioxide and release oxygen, fewer trees mean less of this conversion process. The EPA estimates that for each ton of paper that gets recycled (that's about 40 cases of paper):

- 17 trees are saved.
- 7,000 gallons of water are conserved.
- 3.3 cubic yards of landfill space is saved.
- 1 metric ton less of greenhouse gases are released.
- Enough energy is saved to power a typical American home for 6 months.

That's all good stuff you want to encourage, so vote with your wallet and buy recycled paper. When you do, you increase demand for the product, so companies will make more—and the benefits will grow.

> **Tip** At first, recycled office paper was a bit dull and had a funky texture, but not anymore. Now it's in lots of different colors, weights, and styles, including super-bright whites. But think twice before buying blinding-white paper—it gets that way through bleaching, and dumped bleach is a major cause of water pollution. So when buying recycled paper, look for stuff that's labeled chlorine-free.

When paper is labeled "recycled," it means that some percentage of it comes from recycled materials (same goes for other products). There are two kinds of materials that recycled products can be made from:

- **Preconsumer material** never made it into the hands of consumers. It may come from scraps or byproducts of the manufacturing process that otherwise would have gone to waste, or items like books or newspapers that didn't sell and were returned to the publisher, who recycled them.

- **Postconsumer material** came from someone's recycling bin. This can include junk mail, newspapers, discarded office paper, and so on. Postconsumer material goes beyond paper—the term can also refer to recycled glass or plastic containers, for example.

Note This book was printed on 100% postconsumer recycled paper that was produced using renewable biogas energy.

Office paper is one product that's easy to buy recycled. Here are some others to look for:

- Household paper products like napkins, tissue, toilet paper, and paper towels.

Tip The Natural Resources Defense Council has a helpful guide to home paper products, rated by recycled content and the kind of bleach used, at *www.nrdc.org/land/forests/gtissue.asp*. Better yet, instead of tissues, opt for handkerchiefs you can wash and use again. (Turns out Grandpa was greener than you thought.)

- Plastic outdoor furniture and landscaping items.
- Clothing.
- Retreaded tires.
- Mousepads and doormats made from recycled rubber.
- Pens and pencils made from recycled materials, from denim to rubber to plastic.
- Arts and crafts supplies.

Tip For do-it-yourself recycling, shop thrift and consignment stores (page 99). Reusing others' castoffs is a great way to reduce waste.

Giving Fair Trade a Fair Shake

Big, wealthy companies exploit small producers in poorer countries—isn't that how global trade works? Not according to the international fair trade movement. Instead of being exploitive, they believe, trade between highly developed and less developed countries can benefit both: high-quality products for consumers and a sustainable living for producers. This section examines fair trade in depth so you can make smart buying decisions—another example of how voting with your wallet can make a real difference.

What Is Fair Trade?

Fair trade helps support workers and sustainable practices in developing countries. Instead of buying massive quantities of cheaply produced items at rock-bottom prices, fair-trade importers pay attention to the lives and working conditions of the people who produce the goods they buy, process, and resell, and they typically buy relatively small quantities. For example, such an importer will do business with a farm or cooperative that uses sustainable practices and pays employees a living wage.

> **Note** A *living wage* is a pay rate that lets workers meet their families' basic needs—housing, food, clothing, health care, and so on—in the local community. Because these things cost different amounts in different places, the rate varies, too.

The movement focuses on social, economic, and environmental development. Here are some of its governing principles:

- **Reasonable working conditions.** Fair-trade farms and cooperatives don't exploit workers. They provide safe working conditions and living wages, and don't use child labor.

- **Fair prices.** Instead of focusing only on the bottom line—trying to maximize profit by paying the least they can get away with—fair-trade importers agree to pay local companies prices that cover the cost of sustainable practices (see the next bullet) and living wages for workers.

- **Sustainable methods.** Producers of fair-trade items have to make those goods in a sustainable way. For example, farmers have to minimize or eliminate certain pesticides and use organic fertilizers.

- **Democratic practices.** To become fair-trade certified (as explained in a moment), producers can't discriminate based on race, sex, ethnicity, religion, political views, and so on. Cooperatives need to have democratic structures and consist mainly of small producers who make or grow the products themselves.

- **Local investment.** Companies pay a premium that local producers and co-ops have to use to promote social and economic development that'll benefit their workers.

- **Transparency.** Everyone in the supply chain—producers, importers, processors (such as coffee roasters)—has to prove that they comply with fair-trade principles by letting people outside the organization scrutinize the group's agreements and practices. In other words, they have to be accountable for their practices. Transparency is essential because it lets consumers know that the products they're buying really are fairly traded.

Fortunately, you don't have to personally check up on companies and producers to make sure they're putting these principles to work. That's where the Fairtrade Labelling Organizations International (FLO) steps in. FLO is a partnership of 24 organizations that develops and applies fair-trade standards to make sure producers and importers adhere to them. So when you buy FLO-certified products, you know you're supporting fair trade.

Note In the U.S., the FLO member that approves fair-trade products is TransFair USA (*www.transfairusa.org*). In the U.K., it's the Fairtrade Foundation (*www.fairtrade.org. uk*), and in Canada, it's TransFair Canada (*www.transfair.ca*). Each of these websites has a section that tells you where you can buy certified products.

FLO certifies an ever-growing range of goods. Look for fair-trade certification when you're shopping for:

- Bananas
- Cocoa
- Coffee and tea

Tip When you're shopping for coffee, look for beans that are both fair-trade and shade grown. Many coffee plantations cut down all their trees to make room for coffee bushes—destroying the natural habitat of local critters and migratory birds. *Shade-grown coffee* protects natural habitats because the coffee comes from bushes grown in a forest setting, under trees that are part of the region's ecosystem. One study conducted on Mexican coffee plantations identified over 140 species of birds on shade-grown coffee plantations; on traditional coffee plantations, the researchers found no more than six bird species. For more information on shade-grown coffee, visit the Northwest Shade Coffee Campaign's site at *http://shadecoffee.org*.

- Flowers
- Fresh fruit and fruit juices
- Herbs, spices, and sugar
- Honey
- Rice and other grains
- Wine

Tip To see the items FLO certifies, visit its Products page at *www.fairtrade.net/products.html*.

FLO also certifies **composite products**, which are made of several different things (as opposed to a product like coffee). An example is a chocolate bar, which contains cocoa, sugar, and so on. Depending on where the candy company gets these ingredients, some may be fair trade and others may not. To receive FLO certification, composite products have to meet these standards:

- Liquid items have to contain at least 50% fair-trade ingredients by volume.

- For all other composite products, the significant ingredient (such as cocoa in chocolate) has to be FLO certified and account for at least 20% of the product's weight.

Tip Fair-trade goods aren't limited to just agricultural products. For example, Ten Thousand Villages, which has a website (*www.tenthousandvillages.com*) and lots of bricks-and-mortar stores, sells fairly traded jewelry, home décor, and gifts.

Criticisms of the Fair Trade Movement

Fair trade is a great idea that's gaining international support, but it has its critics. Here are some of the issues they've raised:

- **Fair trade distorts prices by ignoring market principles.** As you learned in economics class, markets are controlled by a simple set of rules: When demand is high and supply low, prices rise; when demand is low and supply high, prices fall. But fair trade makes supply and demand take a back seat to its ideals of sustainability and living wages.

Under normal circumstances, when there's an oversupply of a commodity such as coffee, the price goes down. But if fair-trade importers agree to buy coffee at a certain minimum price, that price correction doesn't happen for fair-trade coffee producers. That can cause prices to plummet for non-fair-trade producers, hurting their livelihoods.

- **Some fair trade isn't all that fair.** Critics say some corporations care about fair trade just because of the public-relations boost it gives them. They charge that such large companies prefer to deal with big farms that mass-produce flowers, coffee, and other crops rather than smaller farms and cooperatives—which means they're buying from farms that are more interested in owners' profits than sustainability and workers' wellbeing. Also, for some of the large corporations that have fair-trade certification, fairly traded goods account for only a tiny percentage of that company's products. Then again, the fact that big companies are interested in fair-trade certification helps the movement and improves the lives of those who work on plantations.

- **Some retailers dupe people who want to buy fair-trade products.** Consumers know that fairly traded products cost more, and many are willing to pay to support sustainable farmers and their families. But *The Economist* magazine has alleged that some retailers overcharge for fair-trade products—in some cases, a measly 10% of the extra amount you pay for a fair-trade product may go to help those who produced it (the other 90% stays in the retailer's pocket).

- **Fair trade doesn't go far enough.** Some argue that the only way to make real strides against poverty in less developed countries is global policy reform, so that international trade rules are fair across the board. Others counter that supporting micro-enterprises makes a real difference peoples' lives *now*, whereas reforming trade policies will take time.

So when is fair trade worth the extra cost—and when is it little more than a gimmick or cynical marketing ploy by companies trying to get money from socially and environmentally conscious consumers? The only way to answer that is to do your research before you buy:

- Is the company FLO certified? Check the website of your country's FLO member organization (page 209) to find out.

- What percentage of fairly traded goods does the company sell? Visit the company's website to see how committed it is to the movement.

Fair-trade goods generally cost more, but for many people, knowing that their purchases support a fairer, greener world is definitely worth a few dollars more.

Tip The National Geographic Society's Green Guide offers a Coffee Label Decoder that explains some of the different labels you'll find on coffee—including Fair Trade Certified, USDA Organic, Rainforest Alliance Certified, and Bird Friendly—along with a list of recommended brands. Check it out at *http://tinyurl.com/bz2ood*.

Compassion in Fashion

When it comes to fashion, green is the new black. Eco-friendly clothing is chic, responsibly produced, and makes more than a style statement—it says something about who you are and what you value.

The clothes on your back can have a big environmental impact. Take a cheap cotton t-shirt. It may have started as cotton grown in Texas or India, then traveled to someplace like China, Honduras, or Uzbekistan to be made into a shirt, then passed through far-flung wholesale and distribution warehouses before landing on the shelf at your local store. Not only did a lot of fossil fuels get used in transporting the shirt, you've got no way of knowing whether it came from farms and factories that share your values: respect for the earth and for workers.

To wear green (no matter what colors are "in" this season), keep these tips in mind:

- **Take care of what you've got.** The greenest clothes are the ones already in your closet. By making them last, you cut back on the virgin materials harvested and processed to make new clothes. Buy timeless classics in neutral colors, and make the most of them. If a shirt loses a button, don't toss the whole shirt—just buy a new button.

Note Cleaning clothes takes even more of a toll on the planet than making them. So avoid dry-cleaning your clothes whenever possible, and see Chapter 1 to learn about earth-friendly laundry supplies you can make (page 25) or buy (page 20).

- **Buy used.** Thrift-store shopping doesn't have to mean hideous bridesmaids dresses and t-shirts advertising bands that last toured in the 1970s. You can find low-priced basics in good condition—including kids' clothes that were outgrown too fast to show much wear; it just might take some hunting to find them. A lot of shoppers treat thrift-store visits like treasure hunts: You never know what you'll run across, and there are often real gems hidden among the polyester pantsuits. And high-end consignment shops sell designer fashions at prices that are almost too good to be true. Page 99 starts you on your thrift-shopping adventure.

Tip Online auction sites like eBay (*www.ebay.com*) also sell good-quality used clothing at rock-bottom prices. If you buy from these sites, check shipping costs and ask the sellers to use minimal packaging.

- **Hold a clothing exchange.** Gather your similar-sized friends together and have everyone bring clothes they're willing to trade. Donate any unclaimed leftovers to charity.

- **Make your own.** If you're handy with a needle and thread, try whipping up your own outfits. Even better, make them from recycled materials you find at thrift stores or get from friends and family—whether bolts of cloth or cast-off clothes, you can piece them together into a totally new garment.

Tip The Threadbanger website (*www.threadbanger.com*) has step-by-step instructions and style tips for do-it-yourself fashionistas.

- **Buy organic.** When it comes to cotton, "organic" means a t-shirt was made from non-GMO (page 185) cotton plants grown in fields that haven't had synthetic fertilizers, pesticides, and weed killers dumped on them for at least three years before harvesting. Also keep an eye out for clothes made from organic flax, linen, and hemp.

Note Cotton covers only 1% of U.S. farmland—but it accounts for about *half* of U.S. pesticide use. Hemp, an alternative source of clothing fiber, requires little or no pesticides and produces about twice as much material as cotton. It's also a great source of fiber for making paper: A single acre of hemp produces the equivalent of four acres of trees.

- **Look for recycled materials.** Like many other products, new clothing can be made from recycled fibers, like recycled cotton socks and fleecewear made from recycled plastic.

- **Consider natural synthetics.** It sounds like an oxymoron, but some fibers are made synthetically from natural substances; they're called *naturally derived man-made fibers*. To make them, manufacturers start with natural materials, like bamboo, corn, soy, or wood pulp. Unlike synthetic fibers such as polyester, clothing made from these fibers is biodegradable, so you can compost it (page 191) when it wears out.

There will likely come a time when thrift-store options and your current duds just won't cut it—maybe the idea of second-hand shoes doesn't appeal or you feel like splurging for a special occasion. In that case, here are some good sources for green clothing and accessories:

- **Autonomie Project** (*www.autonomieproject.com*). This company sells fairly traded, eco-friendly, vegan, sweatshop-free t-shirts, shoes, and accessories.

- **Etsy** (*www.etsy.com*). A marketplace for artisans and crafters to sell their wares, Etsy is a great place to find fashionable handmade and vintage clothing and jewelry.

- **GreenKarat** (*www.greenkarat.com*). Environmentally responsible jewelry sounds like a pipe dream. After all, fine jewelry is made from gems, gold, and platinum—substances mined from the earth and intensively processed. GreenKarat uses recycled metals and manmade stones to create beautiful jewelry that doesn't take a big toll on the planet. Creating jewelry does use energy (although GreenKarat uses only wind-generated electricity), so the company lets customers choose whether to pay a voluntary carbon offset fee to ensure that their purchases are completely carbon neutral. And you can enter an item's tag number on the associated Green Assay website (*www.greenassay.com*) to get info about the jewelry's green characteristics, such as whether gems were ecologically mined, whether the metal came from an ecologically certified refinery, and whether the jeweler used environmentally responsible methods to make the piece.

- **Greenloop** (*www.thegreenloop.com*). Here you'll find organic clothing, shoes, and accessories made from sustainable materials using renewable energy. The company is committed to recycling and reuse, reducing greenhouse gases, supporting organic farming, and manufacturing without sweatshops.

- **Mink Shoes** (*www.minkshoes.com*). If you don't eat animals, you probably don't want to wear their skins, either. Vegan designer Rebecca Brough founded this company because she had a hard time finding fashionable shoes made from animal-friendly materials. Instead of leather, these shoes are made from sustainable and organic materials, handcrafted by Italian artisans.

- **My Green Closet** (*www.mygreencloset.com*). This company uses organic cotton and low-impact dyes to produce cute clothes for kids, all of which is made in the U.S.

- **Nau** (*www.nau.com*). Nau's organic clothing for men and women is available at more than a dozen stores nationwide, or you can order from its website, where you can read about its products and philosophy.

- **Rapanui Organic Clothing** (*www.rapanuiclothing.com*). This company, located in the U.K., uses organic materials and renewable energy to make surfer-inspired clothing for men and women. It donates 5% of its profits to environmental charities.

- **Stewart + Brown** (*www.stewartbrown.com*). Here you'll find trendy clothing made from organic cotton, Mongolian cashmere, factory surplus fabrics, and other sustainable materials. The company gives 1% of its sales to nonprofit environmental groups.

- **StyleWillSaveUs** (*www.stylewillsaveus.com*). An online eco-boutique and more, this U.K.-based site also publishes an entertaining and informative ezine about fashion.

- **Target** (*www.target.com*). This huge retailer is trying to offer green fashions at affordable prices. Not all the clothing Target sells is green, but you'll have a better chance of finding organic cotton clothing here than at some other large retailers. Look, for example, for styles in Rogan Gregory's Loomstate line (*www.loomstate.org*).

- **Terra Plana** (*www.terraplana.com*). This company makes shoes—from trendy pumps to durable sneakers—from natural and recycled materials and vegetable-tanned leather.

- **White Apricot** (*www.whiteapricot.com*). This site sells eco-friendly fashions, jewelry, and beauty products.

Green Health and Beauty Products

Do you know what's in the stuff you slather on your skin, lather into your hair, or paint on your nails? Many beauty and health products are a chemical minefield, and it pays to know what's in them before you make them part of your routine. Obviously, no one today would use the lead-based cosmetics women in ancient Rome used to whiten their complexions. But did you know that as many as 60% of all lipsticks on the market contain some lead? (Don't lick your lips as you ponder that.)

Roman women didn't know that even small amounts of lead can be toxic, building up in the body and causing serious neurological, gastrointestinal, kidney, reproductive, and other problems. Kind of makes you wonder about chemicals that are allowed in health and beauty products today, doesn't it? What problems may crop up down the road because of exposure to amounts currently considered safe?

It's better to be safe—*really* safe—than sorry. Table 7-1 lists ingredients you may find in health and beauty products that have raised concerns about health. Read labels and avoid these substances. (Ironically, you'll find many of these chemicals listed under "inactive ingredients.")

Table 7-1. Iffy Ingredients in Health and Beauty Products

Substance	Commonly Used In	Possible Health Effects
Aluminum	Deodorants (as aluminum chlorohydrate), eye shadows, and in many dyes that color products.	Anemia, brain damage. May be particularly dangerous to people with impaired kidney function.
Coal tar	Anti-itch creams, dandruff shampoos. May be in blue and green dyes used in toothpastes and mouthwashes: watch out for FD&C Blue and FD&C Green 3.	Cancer, respiratory damage, allergic reactions, skin irritation.
Formaldehyde	Hair products, nail products, bug repellants, sunscreens, hand soaps and sanitizers.	Cancer; developmental problems; damage to cardiovascular, reproductive, and neurological systems; allergic reactions; skin irritation.
Fragrance	Most health and beauty products.	You can't tell from this ingredient alone. This is a catch-all term for hundreds of substances, including phthalates (see below).
Hydroquinone (also called benzene-1,4-diol or quinol)	Moisturizers, products to lighten age spots and freckles.	Cancer, kidney damage, neurological damage in lab animals.
Lead, lead acetate (may also contaminate hydrated silica)	Hair dyes, lipsticks.	Cancer, brain, and developmental damage, damage to the neurological and reproductive systems.
Mercury (may be in thimerosal, a preservative)	Moisturizers, lipsticks and lip glosses, mascaras, eyeliners, eyebrow definers.	Cancer, developmental and reproductive problems, damage to the neurological and endocrine systems.

Substance	Commonly Used In	Possible Health Effects
Mineral oils (may be listed as petroleum or liquid paraffin)	Hair products; moisturizers; lotions; anti-aging products; lip glosses, lip balms, and lipsticks; foundations and concealers; eye shadows.	Cancer, skin and eye irritation, allergic reactions, clogged pores.
PABA (para-aminobenzoic acid)	Shampoos and conditioners, body and facial cleansers, moisturizers, shaving creams.	Cancer; developmental, reproductive and neurological damage.
Parabens (may begin with the prefix ethyl-, methyl-, propyl-, butyl-, or isobutyl-)	Hair products, shaving creams, body washes, moisturizers.	Cancer, developmental and reproductive problems, damage to the neurological and endocrine systems.
Phthalates (may appear on labels as "fragrance" or with the prefix dibutyl- or diethylhexyl-)	Nail polishes, nail and cuticle treatments, wart removers. As fragrance, may be in hair products, face and body washes, moisturizers, deodorants.	Cancer; birth defects; developmental, reproductive, and respiratory problems; damage to neurological and endocrine systems; allergic reactions.
Polyethylene glycol	Anti-itch creams, styling gels, facial cleansers, toothpastes, mascaras, vaginal lubricants.	Cancer; reproductive problems; brain, liver, and kidney damage; skin irritation.
p-Phenylenediamine	Hair products.	Cancer, endocrine system disruption, skin irritation.
Sodium lauryl sulfate (also sodium lauryl ether sulfate)	Hair products, toothpastes, tooth whiteners, mouth washes, body and facial washes, moisturizers, foundations.	Cancer; liver damage; damage to cardiovascular, gastrointestinal, endocrine, and reproductive systems; skin irritation.
Triclosan	Antibacterial products (liquid hand soaps, body washes, etc.), facial cleansers, anti-acne products, moisturizers, deodorants, toothpastes, body sprays, lipsticks.	Cancer, birth defects, reproductive and endocrine system damage, skin irritation.
Toulene	Hair colors, hair conditioners, nail polishes.	Cancer, reproductive and developmental problems, immune system damage, allergic reactions.

So how do you find health and beauty products that are safe to use? The Campaign for Safe Cosmetics (*www.safecosmetics.org*, page 156) has done the research for you. It tests products and lists companies that have signed its Compact for Safe Cosmetics, promising to use safe ingredients or replace hazardous ones within three years. More than 1,000 companies have signed. To find one that makes the products you're shopping for, go to *http://tinyurl.com/dzw5up*.

A growing number of companies make natural beauty and grooming products. Read labels, watch out for potentially harmful ingredients (check any you're not sure of at *www.cosmeticsdatabase.com*), and look for businesses that are committed to safe, eco-friendly products. Here are some companies that make products that are safe to use and easy on the environment:

- **Desert Essence** (*www.desertessence.com*) makes organic, fragrance-free skin- and hair-care items.

- **Dr. Hauschka Skin Care** (*www.drhauschka.com*) makes all-natural skin, body, and hair products. On their site, click Ingredient Glossary to get more info about the ingredients they use.

- **Eco-Beauty** (*www.eco-beauty.com*) sells a line of organic skin care for men, women, and babies made by Martina Gebhardt Naturkosmetik, which contain at least 95% organic ingredients.

- **Farmaesthetics** (*www.farmaesthetics.com*) produces 100% natural skin-care products from certified organic herbs, flowers, and grains from American family farms.

- **Future** (*www.futurenatural.com*) offers a full line of natural and organic health and beauty products, including makeup, skin and hair care, bath and body products, and fragrance.

- **John Masters Organics** (*www.johnmasters.com*) features more than 30 organic products for hair, skin, and body. This company also makes an organic pet shampoo that repels fleas and ticks.

- **Juice Beauty** (*www.juicebeauty.com*) creates its products from a patent-pending organic juice base. They sell skin-care products, including cleansers, toners, moisturizers, sun protection, lip balm, and lines for kids and men.

- **Kuumba Made** (*http://kuumbamade.com*) has created all-natural fragrances, essential oils, and bath and body products for more than 25 years.

- **Origins Organics** (*www.origins.com/organics*) carries hair, face, body, and bath products that are certified organic, including massage oils and deodorants.

- **Pangea Organics** (*http://pangeaorganics.com*) makes product lines for skin, body, and lips. Their site includes an ingredient glossary so you can learn more about what goes into the stuff they sell.

- **Suki** (*www.sukipure.com*) offers makeup as well as items for face, body, and hair. You can also shop by concern, such as acne or rosacea.

- **Tarte Cosmetics** (*www.tartecosmetics.com*) makes natural cosmetics that are free of parabens, petrochemicals, phthalates, and synthetic fragrances, and the company uses recyclable or postconsumer recycled material for its packaging.

Tip Many health and beauty products are still tested on animals. The European Union has banned animal tests for cosmetic ingredients, but such testing remains legal in the U.S. If you want to make sure your favorite products haven't been tested on animals, visit the website for the Coalition for Consumer Information on Cosmetics (*www.leapingbunny.org*). Click Consumers Enter, and then click "shopping guide" for a list of companies that have pledged to eliminate animal testing from their products.

Do-It-Yourself Health and Beauty

Organic hair and skin products can get pretty pricey. Fortunately, in many cases, you can whip up your own versions with items you may already have around the house. For example:

- Natural castile soap (page 17) makes a great shampoo. You can thin it with a little water if you like and add a few drops of essential oil to make it smell yummy. These oils may also help with common hair conditions: peppermint oil for oily hair, rosemary oil to add body, jojoba oil for dry hair, and lemon or chamomile oil to brighten blonde hair.

- Blend one small jar of mayonnaise (the real stuff, not salad dressing or a low-fat imitation) with half an avocado to make a deep conditioner. Spread the mixture on your hair, wrap a warm, damp towel around your head, and let the mixture do its thing for 20 minutes before you wash it out. (Half a cup of mayonnaise, all by itself, also makes a good deep conditioner. Spread over hair, leave on for 20 minutes, and then wash out.)

- Here's a conditioner that'll leave your hair soft and smelling wonderful, and fights dandruff: Warm a quarter-cup of coconut oil so that it's liquid (don't let it get too hot), then stir in three tablespoons of lime juice. Apply to hair and leave on for an hour, then shampoo out.

- To get rid of stubborn dandruff, mix equal amounts of apple cider vinegar and water and massage into your scalp after shampooing and conditioning. This vinegar rinse also gives brunettes shiny hair.

- Pour a cup of apple cider vinegar into your bath to soften skin. (Add few drops of your favorite essential oil for relaxing or invigorating aromatherapy.)

- Instead of shaving cream, use liquid castile soap, olive oil, or a phosphate-free dishwashing liquid to shave. And apple cider vinegar makes a great aftershave. (Don't worry: Your skin won't smell like vinegar after it's dry; you can also sweeten the scent by adding a drop of an essential oil you like.)

- Combine a quarter-cup of baby oil with a quarter-cup of olive oil and one tablespoon of lemon juice for an effective makeup remover.

- Honey makes a simple, sweet-smelling facial. Place a warm, damp cloth over your face to open pores, and then spread a couple of tablespoons of honey over your face. Leave on for 15 to 30 minutes, then rinse. If any sticky residue remains, gently rub it off with a damp cloth.

- Avocado makes another all-natural facial: Peel an avocado and mash it into a paste. Spread it onto your skin, leave it for 15 minutes, and then rinse it away.

- This facial is almost good enough to eat: Combine a quarter-cup of organic blueberries with a tablespoon each of honey and olive oil. Apply to your face, leave on for 5 minutes, and then rinse. If you're allergic to any kind of berries though, don't use this recipe.

- To make your own lotion, combine half a cup of oil (try almond, coconut, or grapeseed oil) with two tablespoons of beeswax and heat gently until melted. Add water a little at a time, blending well, until the lotion reaches a consistency that's a little thinner than you want (it will thicken as it cools). Stir in a few drops of essential oil, like rose or lavender (or both), to make it smell even better. Let the lotion cool; adjust ingredients as necessary to get the consistency right.

If the product you want to make isn't in this list, check around online for more recipes. A good place to start is MakeYourCosmetics.com (*www.makeyourcosmetics.com*).

Environmentally Friendly Gifts

Say you've reduced your consumption, as discussed in Chapter 3, to live a more earth-friendly lifestyle and have less stuff to deal with. (Feels good, doesn't it?) But when birthdays and holidays roll around, friends and family still expect gifts. There's nothing wrong with that—getting and giving presents is fun. But instead of playing the usual maybe-they'll-like-it-maybe-they-won't guessing game, you can choose gifts you *know* the planet will like. Here are some ideas:

- **Serve up an eco-friendly dinner.** Make an occasion out of gift giving with a night out on the town. Page 202 has suggestions for finding restaurants that serve organic and locally grown food. Or cook up a delicious dinner yourself from organic and locally grown foods.

- **Give an experience.** A gift doesn't have to be something tangible that'll end up gathering dust on a shelf or in a closet somewhere. Use your imagination to give an *experience* that the recipient will love: a spa day, a hike, a visit to a museum, tickets to a concert or play—whatever. And if you go along, you're giving the gift of your company, too (not to mention sharing the fun).

- **Create coupons.** Parents often appreciate homemade coupon books from their kids that can be redeemed for extra help around the house. With a little thought and creativity, the same idea can work for anyone on your gift list. Dog walking, car washing, lawn mowing, gardening— or anything you're good at that you could do for someone else. (Remember to use recycled paper for your coupons!)

- **Make a donation.** A gift that's both thoughtful and helpful is donating to a charity in the recipient's name. Ask your friend or family member which causes they support, and donate accordingly. Or use the Charity Navigator (*www.charitynavigator.org*), where you can search by category (animals, environment, health, and so on) to find a suitable charity.

> **Tip** Many charities and nonprofits have their own stores, so you can buy a gift and benefit the organization at the same time. For example, the National Geographic Society (*shop.nationalgeographic.com*), the World Wildlife Fund (*http://wwf.org*), and the Sierra Club (*www.sierraclub.org/store*) all sell merchandise as well as memberships. Check your favorite environmental organization's website to see whether they do, too.

- **Make something.** Homemade gifts are always appreciated. Whether it's food, a photo montage, or something else, you know it's environmentally friendly if you made it yourself.

> **Tip** See page 95 for ideas of things you can make out of recycled and reused items.

- **Regift.** When someone gives you a perfectly good item you don't want or can't use, pass it on to someone else who'll appreciate it. That's a gift that really keeps on giving.

- **Shop green.** Browse through this chapter for places where you can buy fair-trade goods (page 209), easy-on-the-earth clothes (page 214), and safe beauty indulgences (page 218). Or use the book's index to find other green products: cleaning supplies as a housewarming gift (page 16), biodegradable diapers for a baby shower (page 150), fun kids' toys (page 158), and a whole lot more.

> **Tip** The National Resources Defense Council's Great Green Gift Guide (*www.nrdc.org/cities/living/ggift.asp*) has fun suggestions from NRDC staffers in a variety of categories, like Nature Lovers, Hot Rods, and Foodies.

Finding Companies That Get It

If you're in the mood for a little online shopping and you Google *eco-friendly* or *organic*, you'll get a list of a gazillion sites that want your business. But there are many companies that aren't fully committed to the green movement's principles. They see green merchandise as a gimmick and are more interested in getting their hands on your cash than they are in saving the planet.

So how do you find retailers that have the same level of commitment caring for the environment as you do? Ask questions: Talk to local retailers and email the customer service departments of online companies. Or check out these sites:

- **1% for the Planet** (*www.onepercentfortheplanet.org*). The idea behind this site is simple: Businesses that join this organization agree to contribute 1% of their profits to an environmental organization registered with 1% for the Planet.

- **Happyhippie.com** (*www.happyhippie.com*). This site has a directory of eco-friendly products and services, as well as green living articles and a member forum.

- **Home Depot Eco Options** (*www.homedepot.com/ecooptions*). Started in 2007, Home Depot's Eco Options initiative helps consumers identify earth-friendly home and building products in these categories: Sustainable Forestry, Energy Efficient, Healthy Home, Clean Air, and Water Conservation.

- **Organic Consumers Association** (*www.organicconsumers.org/btc/BuyingGuide.cfm*). The OCA's Breaking the Chains Buying Guide lists green and organic businesses that sell clothing, food, health and beauty products, items for home and garden, and pet and kids stuff. Listings are by state or country.

- **Planet Green** (*http://planetgreen.discovery.com/buying-guides*). This is the website for the Planet Green cable TV channel. Besides tips for greening your life in various ways, the site's Green Buying Guides cover everything from food to furniture to computers.

- **TreeHugger** (*www.treehugger.com/buygreen*). TreeHugger is a great site for all things green, with helpful articles, reader forums, newsletters, and more. The site also offers guides for buying furniture, clothing, gifts, and more.

8 Going Green: Transportation and Travel

Some people say that when you travel, it's not the destination that's important, but the journey. That's also a good way to think about the impact travel has on the environment. Getting from one place to another is one of the biggest—and fastest growing—sources of greenhouse-gas emissions. According to the U.S. EPA, transportation accounted for 29% of America's greenhouse-gas emissions in 2006, and that's just from cars, planes, and boats moving from place to place—it doesn't include the energy or emissions involved in building vehicles or producing their fuel.

Because transportation is such a big problem for the planet, this chapter helps you become a more responsible traveler. You'll get tips to help you leave your car in the garage or trade it in for a more earth-friendly model. This chapter also explores how to reduce the impact of long-distance travel, whether you're on family vacation or a business junket. Knowing you're traveling in an environmentally responsible way will let you sit back, relax, and enjoy the journey.

Getting Around Without a Car

It used to be the American dream: two cars in every garage and a chicken in every pot. Many people are adapting that dream to the 21st century by making sure the chicken is free-range and having just one car—or none at all. If you want to spend less time in the car or even trade it in for a bike or pair of walking shoes, this section is for you.

Take Public Transportation

Buses, trains, and subways reduce the traffic choking local roads and help you minimize your carbon footprint by cutting back on greenhouse-gas emissions. According to the American Public Transportation Association, U.S. mass transit saves 4.2 billion gallons of fuel and 37 million metric tons of carbon emissions each year. It also provides 1.7 million jobs.

Public transportation has other benefits, too. It saves you time you'd otherwise spend searching for a parking place. And you'll have time to read a book, do a little people-watching, or even take an on-the-road nap as you commute to work or travel around town. Sounds a lot less stressful than weaving in and out of traffic or leaning on the horn when some idiot cuts you off, doesn't it?

If you're used to getting around by car, switching to mass transit takes some getting used to. If you don't use your area's system all that much, take time to learn its ins and outs. Start by taking the bus or train once or twice a week, for example, and work your way up to daily use. You'll get to know the routes and schedules, and before long traveling by public transit will be second nature to you.

Tip Want to know how much you can reduce your carbon footprint by taking the bus, train, or subway? Go to *www.publictransportation.org*, hover your cursor over Interact, and then click Carbon (CO2) Calculator. On the page that opens, type in your car's gas mileage, how many miles you drive per week, and how many of those miles you could travel by mass transit. Then click Calculate to find out how much you could reduce CO_2 emissions.

Here are some ways to get the most out of public transportation:

- **Buy a weekly or monthly pass.** These passes offer better deals than if you pay for each trip individually. (And the more you use it, the better value it is.)

- **Memorize schedules.** Learning when to expect the bus or train you take to work or school saves you from waiting around. Knowing when the next one is due lets you time things so you'll be there right on time to catch it.

- **Study routes.** Check out you local transit authority's website to find the most direct routes to where you need to go. That way you won't have to make many transfers and you'll spend less time traveling.

- **Keep busy.** Taking mass transit frees up lots of time you'd otherwise spend staring at the road. So take advantage of it: Read or listen to a good book, get some work done, or get caught up with the news. You'll be at your destination in no time.

- **Be considerate.** Public transportation is for everyone, and polite passengers make for a much smoother ride. Nobody likes to sit next to someone who's screaming into a cellphone or tucking into a liverwurst-and-onion sandwich. Don't be that person.

Green Tech

Calling All (Pod)cars!

A new kind of vehicle is gaining attention as a way to take the "mass" out of "mass transit." *Podcars*, also called *personal rapid transit* (PRT), are small electric cars (usually four-seaters) that run on electric rails built above roadways, like the kind monorails use. Similar to taxis, podcars come when you call them and take you to your destination without stopping in between, so there's no waiting as others exit and enter the car.

When you get to a podcar station, there may already be a car waiting for you. If not, all you have to do is push a button to summon one, which arrives within a couple of minutes. After you've boarded, you simply tell the podcar where you're going and swipe a card to pay your fare. The doors close, and you're off on an express trip.

Podcars are controlled by computer, so there's no risk of the kinds of human errors that lead to collisions. Because there are no drivers, podcars are also economical to run. (One model has solar cells above the tracks to power the cars.)

Prototype PRT systems are currently being built at Heathrow Airport in London, in Uppsala, Sweden, and in Masdar, Abu Dhabi. To learn more about them, visit *www.personalrapidtransit.com*.

Advanced Transport Systems Ltd.
www.atsltd.co.uk

Tip Here's another way to reduce the amount of time you spend driving: telecommute. Maybe you can work from home a couple days a week instead of going into the office. To help you out, page 250 has strategies for convincing your boss that telecommuting is a great idea.

Put on Your Walking Shoes

People are designed to get around by walking. And when you take a hike instead of taking the car, you leave behind actual footprints instead of a carbon one. Doctors recommend getting 30–60 minutes of exercise each day; a three-mile walk at an easy pace takes about an hour. So when you have errands to do that are only a couple of miles away, lace up those shoes and get moving.

For the best walk, keep these points in mind:

- **Wear the right shoes.** Good walking shoes are definitely not one size fits all. Spend some time finding ones that are comfortable, flexible, and offer good support.

- **Walk safe.** Stay on the sidewalk or, if there isn't one, walk facing traffic (so you can see cars coming). Wear bright colors so drivers can see you and, if you're out at night, wear a reflective vest. Pay attention to your surroundings; be aware of cars, cyclists, and other pedestrians. If you listen to music as you walk, don't crank up the volume—you want to be able to hear approaching cars.

- **Stay hydrated.** To make sure you get enough water, carry your own supply in a water bottle. Get a reusable metal one and avoid BHP-laden plastic (see page 153).

- **Carry a cellphone.** This isn't for chatting all along your route (which distracts you from your surroundings) but to have on hand in case of emergency.

- **Buddy up**. A walking partner makes walks safer and more fun. People who walk together are more likely to walk regularly, too. Find another parent to walk with you as you accompany the kids home from school, for example, or set up a weekly date to run—er, walk—regular errands.

Ride a Bike

If the weather is good and you've got somewhere to go, ditch your car and go by bicycle instead. You'll get some exercise, save gas, and spare the air. You don't even have to be in great shape—start with a mile on level ground, and before long you'll be working your way up to longer distances and more challenging terrain. Many bike commuters find it so much more invigorating and inexpensive than driving that they regularly hop on their bikes to run errands and get to and from work.

The biking movement is on a roll (pun intended). If you want to cycle to and from work, you're in good company. Check out these websites full of tips from like-minded people:

- **Bike Commuters** (*www.bikecommuters.com*).

- **Commute by Bike** (*http://commutebybike.com*).

- **Bicycling Life's Bicycle Commuter's Guide** (*http://tinyurl.com/lt2pa2*).

- **League of American Bicyclists** (*www.bikeleague.org*).

If you're relatively new to two-wheeled travel, here are some ways to make the most of it:

- **Buy the best bike you can afford.** When shopping for a bike, get one that's lightweight, sturdy, comfortable (you won't ride it much if it's not), and suited to your local terrain (flat or hilly, for example). If you'll be riding off-road trails, you'll need different features than if you plan on just pedaling around town. Do your homework before you visit a bike shop so you'll know what you want. Here are a couple of good research sites:

  — **Consumer Reports Bikes Buying Guide** (*http://tinyurl.com/ok38b2*).

  — **Bicycle Buying Guide** (*http://tinyurl.com/nh2f4s*).

  — **The Bicycle Shopping Guide** (*http://bikes.jump-gate.com*).

> **Tip** If you plan on doing some biking after dark, make sure your bike has a good headlight (so you can see) and taillight (so cars can see you).

- **Get a helmet that fits.** A good helmet is a must for frequent riders, and a proper fit makes sure it does its job. When you're trying on helmets, get advice from a the salesperson and keep these tips in mind:

  — When the helmet is level on your head, it should feel snug but not *too* tight. (Don't wear it tilted back.)

  — Fasten the chin strap, and then try to move the helmet backward and forward. If you can push it far enough back to expose your forehead or far enough forward to dip down over your eyes, shorten the straps until the helmet stays put.

  — If you've adjusted the front and back straps but the helmet still moves around too much, try a different model.

- **Outfit yourself with the right clothes.** To stay comfortable and protect yourself from the weather, choose cycling clothes appropriate to your climate. The staff at your local bike shop will have suggestions about what you should wear.

- **Learn basic maintenance.** Do you know how to tune up a bike, patch a flat tire, or fix a slipped chain? Find out how to take care of and fix your bike before you get stranded by the side of the road miles from home.

Tip The League of American Bicyclists has a good primer on bike upkeep: Go to *http://tinyurl.com/5pf2d6*.

- **Learn to ride effectively.** Just because you zoomed around the neighborhood on a BMX or banana bike when you were a kid doesn't mean you know everything about cycling. Most riders, for example, don't really know how to use gears. Consider taking some lessons with a local bike club, or check out About.com's articles on riding basics at *http://bicycling.about.com* (click the left-hand menu's Bike Riding Basics link).

- **Obey the rules of the road.** You've probably seen cyclists riding the wrong way down one-way streets or running red lights. But in most places, bikers are subject to the same traffic laws as cars. Know the cycling laws in your area, and follow them. The American League of Cyclists lists current laws by state: At *www.bikeleague.org*, hover your cursor over the words "Take Action", and then click Legal Program/Bike Laws; on the page that opens, click your state. The group also has list of safe biking tips at *http://tinyurl.com/d2oxfb*.

Note In Canada, bicycle laws vary by province (some require helmets and others don't), but cyclists everywhere have to obey the same traffic laws as motorists. To check U.K. cycling laws, go to *http://tinyurl.com/3x2tfq*. The Australian site Wheels of Justice lists links to Australian cycling laws here: *www.woj.com.au/australian-road-authority-links*.

- **Ride defensively.** Cyclists share the roads with drivers, pedestrians, and other bikes. That means you're likely to encounter drivers who are impatient, rude, or downright dangerous, as well as a host of other hazards. Safety comes from having the right equipment, obeying traffic laws, and knowing how to deal with dodgy situations. For a good guide on safe cycling, go to *http://bicyclesafe.com*.

- **Choose the best route.** Planning your route will make getting around by bike faster, easier, and more fun. These websites can help:

  — **Map My Ride** (*www.mapmyride.com*) is a social network for cyclists where you can find recommended bike trips and meet other cycling enthusiasts.

  — **Bikely** (*www.bikely.com*) is an international site where bikers share their knowledge of good routes. Search for a location, and then look for rides in the category you want, like scenic, commute, off-road, and so on.

Driving Smarter

The previous section has lots of suggestions for getting around without a car. But sometimes you have no choice but to drive. This section tells you how to leave the car in the garage more often, which will save you money and help the environment. According to the U.S. Bureau of Labor Statistics, Americans spend 17% of their household budgets on car-related expenses: car payments, maintenance, insurance, gas, and so on—after housing costs, it's people's biggest expense. (And that number is from a 2004 survey, before gas prices went through the roof; the percentage is likely higher now.) So help your pocketbook—and the planet—by using your car as little as possible. If you can't walk (page 228), bike (page 229), or take public transit (page 226), try one of these strategies:

- **Form a carpool** by finding others who regularly take the same route you do—to commute to work or drop kids off at school, for example—and then take turns driving. This saves money and wear-and-tear on each car, and cuts back on unnecessary driving. If you carpool to work with three other people, for example, you'll drive just once every four workdays.

- **Use a car-sharing program** if you need a car only once in a while, or if you'd simply prefer not to rack up miles on your car for some trips. Car sharing involves renting a car for a short period of time, often by the hour, and gas and insurance are usually included. You use the car only when you need it; the rest of the time, other environmentally conscious drivers get to take their turns. To find out whether your area has such a program, visit The Car Sharing Network at *www.carsharing.net*, which lists cities in North America, Europe, and Asia.

- **Hop in a taxi** to spare your car some wear and tear. Many taxi companies are getting smart and buying hybrids (page 236) for their fleet. When you can, support green business by using these companies.

- **Get better fuel efficiency** to spend less money at the pump and help the environment. In addition to regular tune-ups (which can improve fuel efficiency by as much as 4%), which keep your car running its best, remember these dos and don'ts:

  — **Put air in your tires.** Most people's tires are about 20% softer than they should be. According to *fueleconomy.gov* (a website maintained by the U.S. Department of Energy and the U.S. EPA), inflating tires to the car company's recommended pressure (which is posted on the driver's side door) can improve fuel efficiency by 3%.

Tip Check your tires once a month or so. Even if you've inflated them to recommended amount, tires lose pressure with time and changes in temperature. To get an accurate reading, always check tires when they're cold—that is, before you drive somewhere.

  — **Don't drive with a dirty air filter.** When you do, less air can get through the filter, and that means your car's engine isn't operating efficiently.

Tip Install a permanent air filter, such as the K&N filter, to reduce waste. That way, you clean it when it gets dirty, rather than throwing it out and putting in a new one. Ask about permanent filters at your local auto parts store, or visit *www.knfilters.com*.

  — **Use the recommended motor oil.** If you don't know whether you need 10W-30, 5W-20, or WD-40 (just kidding), check your owner's manual. You can improve your car's gas mileage 1–2% by putting in the right grade.

  — **Minimize idling.** Don't leave the car running while you run into a store. If your car is stopped for more than 30 seconds (in other words, longer than the average red light), turn it off.

- **Don't floor it.** Instead of pressing that pedal all the way down, accelerate gradually—and stick to the speed limit. The faster you go, the faster you burn fuel. Plus you'll enjoy the trip more when you don't have to worry about speed traps.

- **Use cruise control for highway driving.** This nifty invention keeps you at a steady speed, which is more efficient than constantly changing speeds, even slightly. That's why cars get more miles per gallon on highways than they do tooling around town with all those stop signs and red lights.

- **Lighten up.** Not surprisingly, it takes more gas to get a heavier car moving than a lighter one. Keep this in mind when you're car shopping, and check what you're carrying around in the trunk—take out anything you don't need to cart around everywhere you drive.

- **Go aerodynamic.** Wind resistance drags at your car, which means it takes more fuel to keep the car moving forward. So take off any roof racks or car-top carriers that you're not using.

> **Tip** When you're driving around town, turn off the AC and open the windows to get better mileage. But on the highway, the drag created by open windows cancels out the fuel-efficiency benefits of turning off the AC, so close the windows and run the air conditioner to stay comfortable.

- **Plan your trips.** Think before you start your engine. Avoid rush hour whenever possible. Spend some time on MapQuest (*www.mapquest.com*) or Google Maps (*maps.google.com*) to find the fastest route. And group errands so that you can do several at once instead of making lots of trips back and forth.

Green Cars in Every Color

When you're shopping for a new car, you have to decide on more than just style, color, and whether to get satellite radio or a CD player. Going green means looking for a car that's fuel efficient and easier on the environment than some big, heavy gas guzzler. Each gallon of gas your car uses contributes to global warming by releasing carbon dioxide—*20 pounds* worth for each gallon burned—and other greenhouse gases. For the average vehicle, that adds up to six to nine *tons* of carbon dioxide belched into the atmosphere each year. Fortunately, car technology is improving so you now have more earth-friendly choices, as explained in the next few sections.

Fuel-Efficient Cars

Simply put, *fuel efficiency* means you get more miles on less gas, so you save money, burn less fuel, *and* reduce your impact on the environment—it's a win-win-win situation. Special technologies, described in the following sections, can improve efficiency, but if you're looking for a traditional car, ask these questions to get the most MPGs for your money:

- **What size do I need?** Many people buy a bigger car than they really need. Because larger vehicles are heavier, they burn more gas. So think about how much passenger room and cargo space you'll actually use. For example, two parents, a kid, and a typical load of groceries can fit into something smaller than a minivan or SUV.

- **Which models get the most miles per gallon?** Once you've decided on the size you want, compare the mileage ratings for different models in that size range. A good place to compare models (and get tips on fuel efficiency) is *www.fueleconomy.gov*.

- **What kind of transmission should I get?** In general, manual transmissions are more fuel efficient than automatic ones by about 5–10%. (Of course, you need to know how to drive a stick to get this benefit.) Go for a four- or five-speed if it's available.

- **Will I really use four-wheel drive?** Four-wheel or all-wheel drive is great for off-roading and for maximizing control when the road is slippery. But keep in mind that this option increases fuel use by 5–10%. So it's worth assessing whether you really need four-wheel drive.

- **Do I need any bells and whistles?** Car dealers love to pile on the options: auto climate control, power everything (windows, seats, mirrors, and so on), video systems, roof rack, sunroof, and so on. Some of these things can reduce fuel efficiency by adding weight, drawing extra power from the engine, or increasing aerodynamic drag. They also add to the cost, which means you pay more money for a less efficient car.

Hybrids

A typical *hybrid vehicle* gets its power from two sources: a gasoline-powered internal combustion engine and an electric motor. But not all hybrids work the same way. So if you're thinking about getting one, learn these terms before you go shopping:

- **Parallel hybrid.** You might remember the terms "parallel" and "series" from high school science class. In the context of cars, they refer to the way things under the hood are connected. Parallel setups are the most common. In this kind of hybrid, a combustion engine and an electric motor are connected to the transmission. The engine and the motor can run in parallel, meaning the fuel tank supplies gas to the engine, and a set of batteries simultaneously powers an electric motor. So the engine and the electric motor can both run the transmission at the same time. Examples of parallel hybrids include the Toyota Prius and the Ford Escape.

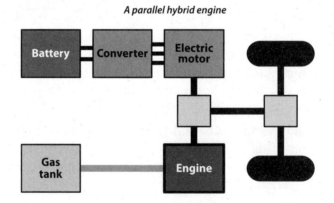

A parallel hybrid engine

Parallel hybrids fit into one of three categories:

- **Full hybrid.** This type of car can run on the combustion engine, the electric motor, or a combination of the two.

- **Assist hybrid.** The electric motor in this kind of setup doesn't have enough juice to move the car all by itself. Instead, the electric motor assists, or boosts, the gas engine.

- **Mild hybrid.** Internal combustion engines move these cars. In general, the electric motor generates power when the car slows down. That power helps run extras like the AC, taking a load off the engine so it can be smaller than in a normal car, which makes the car lighter and increases fuel efficiency.

• **Serial hybrid.** In this arrangement, the gas engine turns a generator that either charges the batteries or powers an electric motor that drives the transmission. That means that the gas engine never directly powers the vehicle. The Chevy Volt, currently being developed, uses serial hybrid technology.

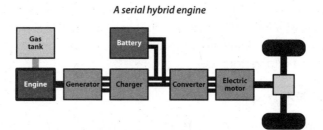

A serial hybrid engine

> **Note** A *plug-in hybrid* (which can be parallel or serial) comes with a plug you can use to charge the car's batteries. When you drive on fully charged batteries, you're not using the gas-powered engine at all. If the batteries need recharging while you're on the road, the gasoline engine kicks in, and the car works like a regular hybrid.

Diesel Engines

Like gas engines, diesel engines use *internal combustion*—a series of small, controlled explosions—to convert the potential energy in fuel into energy that makes your car go. In a conventional engine, the carburetor mixes gasoline and air together, and then spark plugs ignite the mixture. But in a diesel engine, fuel gets sent into a combustion chamber, where hot, compressed air ignites it. This direct fuel injection makes diesel engines more efficient. Although diesel fuel and gasoline are both made from crude oil, diesel is heavier, thicker, and oilier. It also contains more energy than gasoline (about 18% more), and that, combined with the engine's efficiency, lets diesel engines get more miles out of each gallon of fuel.

You probably think of diesel-powered trucks as being smelly, noisy, smoke-belching monsters. That used to be the case, but today's diesels—cars *and* trucks—are a whole new breed. The diesel engine is 20–30% more efficient than the gas-burning internal combustion engines in most cars.

Fuel efficiency is the biggest plus of owning a diesel car. Others include performance (diesel drivers say their cars have a lot more pep) and longevity (it's not unusual for them to keep chugging along for 250,000 miles or more). And as you'll learn in the next section, you can convert a diesel engine to run on vegetable oil.

But these engines have their downsides. They're more expensive than gas-powered cars, and diesel tends to cost more and be harder to find than gas. Though they're quieter than they used to be, diesel engines still tend to make more noise than gas ones, and can be harder to start on cold mornings. But for someone like you who cares about the environment, the biggest issue is emissions. Diesel engines burn dirtier than gas ones, spewing out more smog-forming particulates and nitrogen oxides. But since they're more efficient, they burn less fuel and produce less carbon dioxide. But happily, you can make your diesel *a lot* more environmentally friendly by converting it to veggie fuel.

Veggie Power!

We're used to thinking that cars have to run on the liquefied remains of dinosaurs, but there are other, *renewable* fuel sources. Biodiesel, ethanol, and vegetable oil are all emerging as plant-based options that can reduce our dependence on oil to keep the world moving. The following sections have the details.

Biodiesel

Biodiesel is a clean-burning fuel made from things like vegetable oil (including used cooking oil, called WVO for *waste vegetable oil*), algae, and animal fat. Most biodiesel is made from soybean oil and can be used in most diesel engines without any modifications. You can also mix it with petroleum-based diesel fuel, which is a good idea if you live in a cold climate because biodiesel can be sluggish when the temperature drops. Unlike straight veggie oil (covered in the next section), biodiesel is EPA approved for use as a fuel.

According to the EPA, biodiesel is good for the environment: It reduces greenhouse-gas emissions by 10–50% (depending on the kind of biodiesel used) compared to petroleum-based diesel. Biodiesel cars and trucks also spit out significantly less carbon monoxide, particulate gunk, and sulfates than regular diesel.

The main concern about biodiesel is how much land and resources are needed to produce fuel rather than food. If it's more profitable to grow crops for biodiesel (and other plant-based fuels) than for food, farmers will make the switch—causing food prices to rise. Higher prices for staples like cooking oil and grains would be disastrous in many parts of the world, and could lead to famine.

Planning ahead can help to solve this problem before it gets too big. For example, biodiesel can be made from things like WVO and algae instead. And because biodiesel producers use only soybean oil, the leftover soy meal can be used for food.

Straight vegetable oil (SVO)

Another alternative fuel that's gained momentum is veggie oil, sometimes called *straight vegetable oil* (SVO) to distinguish it from biodiesel. You can convert diesel vehicles using a special kit, so they have two fuel tanks: one for diesel and one for vegetable oil, which is thicker than diesel. Because it's thicker, SVO needs to be warmed up (which thins it) to work properly, so diesel is typically used to start the car. Once the engine is warm, it can switch to using SVO.

Most folks who've converted their cars use WVO they get from restaurants' deep fryers. Many restaurants are happy to give away this used oil, because otherwise they have to pay to dispose of it. (How's that for a step toward zero waste?)

SVO (as well as other biofuels) is also carbon *neutral*: The plants it comes from (like canola, corn, and soy) take in more carbon dioxide from the air than the oil releases when it's burned, which means it doesn't contribute to global warming. And vegetable oil doesn't emit the particulates and nitrogen oxides that diesel does.

Here are some companies that sell vegetable-oil conversion kits:

- Frybrid Vegetable Oil Fuel Systems (*www.frybrid.com*).
- Golden Fuel Systems (*www.goldenfuelsystems.com*).
- Greasecar Vegetable Fuel Systems (*www.greasecar.com*).
- PlantDrive (*www.plantdrive.com*).
- Veg Powered Systems (*www.vegpoweredsystems.com*).

Before you start fooling around under the hood, you should know that, in the U.S. anyway, there are some unresolved legal issues about using SVO as fuel. Unlike biodiesel, the EPA hasn't given it the green light as a fuel, so people who use it in their cars could face stiff fines—up to $32,000 per day—*if* the agency decides to enforce them. Different states also have different regulations about using WVO as a fuel: Some exempt it from fuel taxes; others expect you to pay a road tax. For these reasons, you might want to limit veggie power from SVO to things like tractors that you don't drive on public roads.

Green Tech

Emerging Fuels

More people thinking about the environment has spawned an increase in new technologies to help us get from here to there that look beyond gas- or diesel-guzzling engines. Most current research focuses on alternative fuel sources.

Hydrogen looks promising because it can power electric motors and internal combustion engines. It can be produced domestically, reducing our need for foreign oil. The hydrogen cells that power electric motors don't emit any pollutants and greenhouse gases. Sounds good, but there are several drawbacks. When hydrogen is burned in an internal combustion engine, it produces some nitrogen oxides. Hydrogen is expensive, though, and so are the cars that run on it. And unlike gas, there aren't yet hydrogen stations on every corner, and hydrogen-powered cars need to fill up every 200 miles or so. Most of the hydrogen stations in the U.S. are in California, so folks in other states are kind of out of luck.

A 2006 documentary asked, "Who killed the electric car?" But like Mark Twain's, reports of the electric car's death have been greatly exaggerated. Start-ups like Tesla and Fisker, as well as large, established auto companies, are working to build a viable electric car. Such cars store electricity in a battery and a motor uses that power to turn the wheels. Unlike most hybrids, which recharge the battery as you drive, you have to plug in electric vehicles to recharge them. That's the main thing holding these cars back: They're great for short trips but are limited to a range of 40–50 miles between charges. Advances in technologies like batteries are likely to extend this range. For example, within the next 5 years, improved lithium-ion batteries may help make electric vehicles that can travel about 250 miles between charges a reality.

Long-Distance Travel

Green travel is respectful travel. It means that, wherever you go, you think about:

- **The environment.** Try to find ways to get where you're going that have minimal impact on the planet, such as public transportation.

- **Local people.** Whether you're traveling to the next town over or a far-away place, remember that people live there—and act accordingly. Be friendly, say hello, respect native culture, eat in locally owned restaurants, and buy locally made goods.

- **Your body.** Take care of yourself when you travel, just as you do at home. Don't gorge on junk food, for example, or use toiletries that might contain harmful ingredients.

Whether you're on a business trip or vacation (or combining the two), the tips in this section will help you care for the earth while you explore it.

Before You Go

Green travel starts with planning ahead. Here's how to plan and prepare for your trip:

- **Book earth-friendly accommodations.** Choose a hotel that's in line with your principles to lessen your impact on the environment and support green businesses. Lots of hotels claim to be green, but make sure those claims are true by looking for an independent opinion from an organization like Audubon International's Green Leaf Eco-Rating Program (*http://greenleaf.auduboninternational.org*). Or check out one of these websites:

  - **Best Green Hotels** (*www.environmentallyfriendlyhotels.com*) lets you search for a place to stay by location or hotel name.

  - **"Green" Hotels Association** (*www.greenhotels.com*) lists hotels that have shown a commitment to green practices by joining the association.

  - **Green Lodge** (*www.greenlodge.org*) rates hotels as gold, silver, or bronze, with gold being the most environmentally responsible.

  - **Sustainable Travel International** (*www.sustainabletravelinternational.org*) has an eco-directory you can search by type of lodging, region, and/or keyword.

— **CouchSurfing International** (*www.couchsurfing.org*) lets you skip the hotel and make new friends by matching you up with locals who are willing to let travelers sleep on the couch (or in a spare bedroom). After you've registered, you can make arrangements to stay with other couchsurfers—the site has more than a million members around the world. A system of verification, references, and members vouching for one another helps assure your safety.

Tip Many travel sites—like Expedia, Orbitz, and Travelocity—have guides to green travel, including recommended hotels and tour operators.

- **Do your research.** For example, if you plan to take any tours on your trip, look for guides who are certified as environmentally responsible. (Ask before you book, or take a look at Planeta.com's Guide to Recommended Guides and Tour Operators at *www.planeta.com/worldtravel.html*.)

- **Pack light.** The days of lugging steamer trunks across the ocean are long gone. Choose a lightweight bag and take only what you need. A light bag is easy to carry and puts less weight on the plane, ship, or whatever you're travelling by.

- **Unplug appliances.** Minimize the phantom load (page 61) at home by unplugging anything that doesn't need to stay on while you're gone, like computers, TVs, and microwaves.

- **Turn down the water heater.** There's no reason to heat water if you're not around to use it. So lower the temperature on the water heater to "vacation" or, if it doesn't have that option, to the lowest setting.

- **Go paperless.** Use e-tickets and print your boarding pass at home. That way you can use recycled paper and environmentally friendly ink, and save yourself time at the airport.

Tip When planning your vacation, consider camping. Sleeping in a tent has a smaller carbon footprint than staying in a hotel—and gets you close to the nature you're trying to preserve. Choose a tent over a recreational vehicle (RVs get terrible gas mileage) or trailer (which cause drag so your car burns more gas). You can cook over a camp stove or a small campfire, but don't build any big bonfires, which send lots of smoke and greenhouse gases into the air. Or eat your meals at a restaurant (you're on vacation, after all).

Getting There (and Back)

How you travel is one of the biggest ways you affect the environment when you go somewhere. The Union of Concerned Scientists (UCS, *www.ucsusa. org*) analyzed the impact of various ways of getting around, and came up with some surprising results. For example, a nonstop economy-class flight is greener for one or two travelers than going by car—especially you go more than 500 miles.

When planning your trip, keep these points in mind:

- **Buses are green options.** If you and a friend take a long-distance bus (call it a motor coach if you like) rather than driving to your destination, you'll cut your trip's carbon footprint almost in half. And taking a motor coach instead of flying reduces your trip's footprint by as much as 75%. It'll take longer to get there, but enjoy the relaxed pace and watching the countryside roll by.

- **Take the train.** Another good option for long-distance travel is going by train. According to Friends of the Earth, flying creates 4–5 times the pollution of taking a train.

- **Don't drive during rush hour.** Stop-and-go traffic is more than frustrating, it means worse fuel efficiency. Time trips for when you'll be able to cruise along the highway without hitting traffic.

- **For group travel, drive a fuel-efficient car.** When you're traveling with friends and don't want to go by bus or train, your best choice is a fuel-efficient car (page 235). (That means leave the gas-hog of an SUV in the garage.) If none of you own a car that gets good gas mileage, consider renting a hybrid (page 236) for the trip.

- **Avoid flying first class.** Yes, first class is roomier than economy—and that's the problem. Those bigger seats make your trip less efficient. According to UCS, when you sit in a wider seat with more legroom, your carbon footprint is up to *twice* as big as someone flying coach.

- **Take nonstop flights.** You probably already prefer nonstop flights to sprinting across airports, trying to make connections. But flying nonstop also makes good environmental sense because taking off, landing, and fueling the plane, loading and unloading bags, and all the other stuff they do on the ground all produce a lot of carbon. The UCS says a 1,000-mile nonstop flight from New York to Orlando is almost 35% more carbon-efficient than a two-connection trip between those two cities.

- **Fly fewer miles.** Sometimes you can't get a direct flight to your destination. In that case, compare the mileage of the options you're presented (most travel websites give you this info). The fewer miles you fly, the smaller your carbon footprint.

- **Pick the best plane.** In general, regional jets and narrower planes are more fuel-efficient than wide-bodied planes. Your travel agent or the website where you book your trip will tell you what kind of planes fly the routes you're considering. Once you know your options, download the UCS's Getting There Greener report from *http://tinyurl.com/5uzj9u*. Appendix B lists emissions for different planes so you can choose the most efficient one.

- **Support green airlines.** Some airlines offer only economy seats, which reduces the carbon footprint of each flight. When you can, spend your travel dollars with these carriers.

> **Tip** If your trip is going to have a bigger carbon footprint than you'd like, consider buying a carbon offset (page 259) to reduce your impact. Or offset the carbon the natural way by planting a few trees, which take in carbon dioxide and release oxygen.

During Your Stay

Getting there is half the battle, but once you arrive at your destination, you want to be a good guest. Tread lightly upon the earth and respect the people and environment you're visiting. Use these ideas as guidelines:

- **Take public transportation.** Taking the bus or subway lets you experience the area as the locals do—and it saves you the expense and greenhouse-gas emissions of a rental car.

- **Share a taxi.** When you take a cab, split it with someone who's going your way. You'll cut the environmental impact of the trip in half.

- **Take a stroll.** Page 228 explains why walking is a good for both you and the environment, so travel by foot whenever possible. If you're a tourist, take a walking tour instead of one that goes by bus. Of course, use common sense when walking in an unfamiliar place—don't walk alone or late at night, and take a map so you won't get lost.

- **Air-dry towels at the hotel.** You probably don't insist on freshly laundered towels every day at home, and you don't need them at a hotel, either. If the hotel has a linen program, join in it by hanging up used towels instead of leaving them in a heap on the floor. If the hotel doesn't have such a program, ask the front desk to tell housekeeping that you don't need the towels and sheets changed every day.

> **Tip** Because all hotel towels look alike, keep track of whose towel is whose by packing diaper pins with different colored or shaped heads and putting a pin on the corner of each towel. Just don't forget to remove the pins before you leave!

- **Use your own toiletries.** Page 220 tells you how to find (or make) safe, environmentally responsible shampoo, conditioner, and other health and beauty products. So instead of wondering what's in the little bottles at the hotel, bring your own. And don't open those little bottles, even for a sniff—if you do, the hotel will throw them away when you leave.

- **Turn off the lights.** When you go out to explore your destination, turn off the lights in your hotel room. And adjust the temperature when you're not in the room; you don't need to keep the AC or heater going full blast when no one's there.

- **Check out over the TV.** Many hotels let you review charges and check out through the in-room TV, which helps you save time and paper.

- **Say yes to local flavor.** What's the point in traveling if you're just going to patronize the same chain stores and restaurants you go to at home? While you're on the road, seek out neighborhood businesses to support the local economy. Buy native handicrafts as souvenirs (instead of imported junk), preferably directly from the artisan who made them.

> **Tip** Flip to page 202 to for tips on finding organic restaurants when you travel.

Ecotourism

Because of the demand for green travel, a whole industry has sprung up around *ecotourism*—responsible travel to areas of natural beauty or amazing plants and animals—that seeks to protect the environment and minimize adverse effects of travel. Ecotourism often involves viewing wildlife, volunteering, interacting with local people, and enjoying chances to grow as a person and expand your sense of the world.

But ecotourism has its critics. Some companies want to benefit from the buzzword without making the environmental commitment that word implies. For example, poorly managed tour operators may harm the areas its patrons want to protect by increasing traffic or disrupting the ecobalance of previously off-the-beaten-track areas. And some companies are more concerned about their profits than about aiding local people in the areas they visit.

> **Tip** Instead of going away for vacation, consider a *staycation*. That's when you stay home and explore your hometown—try a new restaurant, hike a local park, or visit that museum you've been meaning to check out. Spending your vacation at home saves you the hassle and expense of travel, reduces your carbon footprint, and lets you see your town or city with fresh eyes. Just remember that you're on vacation—don't worry about housework or check your email, but *do* plan the kinds of activities you'd enjoy if you were away from home.

So how do you find a responsible ecotourism operator? Make sure any company you're considering:

- Promotes ecosystems to conserve biological diversity.
- Respects communities by investing in the local economy and involving native people in decisions.
- Increases environmental and cultural knowledge.
- Minimizes waste.
- Follows sustainable practices to reduce its environmental impact.

> **Tip** Before you book a trip, ask to see your tour operator's policy on responsible tourism and sustainable practices. If the policy doesn't live up to your expectations (or if the company doesn't have one at all), keep looking.

Here are some sites that can help you choose a reputable ecotourism company:

- **The Charity Guide** (*www.charityguide.org*). Click the left-hand "on a volunteer vacation" link, and then choose an interest (such as animal welfare, environment, or poverty) to see volunteer opportunities in that category.

- **Conservation International** (*www.conservation.org*). Click the left-hand Ecotourism link to see this group's guide to ecotourism.

- **Ecoclub, the International Ecotourism Club** (*www.ecoclub.com*). This social networking site has forums and blogs where you can get first-hand info about tours and destinations you're considering.

- **The International Ecotourism Society** (*www.ecotourism.org*). Click the Your Travel Choice link, and then click Ecotourism Explorer to find tour operators, hotels, and so on that are TIES members.

- **The Rainforest Alliance's Eco-Index Sustainable Tourism** (*http://eco-indextourism.org*). This site specializes in Latin-American and Caribbean ecotours.

- **VolunteerMatch** (*www.volunteermatch.org*). To find volunteer opportunities in the U.S., type in a location and interest (such as ***environment***) and you get a list of organizations looking for volunteers in that area.

> **Note** Visiting large cities and traditional tourist destinations—like London or a theme park—may have less of an environmental impact than an ecotour because these sites are set up to handle tourists. Seldom-visited areas, on the other hand, may be harmed by an influx of tourists.

9 Green Business Is Good Business

Lots of people spend nearly as much time at the office as they do at home—you might even be one of 'em. You've made earth-friendly improvements at home, so why not do the same at work? This chapter suggests ways to make your workplace greener, from stuff you can do at your desk to company-wide policy changes you can suggest. In business, it's all about the bottom line, and going green can save your company money by reducing operating costs, using fewer supplies, and cutting back on expensive travel. And the goodwill you generate in your industry and community might just attract new customers.

> **Tip** Even if you're not a bigwig in your company, you can influence company policy. Research greener alternatives to the way your company does things, then write up a proposal and present it to management.

Greening the Workplace

The U.S. EPA says that the energy required for just one worker in an office building in a single workday causes *twice* as many greenhouse-gas emissions (for things like heating and cooling, and powering lights, computers, and copiers, and so on) as that worker's commute. Clearly, businesses can do better. There are lots of things you can do to make your workplace a healthier, more environmentally friendly place. This section gets you started with ideas for doing things greener at work.

Telecommuting

Chapter 8 has all kinds of tips for greening your commute, but the greenest option is to avoid commuting altogether. *Telecommuting*, working remotely from home, is a great way to save time, money, and help the planet. With high-speed Internet, video- and Web conferencing, and fast file transfers, many people have no reason to trudge across town every day to work in cramped cubicles. (Obviously, it depends on the industry you're in.) Some work from home a couple of days each month or one day a week, while others are full-time telecommuters who rarely put in any face time at the office.

> **Note** Telecommuting just twice a week will save you 40% of the money you spend on gas driving to and from work—not to mention cutting back on your greenhouse gas emissions.

To telecommute successfully, you need the right equipment (and permission from your boss, of course). You probably already have most of what you need:

- **A computer.** Ask if you can use a company laptop at home.
- **A fast Internet connection.** Old-style dial-up is just too slow for telecommuting.
- **A dedicated phone line or cellphone.** You don't want to miss work calls because your kid is chatting with friends. If your company issues you a cellphone, use it when you work from home.
- **A fax machine or fax/printer/copier combo.** Of course, if you convince the powers that be to go paperless (page 253), you can skip this.

Tip Don't want to buy a fax machine? Try eFax (*www.efax.com*), which uses email to send and receive faxes. You pay monthly fee, which includes a certain number of free pages each month (depending on the plan you choose).

- **A webcam.** If you have to attend videoconferences, you need a way to transmit your smiling face to the meeting. (Just remember to brush your hair before you log on.)

- **The right software.** Ask your IT department what programs you'll need to work from home. You've probably already thought about the basics like a word processor, spreadsheet program, and so on, but make sure you have everything you need for web-conferencing, connecting to company databases, and anything else you use.

- **Dedicated space.** You need a room where you can close the door and *work*. If you try to do your job at the kitchen table or in a corner of the family room, you'll run into too many distractions. And make sure your family knows that when the door is closed, you need to be left in peace.

Tip A home office can give you a tax break, too. To qualify, the office has to be your primary workplace and be used only for work. Ask your accountant or tax preparer about claiming a home-office deduction, or visit *www.irs.gov* and, in the upper-right Search box, type *home office*.

In addition to the right equipment, you need the right personality. Telecommuting isn't for everyone. You have to be motivated, organized, and able to work without direct supervision. You also need to know when to call it a day—with no coworkers stopping by your desk to say goodnight on their way home, it's easy to work longer hours than you would at the office. And telecommuting can be lonely: If water-cooler gossip sessions are the highlights of your day, you'll probably feel isolated at home.

Tip Not sure what your company's telecommuting policy is? Make an appointment to talk with someone in HR to find out.

If your home office is set up and you've got the temperament, the next step is talking your boss. When you do, be ready with these arguments for telecommuting:

- **It increases productivity.** There's a myth that people who work from home slack off—get up late, work in their pajamas, take more breaks, and so on. Although some telecommuters do work in their PJs, they also work hard. In a 2008 survey, 67% of respondents cited increased productivity as the number one benefit of telecommuting. Several factors help boost your output at home, including using the time you'd otherwise spend sitting in traffic to actually get work done. And there are often fewer distractions at home than in an office full of people.

- **It saves money.** When you work from home, you use one less company desk, chair, phone, computer, and so on—and you cut the company's energy costs. Couple that with increased productivity and telecommuting looks good for the bottom line.

- **It improves morale.** Firms that let employees telecommute report fewer sick days, less stressed-out workers, and higher retention rates than other companies. (If your company doesn't allow telecommuting, this argument might help change that.)

- **It's good for the planet.** Showing a commitment to doing business in an environmentally responsible way can be good PR for your company.

- **It makes companies more competitive.** Outfits that allows telecommuting have an easier time finding, recruiting, and retaining qualified staff, since employees can work from anywhere—even if they live hundreds of miles away from the office.

> **Note:** In 2008, the American Electronics Association found that 45 million Americans telecommute at least one day a week.

- **You're ready.** Make sure you have everything in place to start working from home, and then fill your boss in on the details, emphasizing that there won't be any downtime—you're all set up to start working from home right away.

- **You can try it first, then assess.** Offer to telecommute for a trial period, and then sit down with your boss to evaluate how it went. Be sure to do an extra terrific, bang-up job during the trial period.

Reducing Office Waste

People have talked about paperless offices for years. Although advances in technology—including email, databases, and file-sharing sites—have reduced the amount of paper companies use, they're still far from paperless. A typical office generates about one-and-a-half pounds of waste paper per employee each day. According to the Clean Air Council, the amount of paper thrown out by U.S. businesses in a year could build a 12-foot-high wall stretching from Los Angeles to New York City. Cutting paper use by a measly 10% would reduce greenhouse-gas emissions by 1.6 million tons—equivalent to taking 280,000 cars off the road.

Changing those statistics happens one sheet at a time. If you start today, making even one small change, you can reduce waste, conserve energy and resources—and save your company money while you're at it. Here are some tips to get you started:

- **Save energy at your desk.** Set your computer and monitor to power down when you're not using them. When you head home at night, turn off your computer, monitor, printer, and so on instead of leaving them on overnight. One easy way to do this is to plug everything into one power strip with an on/off switch—just turn off the strip at the end of the day. Or get a smart power strip (page 62).

- **Turn off the lights.** Last one out of the office? Don't forget to flip the lights off on your way out the door. And if you use a desk lamp, use a CFL (page 69) instead of an incandescent bulb.

- **Unplug.** After you charge your cellphone, laptop, or other mobile device, unplug the charger so it won't waste energy while it's not doing anything. Also, look for chargers and adapters with the Energy Star label; they use about a third less energy than other models.

- **Go paperless.** Even if your company isn't ready to go *completely* paperless, you can still save paper at work. Before you print out an email or make a copy of a memo, think about whether you really need a paper version. Instead of printing, read onscreen, save files on your computer (don't forget to back them up!), and email documents or store them on file-sharing sites like SharePoint or Google Docs. Put employee manuals and info on the company's website. And when you truly need paper copies, print double sided.

Note The average American office worker uses 10,000 sheets of paper each year. Look around your office. If each person cut their paper use by half, think about how much paper would that save.

- **Recycle.** How often do people unthinkingly throw paper away instead of dropping it in a recycling bin? If your company has a recycling program, use it for paper, plastics, aluminum cans and foil, glass bottles, printer cartridges, cellphones, and more. If your company doesn't have such a program, look into starting one. Recycle911.com has a helpful guide for doing that: Go to *http://business.earth911.com*, click Green Guides, and then click "Start a Recycling Program at Work".

> **Tip** Make sure recycling bins are easy to find and use. Put bins near the copier, printer, and at each desk. In the break room, place bins labeled for plastic, metal, and glass where people will see them, along with clear instructions for what can and can't go into each one. (You'd be surprised how many people still have no clue about recycling.)

- **Buy green office supplies.** Look for recycled paper that's made using an earth-friendly process (page 205). And refilled printer cartridges are cheaper than brand-new ones. You can also buy recycled pens and pencils, folders, binders, furniture, and more. Think outside the cubicle, too—cloth or recycled paper towels for the kitchen and restrooms, reusable coffee filters for the break room, biodegradable cups and utensils.

> **Tip** Check out the EPA's Comprehensive Procurement Guide (*www.epa.gov/cpg*) to see its recommendations for recycled office supplies.

- **Reuse.** Using stuff more than once (page 94) is just as important at work as it is at home. Every time you reuse something instead of throwing it away, you make your office a little more earth-friendly. So instead of grabbing a fresh notepad from the supply closet, reuse paper that has something printed on one side. And use the blank sides of previously printed paper when you need to print a draft of a document you're working on. Reuse envelopes for in-office correspondence (or better yet, send an email). When a shipment arrives, save and reuse the box and packing materials, or see whether the shipper will take them back for reuse or credit. Just about anything in the office is a candidate for reuse: furniture, relabeled folders, shredded paper (for cushioning shipments)—use your imagination.

- **Mug it up.** Instead of using disposable cups for your coffee, bring in your own mug. On the same note, forgo paper plates and throw-away utensils for ones you can wash and reuse.

- **Just say no to disposable water bottles.** Plastic bottles you use once and then throw away raise concerns about both health (page 153) and waste (page 78). (According to the group Refill Not Landfill, Americans drank 8.3 *billion* gallons of bottled water in 2006—that's a lot of empty containers!) Instead of bringing bottled water into the office, get a reusable container and fill it up at the water cooler or drinking fountain. If you do drink a bottle of water, drop it in the recycling bin when it's empty.

Staying Healthy on the Job

People in developed countries spend 75–90% of their lives indoors. And, as page 10 points out, indoor air can be a soup of VOCs, making it more polluted than outside air. Chapter 1 explains how to make your home healthier, so browse that chapter for tips you can also apply at work. Here are some more ways to keep your workplace healthy:

- **Let the air flow.** Don't let stacks of paper, cabinets, or cubicle walls block vents that circulate air through the building. With clear vents, you breathe fresher air, and the building's ventilation system doesn't have to work as hard, so you save energy, too.

- **Buy a plant.** Plants freshen the air by absorbing indoor air pollution and giving off oxygen. Recent studies have shown that two plants in 12"–14" containers can significantly decrease VOCs (page 12) in a 10' × 10' room. So you'll breathe easier if you keep a plant (or several) on or near your desk.

> **Tip** Some of the most effective VOC-absorbing plants are rubber plants, English ivy, Ficus alii, Boston ivy, Boston ferns, spider plants, bamboo palms, and lady palms.

- **Lobby for a clean-air policy.** Many people are sensitive to perfumes and colognes, which are a real problem in offices where people spend hours at close quarters. Ask HR to create guidelines for use of perfumes, colognes, and aerosol sprays; VOCs (page 12) such as cleaning products; and smoking (many workplaces have banned indoor smoking, but you may still have to walk through a haze of smoke when you leave the building).

- **Campaign for green cleaning.** As page 10 explains, many common cleaning products contribute to indoor air pollution and can harm people's health. There's no need to spend 40 hours a week inhaling potentially harmful chemicals when there are effective green alternatives. Propose that your company hire an environmentally friendly janitorial firm (do your research so you can suggest specific companies in your proposal), or request that the current cleaners use green products.

- **Minimize off-gassing.** When it's time to spruce up the office, try to avoid VOCs. New furniture, paint, and carpeting all contain VOCs (see the box on page 12) that *off-gas*, gradually releasing vapors from chemicals used to make them.

- **Eat healthy at work.** It's cheaper and healthier to pack your own lunch than to order fast food (and can save you from driving to a restaurant at lunchtime). When you bring your own food, you know what's in it and you can make the same healthy choices you make at home (Chapter 6). Instead of brown-bagging it and then throwing the bag away, pack your lunch in a reusable bag with reusable containers and utensils—even a cloth napkin you can take home and wash.

- **If you order out, make it a group order.** Food delivered to the office brings with it a lot of wasteful packaging and probably involves a car trip. Minimize packaging and emissions by asking coworkers if they'd like to get in on the order, so there's just one delivery instead of several. And tell the restaurant that you don't need napkins, utensils, or anything else that'll get thrown away.

Greener Business Travel

Businesspeople cover a lot of ground, making more than 200 million trips each year in the U.S. alone, a third of those by plane. And with air travel growing by nearly 5% a year, it's also the fastest-growing source of carbon dioxide emissions. So it's important to make the trips you take for work as green as possible.

Tip Chapter 8 is all about traveling greener, and many of the tips apply to business travel, as well, so page through it to see how to go green when you're on the road (or in the air).

Green-Collar Jobs

What's a "green-collar" job, and what industries are creating them?

It used to be that jobs were broken down into two main categories, defined by the kind of shirt workers in each category usually wore:

- **White collar** referred to salaried managers and professionals, who wore dress shirts and neckties to work.
- **Blue collar** described the jobs of the tradesmen and laborers who got paid by the hour and wore uniforms or denim work shirts.

As more women entered the workforce, the term "pink collar" came to describe jobs traditionally held by women, like typists and secretaries. And now that people are realizing the importance of living in a sustainable, environmentally responsible way, a new color is emerging: green.

A *green-collar* job is one in the environmental sector. These positions cross the old boundaries of salary vs. hourly wage, professional vs. labor, men vs. women. Workers in these jobs fight pollution, reduce waste, and help the environment while earning a living wage.

Here are some of the industries that provide green collar jobs; a few might surprise you:

- **Alternative energy.** Manufacturing, selling, and installing solar panels, wind turbines, and hydroelectric power systems; researching and developing alternative energy sources and fuels.
- **Green building.** Architecture, environmentally responsible construction, inspecting and certifying LEED (page 118) buildings; auditing home energy use.
- **Green transportation.** Researching and developing energy-efficient vehicles (page 234); manufacturing, selling, and repairing those vehicles and related products; working for public transit authorities; developing, promoting, and selling alternative transportation, from bicycles to podcars to car-sharing programs.
- **Sustainable food production.** Organic farming, nurseries, and garden suppliers; restaurants committed to supporting local farms.
- **Environmental protection.** Environmental activism and law; recycling and environmentally responsible waste management; industrial composting; hazardous materials clean-up; habitat or ecological restoration.
- **Green business services.** Paperless payroll companies; green Web hosting; environmentally friendly printing services; ethical marketing.

If you're looking for a job, check out the job boards at Tree Hugger (*http://jobs.treehugger.com*), Greenjobs (*www.greenjobs.com*), and the Green Jobs Network (*www.greenjobs.net*).

The greenest trip, of course, is the one you don't take. So before you book a flight, think about whether it's really necessary. Could you accomplish the same thing with a videoconference or online meeting instead? Could one or two of the people traveling stay home? Are there other ways to learn the info and enjoy the networking opportunities you'd get at that distant conference? Cutting back on business travel reduces your company's carbon footprint and cuts on-the-road costs—meals, hotel, car rental, taxis, and so on.

When you *have* to travel, there are greener, cheaper ways to go:

- **Instead of flying, take a bus or train.** Especially for trips under 500 miles, taking a train or bus will use less fuel and produce fewer greenhouse-gas emissions than hopping on a plane. Staying on the ground might even save you time, since you don't have to go through a security line or arrive early to hang around the boarding area waiting for your flight. And because most train and bus stations are closer to city centers than airports, you'll spend less time getting where you're going.

- **Fly coach.** Yes, business class is more comfortable and yes, the company is picking up the tab. But the extra seat space and legroom you get in business or first class increases the trip's carbon footprint by up to 100%.

- **Line up back-to-back trips.** If you need to make several trips in a short time frame, try to make them back to back, instead of going home for a day or two between them. And if you can, try to get nonstop flights—takeoffs and landings are the biggest fuel hogs of a flight.

- **Carry one bag.** Packing light (page 242) saves bag-checking fees and reduces the weight that the plane has to carry—and that you have to lug around.

- **Pick green hotels.** Flip to page 241 for tips on choosing a green hotel and using less energy during your stay.

- **Go hybrid.** When you're renting a car or hailing a taxi, choose a fuel-efficient hybrid whenever you can. (And don't rent a bigger car than you need.) If you hire a car service to chauffeur you or some VIPs around town, look for one that has hybrids in its fleet. DrivenEco (*www.driveneco.com*) is a green limo service with more than a dozen locations throughout the U.S., or consider one of these:

    — Austin, TX: Clean Air Limo (*http://cleanairlimo.com*).

    — Hollywood/Los Angeles, CA: Green SUV (*www.greensuv.com*).

— London, U.K.: Greentomatocars (*www.greentomatocars.com*).

— New Jersey/New York city: Green Fleet Car Service (*www.green-fleetlimo.com*).

— New York, NY: NYC Green Car (*http://nycgreencar.com*).

— New York, NY: OZOcar (*http://ozocar.com*).

— San Francisco, CA: (*www.greencarlimo.com*).

> **Note** You can find all the links listed above on this book's Missing CD page at *www.missingmanuals.com*.

- **Use a green travel agency.** If your business relies on an agent to arrange business trips, make sure yours is committed to protecting the earth. The American Society of Travel Agents (ASTA) has a green program for its members that educates them and keeps them up-to-date on green travel trends. Participating agents display the ASTA Green Member logo, so look for that when choosing an agency.

Buying Carbon Offsets

Some companies stomp all over the planet with an awfully big carbon footprint. To mitigate the effects of their greenhouse gas–emitting activities, companies large and small—as well as individuals—are purchasing *carbon offsets*. As the name implies, carbon offsets are investments used to help remove carbon dioxide (and other greenhouse gases) from the atmosphere.

So how do they work? You buy a carbon offset from a third-party company (some are nonprofit, others for-profit), paying a set price for each ton of greenhouse-gas emissions you want to counteract. Typically, you can buy offsets by the activity you want to balance out (the industry terms for this is making the activity *emission neutral*), such as a flight, or you can simply pick the amount you want to pay. The company then invests your money in verified carbon offset projects like renewable energy (Chapter 10 tells you more about what that means); planting trees to replace forests, absorb pollution, and release oxygen; energy conservation programs; environmental education; and methane destruction (capturing landfill gas and using it for energy).

Of course, the best way to reduce your carbon footprint is not to make one in the first place, and this book is packed with advice to help you do just that. The fewer emissions you produce, the fewer there are to counteract. Carbon offsets work best for activities you can't avoid or mitigate on your own, like if you have to go to a conference or sales meeting halfway across the country. In that case, at least you can buy offsets to mitigate the trip's impact on the environment.

There are lots of organizations out there that would love to sell you carbon offsets—and not all of them are legit. To make sure your money will really reduce your carbon footprint (and not line some scammer's pockets), check out these sites:

- **The Environmental Defense Fund** (EDF) has a list of offset projects that meet EDF criteria, including independent verification of offset claims and permanence of the carbon reduction. Check it out at *www.carbonoffsetlist.org*.

- **Ecobusinesslinks.com** has compiled an easy-to-read table that gives the offset provider's name (and links to its website), price per ton of CO_2 offset, whether the provider is nonprofit, the kinds of projects it invests in, and who certifies it. To see the table, go to *http://tinyurl.com/nvbhw*.

- **The Voluntary Carbon Standard** (*www.v-c-s.org*) provides a set of criteria for legitimate carbon offsets. To make the cut, "offsets must be real (have happened), additional (beyond business-as-usual activities), measurable, permanent (not temporarily displace emissions), independently verified, and unique (not used more than once to offset emissions)." To learn about VCS-approved offset programs, visit *http://vcsprojectdatabase.com*.

Offsets sound like a great idea—and there's no doubt that they're doing some good. They make people more aware of their carbon footprints and fund worthy environmental projects. But they have their critics. One major complaint is that offsets give the impression that you can buy your way out of irresponsible activities. There's a danger that people and companies will treat offsets as license to endanger the environment. But that argument is like saying that giving money to an anti-drunk-driving program gives you permission to drive drunk.

The most effective way to reduce your carbon footprint is to change how you do things and become more environmentally responsible. You can't simply throw money at the problem and hope it'll go away. When companies—and individuals—stop polluting, we can stop worrying about how to clean up that pollution.

Corporate Giving

Carbon offsets are one way to put your money where your environmental consciousness is. There are also lots of nonprofits doing work that your company can support through corporate giving. Even if you're not the CFO, you can still write up a proposal for corporate giving and present it to management. When you share the wealth with organizations that are helping preserve the environment, you're supporting their full-time commitment to saving the planet. And you might get a little good karma in return.

Tip To find a nonprofit that matches your interests and values, visit Charity Navigator (*www.charitynavigator.org*), an independent evaluator, and search its database of more than 5,000 organizations.

Your company has tons of great charities to choose from. Here's a sampling:

- **The Alliance for Climate Protection** (*http://climateprotect.org*), led by Al Gore, supports projects related to clean energy.

- **Conservation International** (*www.conservation.org*) aims to conserve biodiversity and promote balance between society and nature.

- **The Conservation Fund** (*www.conservationfund.org*) has conserved land and water resources throughout the U.S.—more than 6 million acres so far.

- **Defenders of Wildlife** (*www.defenders.org*), as its name implies, helps protect animals and plants in their natural habitats.

- **Earth Day Network** (*http://earthday.org*) makes every day Earth Day by promoting environmental activism through education, community mobilization, clean-water projects, and more.

- **Environmental Defense Fund** (*www.edf.org*) has worked since 1967 to protect the environment and promote good health.

- **Greenpeace** (*www.greenpeace.org*) has promoted conservation and combated environmental destruction through nonviolent confrontation since 1971.

- **National Audubon Society** (*www.audubon.org*) promotes biodiversity by helping conserve natural habitats.

- **National Wildlife Federation** (*www.nwf.org*) protects wildlife for future generations.

- **Natural Resources Defense Council** (*www.nrdc.org*) uses its staff of 300+ lawyers, scientists, and policy experts—with support from its 1.2 million members—to protect the environment.

- **The Nature Conservancy** (*www.nature.org*) works internationally to conserve and protect land and water, including 119 million acres of land and 500 rivers so far.

- **Rainforest Alliance** (*www.rainforest-alliance.org*) focuses on preserving biodiversity and promoting sustainable livelihoods in the world's rainforests.

- **Sierra Club** (*www.sierraclub.org*), founded in 1892, promotes healthy communities, fights global warming, and conserves wildlife habitats.

- **World Wildlife Fund** (*www.worldwildlife.org*) has 5 million members worldwide and works to promote conservation, sustainable use of natural resources, and reducing pollution.

Don't overlook local opportunities to make a difference—many of the organizations on this list have chapters in your community. Donate to these chapters or organize a group of coworkers to volunteer. You can likely find groups that could use your help counting birds, planting trees, and cleaning up parks or shorelines, for example. Your company might also donate money to sponsor an event, such as a fundraiser.

> **Tip** Here's a way to give to your favorite charity as you go about your tasks at work: Instead of whatever search engine you now use to find stuff on the Web, try GoodSearch.com (*www.goodsearch.com*), a search engine powered by Yahoo. You tell the site which group you want to support, and then search for info as you would with any search engine. Each time you search, GoodSearch.com donates money to the charity you chose.

10 Alternative and Renewable Energy

Ever since the Industrial Revolution, the world has been hungry for energy. A hundred years ago, developing technologies relied on fossil fuels—and that reliance has only grown with time. Today, most power plants burn coal, oil, or natural gas; cars run on oceans of gasoline; and people heat their homes with oil or gas. But fossil fuels won't last forever, and their overuse poses serious environmental problems. We need new technologies to supply our energy without taking such a heavy toll on the planet.

There are lots of reasons to be optimistic about the future. We're at an exciting and historic crossroads: Conventional power sources such as fossil fuels are making room for carbon-neutral, earth-friendly alternatives. This chapter gives an overview of renewable energy and some of the emerging technologies.

Why We Need New Energy Sources

As you've no doubt heard, the climate is changing—largely due to human activity. *Global warming* refers to an average increase in the temperature on the earth's surface and in the *troposphere*, the atmosphere's lowest layer. This warming contributes to climate changes, which can have a host of consequences, like shrinking polar ice caps, rising sea levels, and changes in weather patterns that can affect crops and even drive some species to extinction.

A big cause of global warming are the *greenhouses gases* that get released when people burn fossil fuels like coal, petroleum, and natural gas. These gases—which include carbon dioxide (CO_2), methane, and water vapor—aren't bad in themselves. Every time you take a breath, you exhale CO_2, which plants take in and then give off oxygen. This cycle works great—when it's in balance. But increased fossil fuel consumption and deforestation has thrown the cycle out of whack.

With too many greenhouse gases, radiation from the sun gets into the atmosphere but can't leave because the gases absorb and then reemit it, which raises the earth's temperature. This *greenhouse effect* traps heat in the troposphere. Like greenhouse gases, this effect isn't bad in itself—it lets the earth support life—but too much of it is causing global warming and messing up the climate.

According to the U.S. EPA, average temperatures worldwide could increase from 3.2–7.2° F (about 2–4° C) above 1990 levels in less than a hundred years. When you're shoveling snow on a frigid morning, heating things up a bit might seem great. But global warming can cause lots of problems, like the spread of diseases (as host insects expand their range); extreme weather like hurricanes, tornadoes, flooding, and drought; extinction of plants and animals; and food and water shortages.

One way for you to reduce greenhouse-gas emissions is by using less energy—and this book is full of ways to do that. If everyone made a few small, simple changes, we'd all use less power and spew less pollution into the atmosphere. But we need bigger changes, too. The U.S. Energy Information Administration says that 86% of the power produced in the U.S. comes from fossil fuels, and only a measly 6% from renewable sources. To reduce global warming, the government needs to invest in research and practical applications for energy that's clean, sustainable, and renewable.

> **Note** *Acid rain* is another serious problem caused by burning fossil fuels. The culprits are sulfur dioxide and nitrogen oxides, which react with water vapor and other gases to produce sulfuric acid and nitric acid. These acids upset the balance of rivers, lakes, and soil and damage trees, buildings, statues, and even human health by damaging lungs if inhaled.

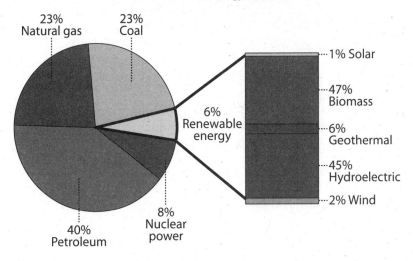

Where America's energy comes from

23%
Natural gas

23%
Coal

6%
Renewable
energy

40%
Petroleum

8%
Nuclear
power

1% Solar

47%
Biomass

6%
Geothermal

45%
Hydroelectric

2% Wind

Wind Energy

Harnessing the power of the wind is nothing new—people have been doing it for more than a thousand years. Ninth-century Persians used windmills to pump water and grind grain, and twelfth-century Europeans built
the kind of windmills you see in the Netherlands today. These ancient
windmills used rotating blades or sails to convert wind into mechanical
energy that powered machines.

Modern wind generators are similar: The wind turns the blades of a turbine, which spins a shaft that drives a generator, which produces electricity. These turbines, which are usually on top of towers at least 150 feet
tall, can power individual homes or buildings (page 127) or they can be

grouped into *wind farms* (sometimes called *wind power plants*)
and supply energy to a power
grid. In such a farm, clusters of
turbines are positioned to catch
the site's prevailing wind, preferably one that's strong and
steady year round, averaging
more than 10 miles per hour.
You'll find wind farms in fields,
on ridges, even at sea.

Advantages

Wind energy is clean, which means it generates electricity without emitting any greenhouse gases, particulates, or other pollutants. It's renewable since it doesn't rely on a finite resource like oil, coal, or natural gas. And that points to another advantage: operating cost. Conventional power plants have to buy the fuel they use to generate electricity, whereas wind energy is basically free. Of course, it costs money to set up wind farms and connect them to the grid, but these costs decline with time—once a farm is up and running, it's cheap to maintain.

In the U.S. today, wind power generates enough electricity to power three million homes. That's about 15,000 megawatt hours (page 49)—and each of those wind-produced megawatt hours keep 1,220 pounds of CO_2 from being released into the atmosphere. If America got just 20% of its electricity from wind, that would be like taking more than 70 million cars off the road.

Disadvantages and Concerns

Utility-scale wind energy—that is, wind farms as power plants—has generated a bit of controversy. Some of the opposition comes from folks who don't want to live near a large-scale wind farm, and others who mistrust new technologies or don't like change. Here are some of the concerns people have raised (and rebuttals to a few common myths about wind power):

- **Claim: The wind is too intermittent—we need a constant power supply.** True, one of the biggest challenges of wind energy is that breezes come and go, and they're not always blowing when there's a lot of demand for electricity. So we need backup power sources.

  One solution would be to store the energy produced when the wind *is* blowing, and then release that energy when the wind dies down. That requires batteries, and right now we don't have the technology to easily store this energy. But researchers are working on better storage methods, including high-tech batteries, hydrogen fuel cells, supercapacitors, and compressed air storage (which uses wind energy to compress air in an underground chamber, from which the air can be released later and used to turn a gas turbine).

- **Claim: Wind energy doesn't reduce overall greenhouse-gas emissions.** How can this be, you may wonder. Isn't wind energy 100% free of greenhouse-gas emissions? Yes, it is. Like the previous claim, this one stems from concerns about the wind's intermittency. This argument suggests that we need fossil fuel–powered plants as a backup when the wind isn't strong enough, and these plants end up emitting just as much pollution as they would if they were supplying *all* the power.

This claim is mistaken. In the first place, we don't need a backup just because of wind power—the national grid needs it whether or not wind power is part of the system. And according to an analysis by Yes2Wind (a joint project of Friends of the Earth, Greenpeace, and the World Wildlife Fund), "even if the backup was the dirtiest option—coal power—at 10% wind power on the system, only 1% of the CO_2 saved by the wind would be emitted from the back-up—and 99% is saved" (*www.yes2wind.com/44_faq.html*). So even with a "dirty" backup power source, wind power still helps reduce greenhouse gases.

Note Denmark is a global leader in wind power. It began developing utility-scale wind power more than 30 years ago, and in 2007, nearly 20% of the country's electricity came from the wind. Since 1990, Denmark's CO_2 emissions have dropped by 13%, even though energy consumption went up by nearly 7% during the same period.

- **Claim: Wind energy is more expensive than traditionally produced power.** Creating a wind farm does have a lot of up-front costs (so does building a power plant). But as technology advances and wind farms proliferate, the cost is coming down. For example, a 2008 report from the American Geological Institute found that larger wind turbines have brought down the cost of wind power. The report states, "Current costs [in December 2008] are around 3.5–4 cents per kilowatt hour, less expensive than coal, oil, nuclear, and most natural gas-fired generation."

- **Claim: Wind turbines are noisy.** This used to be a problem, but it's gotten better. New turbines produce much less noise than earlier models.

- **Claim: Wind farms make people sick.** The concern here is the low-frequency noise the turbines generate. Studies have found that people living within a mile of such farms report more frequent headaches, dizziness, insomnia, and depression than those living farther away. Called *wind turbine syndrome*, the problem has been reported in several countries. Scientists need to do more studies, but several researchers have suggested putting wind farms at least a mile away from homes, schools, and hospitals.

- **Claim: Wind farms are an eyesore.** This one's in the eye of the beholder: Some people think wind turbines are ugly; others see them as fascinating kinetic sculptures. People have also called power lines and cellphone towers eyesores yet accepted them as necessities of modern life. The sight of turbines on the horizon is a small price to pay for the clean energy they generate. And besides, conventional power plants aren't exactly what you'd call picturesque.

- **Claim: Wind turbines kill wildlife.** This is one of the most common objections you'll hear: that birds can't perceive the turbines and fly into the rotating blades. Although this can happen, recent designs have greatly reduced the risk. It's also worth putting those bird deaths in perspective: In the U.S. each year, power lines kill at least 130 million birds, cars kill another 60–80 million, and cats (wild and domesticated) kill nearly 40 million. Compare those numbers with a 2001 study by the National Wind Coordinating Committee, which found that an average wind turbine kills fewer than two birds per year (1.83, to be exact). The report estimates that, at worst, only 1 out of every 5,000 bird deaths is due to wind turbines.

> **Note** The National Audubon Society, whose mission is to protect birds and wildlife, supports wind power. The group recommends careful attention to state and federal guidelines on the location and operation of wind farms to mitigate their impact on wildlife. You can read the society's position on wind farms at *www. audubon.org/campaign/windPowerQA.html.* (This link and all the others in these pages are posted on this book's Missing CD page at *www.missingmanuals.com.*)

Solar Energy

That big ball of fire that rises in the east and sets in the west each day is a powerful energy source. And it beams its rays everywhere on Earth—for free. There are three main ways to harness the sun's energy:

- **Photovoltaic (PV) cells.** Explained in detail in the box on page 125, these cells convert sunlight directly into electricity. They can be small enough to recharge your cellphone or (combined into arrays of panels) large enough to produce energy for the national grid.

A photovoltaic solar power plant in Nevada

- **Solar thermal collectors.** Described on page 124, these panels absorb heat from the sun during the day and release it as needed. They use the collected heat to warm up swimming pools, for example, or heat water that's sent through pipes to warm a building or even a whole neighborhood. The heat can also create steam that drives a generator to produce electricity.

- **Solar dishes and other concentrating technologies.** This category includes different kinds of high-temperature solar thermal collectors. A solar dish, for example, uses reflectors to collect solar energy and concentrate it into a single beam. The beam is focused onto a heat engine, which drives a generator to create electricity.

A solar dish in New Mexico

Advantages

Solar power has a lot going for it. Like wind energy, it's free, it's renewable, and it's clean—it doesn't emit greenhouse gases, particulates, or other pollutants. In addition, solar power is:

- **Quiet.** If you're worried about noisy wind turbines, you'll be glad to know that solar technologies are silent.

- **Low-maintenance.** Solar panels and collectors don't need much in the way of maintenance or repair, and they last a long time.

- **Scalable.** As energy needs increase, you can add more panels or collectors.

Disadvantages

Alas, solar energy isn't perfect. It has a few drawbacks, including:

- **Land use and environmental impact.** Utility-scale solar power plants take up a lot of room because they require hundreds (or even thousands) of acres to hold all those solar cells and collectors. Such development can harm wildlife habitats and biodiversity. Many environmentalists would rather see people use less power than use large tracts of land to build a power plant, solar or otherwise.

- **Start-up costs.** Although solar power plants can pay for themselves over time (and advances in technology have been bringing costs down), setting them up is expensive.

- **Intermittency.** The sun doesn't shine all the time, so solar cells and collectors can't generate electricity around the clock, but people need power at night, too. Also, solar energy works best in places that get lots of sun; areas with air pollution or lots of cloudy days won't reap the same benefits from solar power.

Water Power

As mentioned on page 128, moving water is another clean and renewable energy source whose history goes back to ancient times. Villages and towns sprang up next to rivers because they provided water, transportation, and energy to power mills.

Hydropower remains an important source of energy. According to the U.S. Department of Energy, American hydroelectric plants can generate enough electricity to supply 28 million households with power—that's enough to save about 500 million barrels of oil. Hydropower accounts for more than 70% of the electricity generated from renewable sources in the U.S. Other countries do even better: Brazil, Canada, Norway, and Venezuela all get most of their electricity from water.

In a hydroelectric plant, water gets diverted from a river, flows through a pipe (called a **penstock**), and turns the blades of a turbine as it flows back to the river. The turbine spins a generator, which produces the electricity. There are two kinds of hydroelectric plants:

- **Dams.** As you know, dams store water by blocking a river and creating a reservoir. The stored water drives a water turbine and powers a generator to create electricity. When demand for energy is high, the dam can let more water through to generate more electricity.

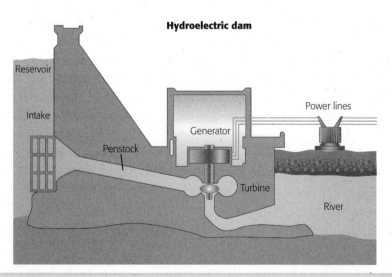

Hydroelectric dam

Reservoir

Intake

Penstock

Generator

Power lines

Turbine

River

- **Run-of-the-river systems.**
  This kind of plant takes
  advantage of water that's
  flowing from higher to
  lower ground. Instead of
  storing water, it uses the
  force of the flowing water
  to turn turbines and
  generate electricity.

A run-of-the-river hydroelectric plant

> **Note** Not all dams produce electricity. Many were built for irrigation and flood control, and can't generate hydroelectric power.

Advantages

Like the other kinds of renewable energy discussed so far in this chapter, hydropower plants don't burn fossil fuels, so they don't belch greenhouse gases and other pollutants into the air. And the river water that turns the turbines is free. Once such a plant is built, it doesn't cost much to maintain and operate. Hydroelectric power has been around for a long time, too, so it's a proven technology that's already in place in many areas.

Disadvantages

You won't be surprised to hear that building hydroelectric plants is pricey. And because they only work when there's water, a disruption of the water cycle (like a drought) means they can't generate as much electricity. Before a company or government invests in building such a plant, it needs to make sure that the plant can earn back its startup costs.

Other concerns center around hydroelectric power's effect on the environment. Building a dam and creating a reservoir means flooding an area where birds, animals, plants, and even people already live. Habitats and biodiversity can be harmed, both upstream and downstream, so it's important to study the impact of a proposed site carefully. Hydroelectric plants can also affect a river's water quality and harm its fish by, for example, blocking the path to their spawning grounds.

> **Note** Some hydroelectric plants have installed *fish ladders*, a series of pools arranged like a staircase so that fish can bypass the dam or other structure and make their way upstream.

Making Waves with Ocean Power

Oceans cover nearly three-quarters of the earth. And if you've ever sat on the beach, watching waves crash into the shore, you've seen some of the power of this vast resource. The ocean has great potential as a source of clean, renewable energy. Here are some of the techniques people are developing to capture the ocean's power:

- **Harnessing the tides.** With this method, the tides turn turbines—which generates electricity—as they flow in and then out to sea. The main problem here is that the movement of the tides doesn't always coincide with peak energy demands.

- **Flowing with the currents.** Tidal stream generators make power using the movement of ocean currents to turn turbines. The water has to be moving at a speed of at least 2 knots.

- **Catching some waves.** The relentless power of ocean waves could be a significant source of energy. Current technology produces electricity using generators that are either linked to buoys or turned by air displaced by the rolling waves.

Although ocean power looks really promising, it's still in the early stages of development. Right now, it's more expensive and produces less electricity than other technologies. According to a story in the *Wall Street Journal*, for example, a typical ocean power project can generate about 2 megawatts of electricity—compared to *200* megawatts from a typical wind farm or *600* megawatts from a coal-burning power plant. But the goal is to improve current technologies and make ocean power a viable energy source.

Geothermal Plants

Geothermal energy taps into the heat stored in the earth and uses it for things like heating and cooling (page 126) or generating electricity. In a geothermal power plant, a deep well goes down a mile or more into the earth, where the temperature is *much* hotter than at the surface.

There are three kinds of geothermal plants:

- **Dry steam plants** use geothermal steam to turn turbines and produce electricity.

> **Note** Some sites use water to produce steam. Engineers drill two deep holes and then use explosives or high-pressure water to break up the rock and create a reservoir at the bottom of the holes. To generate electricity, the plant pumps water down one hole. The earth heats the water, and steam rises through the other hole to turn the plant's turbines.

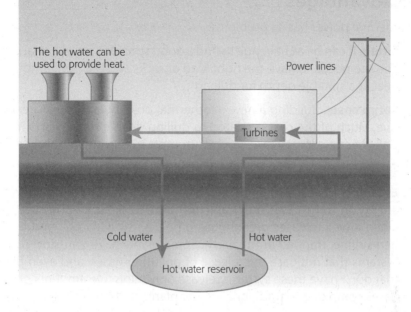

The hot water can be used to provide heat.

Power lines

Turbines

Cold water

Hot water

Hot water reservoir

- **Flash steam plants** create steam by tapping into very hot, highly pressurized water that's deep underground and pulling it into lower-pressure tanks. This creates the steam that drives the turbines.

- **Binary cycle plants** take moderately hot water that's been heated by the earth and pass it by a second fluid that has a lower boiling point than water. The fluid vaporizes and drives turbines to generate power.

Advantages

Geothermal power is clean—it gives off little or no greenhouse gases or other pollutants—and operates without using fossil fuels. And it's got something going for it that the other technologies mentioned so far don't have: reliability. The earth's underground temperature remains constant, so geothermal plants produce electricity, on average, 95% of the time.

Compared to other kinds of power plants, geothermal plants are relatively small, and once they're built, they require little maintenance and cost almost nothing to run.

Disadvantages

Geothermal power has its problems:

- **Siting.** It can be a challenge to find a good spot for a geothermal plant. The site needs to have the right kind of rocks and the right amount of heat at a suitable depth for drilling.

- **Setup costs.** Building a new geothermal power plant is really expensive. Much of the cost is related to drilling deep into the earth, especially because it may take several attempts to find an appropriate site.

- **Tapped-out sites.** The wells at a particular plant may go dry or cool down.

- **Escaping gases.** Although most geothermal plants produce clean energy, in some cases they can contribute to pollution. This happens when a well releases greenhouse gases, particularly CO_2 and hydrogen sulfide, trapped in the earth. Some plants have emission-control systems that mitigate the release of polluting gases, and even plants that don't have these systems release only miniscule amounts of such gases compared to traditional power plants that burn fossil fuels.

- **Sludge.** Some geothermal plants produce *sludge*, rocks and sediment that need to be disposed of at an approved site. But on the plus side, some of the stuff in sludge, like zinc, silica, and sulfur, can be separated from the other materials and sold.

Bioenergy

As page 129 explains, *biomass* is a renewable fuel source made from organic material (in this case, *organic* means material that was once alive or was derived from a living thing). Biomass can come from many different sources including both plant and animal material like wood and wood residue (bark, sawdust, and so on), municipal solid waste, sewage sludge, agricultural waste, and crops grown for energy.

Biomass power plants can produce electricity in one of two ways:

- **Direct combustion.** These plants burn biomass in boilers, which create steam that drives generators. These generators are just like the ones that produce electricity in traditional, fossil fuel–powered plants.

- **Gasification.** This method coverts biomass into methane, which is then burned to run generators.

Biomass is the most widely used renewable energy source in the U.S., currently accounting for about 3% of the total energy produced in the country. Biomass is also used to heat homes, power vehicles, and produce biodegradable plastics, among other things.

Advantages

There are several reasons why biomass has broken ahead of the pack and become the most widely used renewable energy source:

- **A step toward zero waste.** A lot of biomass comes from waste: agricultural, industrial, and municipal. Generating power from otherwise undesirable refuse reduces the amount of waste and protects natural resources.

- **Endlessly renewable.** Unlike fossil fuels, the supply of biomass is unlimited—whether it comes from waste, byproducts, or crops. And biomass can be produced domestically, so there's no need to import it.

- **Carbon neutral.** Although burning biomass releases CO_2 and other greenhouse gases, planting crops to grow biomass offsets those emissions, because the plants absorb CO_2 and give off oxygen.

- **Flexible.** Unlike other sources of renewable energy, biomass can be converted into liquid fuel, such as ethanol and biodiesel (page 238).

Disadvantages

There are some downsides to using biomass, including:

- **Air pollution.** Biomass emits greenhouse gases when it's used to generate fuel. If the carbon isn't offset by replanting crops, biomass contributes to global warming. Direct burning of biomass also releases particulates, although these can be minimized with an emission control system.

- **Energy use.** It takes energy to plant, grow, harvest, and transport the crops used for biomass. Unless these activities are done responsibly, biomass can use up more energy than it produces.

- **Land use.** Thanks to the world's ever-growing appetite for energy, more and more land is being devoted to growing biomass crops. But what about land that's needed to grow food? Some activists are concerned about reduced food production.

Hydrogen Fuel Cells

As you may remember from chemistry class, hydrogen is the first element in the periodic table. It's the simplest molecule with just one proton and one electron, and it's the most abundant element in the universe. It's also what stars are made of: At the center of our sun, hydrogen atoms combine to form helium, giving off radiant energy in the process.

Hydrogen is an energy carrier, like electricity. If your home's electricity is generated by a traditional power plant, that energy comes from burning a fossil fuel, such as coal. But when you want to turn on a light, you don't have to light up a coal stove—you just flip a light switch and electricity delivers the energy from the power plant to your light bulb. Similarly, hydrogen can carry energy that's produced by something else, and can also store that energy.

Hydrogen fuel cells are batteries that store energy and convert it into electricity, generating only water and heat in the process, so the energy is very clean. Fuel cells have no moving parts, and they're small so they need to be stacked to produce a significant amount of energy. These cells currently cost a lot to make, which has limited their practical applications—although you can find hydrogen fuel cells powering everything from laptops to cars to the space shuttle. They also provide emergency backup power to hospitals and police stations, as well as in remote locations, such as middle-of-nowhere cellphone towers.

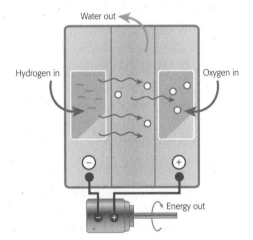

Making hydrogen is a bit of a challenge. Right now, the process is energy-intensive and expensive. The most common method makes hydrogen by burning natural gas—but that also releases greenhouse gases. Another option is electrolysis, which uses electricity to split water molecules into hydrogen and oxygen, but this method is expensive and requires a lot of energy.

Although hydrogen holds a lot of promise for clean, renewable energy, the current high cost of fuel cells, along with the need for an infrastructure to produce, store, and transport hydrogen, presents significant obstacles.

Note Nuclear power plants also produce electricity without emitting greenhouse gases—but they produce radioactive waste that has to be treated and disposed of. A single nuclear power plant produces about 20 metric tons of such waste each year, and storing it safely presents a problem because it takes tens of thousands of years for the radioactivity to decay to a safe level. And past accidents at nuclear power plants in Three Mile Island, Pennsylvania, and Chernobyl, Russia, have caused many to doubt the safety of nuclear power.

11 Getting Involved

One person *can* change the world, and if you've made some of the changes suggested in this book, you've already made a difference. But there's strength in numbers, so this chapter explains how to join forces with others to make changes on a local, national, or even global scale. You'll learn how to get started, but then you have to take it from there.

Activism Begins with You

"Think globally, act locally" has long been a rallying cry of the sustainable-living movement. When you walk instead of driving, enjoy a cup of fair-trade coffee, or replace energy-wasting light bulbs with CFLs, you're making changes that contribute to a better world for all. Small changes add up—the more people who live gently on the earth, the bigger the benefit.

One way to make those good deeds multiply is to get together with other, likeminded people and work for a common cause. There's power in numbers, whether it's half a dozen people picking up trash in a local park or an international organization with millions of members working to conserve natural habitats. After you've made adjustments in your own life and home, look outward. There are lots of ways for you to get involved in ongoing efforts to save the planet.

Your Local Community

Going green in your community makes your city or town a nicer place to live. It brings neighbors together for a common purpose, makes earth-friendly improvements right in your own backyard, and spreads the word about the benefits of going green.

There are many local projects you can join or initiate. Here are some ideas to get you started:

- **Plant a tree (or several).** Help to offset carbon emissions and clean the air in your town by getting folks together to plant trees. For advice on planning a tree-planting event, visit the Arbor Day Foundation (*www.arborday.org*) or Trees Forever (*http://treesforever.org*).

> **Tip** Your area may already have a city forester; call city hall to find out. If you do have one, call the forester's office and ask if you can volunteer or make a donation.

- **Beautify your community.** Many places have community beautification programs that plant and care for flowers and shrubs in public spaces. Sometimes these programs are sponsored by local businesses or maintained by neighborhood garden clubs. Check with your city to see whether there's such a program in your area so you can volunteer. If not, start one.

- **Pick up trash.** Get a group together to clean up a local park or other outdoor space. Check with city hall to find out which park needs it most and to learn the best way to dispose of the garbage you collect. You may be able to get the local landfill, a waste management company, or a retailer to donate trash bags. Consider getting schools or scout troops involved too.

> **Note** Check with your state highway department about taking responsibility for regularly cleaning up a stretch of road. And don't forget about safety: Make sure everyone who helps with roadside cleanup wears a fluorescent vest, and don't schedule cleanups at twilight, when it's hard for motorists to see.

- **Clean up waterways.** Nothing spoils a day by the water like floating trash or garbage washed up on shore. Organize your own cleanup day, or participate in the Ocean Conservancy's International Coastal Clean-up, which takes place each September. You don't even have to live near the ocean to participate in this event—rivers and lakes need cleaning, too—and it feels great to know you're part of a coordinated cleanup that's happening all over the world. To learn more, go to *http://tinyurl.com/afr2ws*.

- **Start a recycling program.** You can do this at work (page 254), your kids' school, your church, your apartment building—look around and see where recycling would do some good. Earth911.com has a step-by-step guide for getting such a program off the ground at *http://earth911.com/recycling/start-recycling-program*. If your city, town, or county doesn't offer curbside recycling, start a citizen's action group to advocate for it: Find likeminded people, write a petition, and hit the streets to gather signatures.

- **Create a community garden.** As discussed in Chapter 6, these gardens are a great way to green urban spaces and encourage organic garden-ing. You'll need to buy (or convince someone to donate) a sizeable plot of land, form a steering committee, and then decide on rules.

- **Build affordable housing.** The international program Habitat for Human-ity builds inexpensive housing throughout the world, with a focus on en-ergy efficiency and sustainability. Visit *www.habitat.org*, click Get Involved, and then click Volunteer Locally to search for a program near you.

> **Tip** Head to this book's Missing CD page at *www.missingmanuals.com*, which includes all the links listed here.

If you want to gather a group for a green project, follow these steps:

1. **Define the project's scope.** Do you want to do a one-day spring cleanup of a local park or creek? Or do you want to have an ongoing project like planting and caring for flowers and shrubs in public areas, which requires people to commit to coming together several times or meeting regularly?

> **Tip** Check with your town or city to find out whether you need to get official permission for the project you have in mind. For example, if you want to build affordable green housing in your community, you'll need to get the necessary building permits.

2. **Get the word out.** Make sure that your community knows about your project or group. Put notices in local newspapers, tack flyers onto community bulletin boards, and advertise online on sites like Craigslist.org. Set up a special email account for your project (you can do this at a site like *http://mail.google.com* or *http://mail.yahoo.com*) and collect email addresses so you can send out notices. Announce your project well in advance, and remind people as the date approaches.

3. **Get organized.** Volunteers need to know their roles and responsibilities or your project will turn into chaos. This step might be as simple as deciding who'll pick up trash in which section of the park, or as involved as electing officers and forming committees.

4. **Raise funds and solicit donations.** This isn't necessary for all projects, but for large or ongoing ones, you may need more than volunteers' time. Ask local businesses for donations, and research grants. Your city, county, state, or the federal government may have money available for green projects and organizations.

5. **Get the word out—again.** Doing good is good in itself. But it's even better when you have widespread support throughout your community. Contact your local newspaper and TV and radio stations to get some press. Visit community groups and schools to talk up what you're doing, and offer information sessions at the local library or other venue. You'll recruit more members and generate goodwill.

> **Tip** The U.S. EPA offers advice and an action plan for people who want to make their communities greener. Check it out at *www.epa.gov/greenkit*.

Online Communities

You can connect with thousands of environmentally conscious people from all over the world without leaving your house. When you join an online community that's committed to spreading the word about green, healthy living, you'll make new friends, get ideas, and have fun, too. Here's a sampling of online communities with a green focus:

- **Care2** (*www.care2.com*). This site, which focuses on green and healthy living, has more than 10 million members, so you'll have lots of like-minded company when you join it (registration is free). It has tons of free articles on all aspects of green living and dozens of petitions you can sign. You can also look for green jobs and volunteer opportunities in your area. When you register, you can set up your own page on the site, create or join a special-interest group, or start a blog.

- **GenGreen Life** (*www.gengreenlife.com*). Here, the emphasis is on your local area, with a directory that helps you find green businesses near you. Tens of thousands of listings cover everything from alternative energy and carbon offsets to recycling and waste management to food and dining. List your earth-friendly business here or create a free personal account. With an account, you can post reviews of businesses, sign up for GenGreen Life's newsletter, join and create groups, and more.

- **Huddler's Green Home** Community (*http://greenhome.huddler.com*). This online community for friends of the Earth lets you submit product reviews, write articles, and participate in public forums.

- **Planet Green** (*http://planetgreen.discovery.com*). This site is run by Discovery Communications (which owns the Discovery Channel and the TreeHugger site listed next). If you watch Planet Green TV, you'll like this companion site. It's got a schedule letting you know what's on and pages for the channel's shows. There are lots of articles on green living here, as well as forums about all aspects of green living.

- **TreeHugger** (*www.treehugger.com*). This site, which shares its forums with Planet Green, is loaded with ideas and tips for green living, the latest environment-related news, product reviews, and a whole lot more.

- **WiserEarth** (*www.wiserearth.org*). This site's slogan is "Connecting You to Communities of Action," and that's just what it does. It's both a community site and a community directory, listing more than 100,000 organizations worldwide that are working for social and environmental change.

Tip While you're online, try the Green Maven search engine (*www.greenmaven.com*) to help you find greenest websites. Instead of searching the billions and billions of sites on the Web, Green Maven scours green sites only, giving better targeted results. Those green sites are listed in a Green Directory you can browse.

National and International Organizations

The good news: There are tons of nonprofits working hard to protect wild-life, conserve natural habitats, protect biodiversity, influence environmental policy, fight climate change, and generally protect the planet. The bad news: There are too many worthy organizations to list here. This section lists a number of active, well-known groups that help you volunteer, join forces with others, or donate to a worthy cause. But this list barely scratches the surface. You can find more at Charity Navigator (*www.charitynavigator.org*), which evaluates a wide range of nonprofits, including those with an environmental focus.

Here are some groups to consider supporting with your time, money, or both:

- **Animal Protection and Habitat Conservation:**
    - Amazon Conservation Team (*www.amazonteam.org*)
    - Amazon Watch (*www.amazonwatch.org*)
    - Audubon Society (*www.audubon.org*)
    - Birdlife International (*www.birdlife.org*)
    - Conservation International (*www.conservation.org*)
    - Defenders of Wildlife (*www.defenders.org*)
    - Ecology Fund.com (*www.ecologyfund.com*)
    - Forests and European Union Resource Network (*www.fern.org*)
    - Grey Seal Conservation Society (*www.greyseal.net*)
    - National Wildlife Federation (*www.nwf.org*)
    - Natural Resources Defense Council (*www.nrdc.org*)
    - Nature Conservancy (*www.nature.org*)
    - Rainforest Action Network (*www.ran.org*)
    - Rainforest Alliance (*www.rainforest-alliance.org*)
    - Sierra Club (*www.sierraclub.org*)
    - Wilderness Society (*http://wilderness.org*)
    - World Wildlife Fund (*www.worldwildlife.org*)

- **Climate Change and Global Warming:**
  - Clean Air Cool Planet (*www.cleanair-coolplanet.org*)
  - Climate Group (*www.theclimategroup.org*)
  - We Can Solve It (*www.wecansolveit.org*)
- **Environmental Education and Outreach:**
  - ecoAmerica (*www.ecoamerica.net*)
  - Foundation for Environmental Education (*www.fee-international.org*)
  - Focus the Nation (*www.focusthenation.org*)
  - Slate Foundation (*www.theslatefoundation.org*)
  - Student Environmental Action Coalition (*www.seac.org*)
- **Environmental Law and Policy:**
  - Center for International Environmental Law (*www.ciel.org*)
  - Earth Justice (*www.earthjustice.org*)
  - Environmental Law Alliance Worldwide (*www.elaw.org*)
  - Rocky Mountain Institute (*www.rmi.org*)
- **Oceans and Water Conservation:**
  - American Rivers (*www.americanrivers.org*)
  - Blue Ocean Institute (*www.blueocean.org*)
  - MarineBio (*http://marineio.org*)
  - Ocean Alliance (*www.oceanalliance.org*)
  - Ocean Conservancy (*www.oceanconservancy.org*)
  - Ocean Conservation Society (*www.oceanconservation.org*)
  - Oceana (*www.oceana.org*)
  - Waterkeeper Alliance (*www.waterkeeper.org*)

Environmentally Responsible Investing

Whether you're saving for retirement or growing your nest egg, you want to invest your hard-earned money in companies that respect the environment. *Socially responsible investing* (SRI) has been around for a while. It's a strategy that takes investors' ethics and values into consideration, with the two-pronged goal of getting a good financial return *and* supporting companies that do some good in the world.

SRI focuses on companies that work in an environmentally responsible way, respect human rights and indigenous peoples, and deal fairly with employees and consumers. Some—but not all—SRI funds also avoid companies involved in controversial industries like tobacco, alcohol, weapons, and gambling. So if you object to certain kinds of businesses, be sure to research the SRI funds you're considering to make sure you're not investing in something you oppose.

There are several ways you can invest responsibly:

- **Mutual funds.** Socially responsible mutual funds are made up of securities from companies that act in accordance with certain ethical, moral, or religious values. Green mutual funds hold stock in businesses that protect the environment and/or in forward-looking companies that are working on solutions to environmental problems, such as clean energy. To start your research into green and socially responsible mutual funds, spend some time on the Social Investment Forum (*www.socialinvest.org*), a nonprofit association of financial services professionals and companies. Another helpful site is SocialFunds (*www.socialfunds.com*), which has thousands of pages on mutual funds, community investing, sustainability reports on specific companies, news, and more.

> **Tip** Investopedia, a Forbes website, has an entire section with articles, opinions, and tips on green investing. Visit it at *http://tinyurl.com/mflm9w*.

- **Individual stocks.** Many green-minded investors prefer to screen and select their investments individually, rather than going with a mutual fund. When you do your own research (instead of relying on someone else to pick stocks for you), you know you're choosing companies that are in line with your values and get a sense of satisfaction from making your own investment decisions. In addition, you'll pay less in fees and you may even get a higher return, because many mutual funds fail to outperform the major market indexes. (Of course, as the box on page 285 explains, there's a potential for greater losses, as well.)

Stocks vs. Mutual Funds

New investors are often bewildered by all the options out there. A common source of confusion is the difference between stocks and mutual funds.

First, you need to know what a *stock* is: To raise money, companies sell shares of stock, which are little pieces of the company. In other words, you're giving the company money to help run its operations. If a business sells 10,000 shares to investors and you buy 100, for example, you're the proud owner of 1% of that company. Most investors buy shares hoping that the company will do well and the stocks will go up in value. You can buy individual stocks, selecting a company and purchasing a specific number of shares. A collection of stocks is called a *portfolio*.

To buy shares in a company, you need a stockbroker to help you. The broker can be someone who works for a financial firm, or you can manage your portfolio using an online stockbroker like E*Trade (*www.etrade.com*) or TD Ameritrade (*www.tdameritrade.com*).

When you invest in a *mutual fund*, you're pooling your money with other investors so that the fund manager can invest that money in a portfolio of stocks and other securities (like bonds and money-market funds). The fund manager picks the stocks and balances the portfolio.

Which is better? The answer depends on how much time and money you're willing to devote to your investments. Choosing individual stocks and managing your own portfolio takes time and skill: You have to research companies and be able to analyze them and their potential for growth. You also need to watch the stocks in your portfolio so you can step in and manage them. Buying individual stocks can be expensive, too. When you pool your money with thousands of other investors in a mutual fund, on the other hand, the starting threshold is lower—often just a few hundred dollars.

Individual stocks can have greater gains—and greater losses. A mutual fund includes numerous stocks and other kinds of securities. The idea behind this diversity is to provide some stability. If one stock shoots up, other stocks in the fund that aren't performing quite so well mitigate that rise, so the fund's value doesn't increase as much as the individual stock's does. But this works both ways: When a stock drops in price, the other securities in the fund help to cushion that fall.

- **Community investing.** If you want to be sure your investment is helping communities, consider investing in a *community development financial institution* (CDFI), which loans money to people and organizations that have don't have access to traditional loans. This money can be used to start or grow a small business, buy or improve housing, get an education, and so on. Many CDFIs provide *micro-loans*, small amounts of money to help individual entrepreneurs who don't qualify for other loans. Two CDFIs to check out are Self-Help (*www.self-help.org*) and Clearing House CDFI (*www.clearinghousecdfi.com*).

Tip Kiva is a website that matches investors with specific projects by partnering with microlending institutions around the world. Here's how it works: When you visit *www.kiva.org*, click the Lend button to browse entrepreneurs from around the world who need funds. (You can also search by the requestor's gender, type of loan, or region.) For each loan request, you can read about the amount needed, what the borrower will use it for, and the loan partner's default and delinquency rates. When you find a project you want to invest in, you choose the amount (which can be as little as $25) and pay using PayPal or a credit card. Over time, the borrower repays the loan, and you can keep those funds or invest them in another project.

Investing in the stock market can be a roller-coaster ride, and green businesses are just as subject to its ups and downs as any other company. Never invest money you can't afford to lose. And before you buy a stock or fund, do your research. Check how a stock or fund has performed over time (not just last quarter or last year) and compare it to other funds and stock market indexes such as the Dow Jones and NASDAQ. A great resource for researching stocks and mutual funds is Morningstar (*www.morningstar.com*), which offers analysis and evaluation of stocks and funds, including their risk levels. Or check out MSN's Money Central: *http://moneycentral.msn.com/investor/home.aspx*. And to see how a particular company measures up in terms of climate change, take a look at Climate Counts (*http://climatecounts.org*), which rates companies' commitment to fighting global warming.

Note When evaluating companies, watch out for *greenwashing*—that's when businesses try to make their practices look greener than they actually are. Some companies run misleading ad campaigns, for example, in hopes of getting good PR they don't deserve. Other greenwashing practices include making false claims, such as saying that a product is organic when it hasn't been certified as such, and exaggerating green initiatives. Some companies spend millions more on ads to prove how green they are than on actually cleaning up their act. If you're wondering whether a particular company is a greenwasher, check Greenpeace's Greenwashing site (*http://stopgreenwash.org*) or the Greenwashing Index (*www.greenwashingindex.com*).

Index

D

E

F

Institute for Local Self-Reliance (ILSR),
205
insulation (green homes), **121**, **134**, **138**
internal combustion, **237**
international organizations, **282–283**
investing
Investopedia, **284**
socially responsible (SRI), **283**

J

job health tips, **255–256**
joules, defined, **49**
junk mail, **92–94**

K

Kazarie Worm Farm, **195**
kilowatt hour, defined, **49**
kitchens
chemicals in cleaning products, **10**
cleaning, **20–22**
reducing water usage in, **67**
Kiva, **286**

L

landfills, **79–82**
landscaping, **32**, **124**
laundry
chemicals in cleaning products, **11**
efficiency tips, **59–63**
green cleaning of, **25–27**
laundry room efficiency, **67**
lawns
mowing, **39**
natural care of, **31–36**
overview of, **28–29**
pesticide dangers and, **29–30**
watering, **37**, **64**
leachate, **80**
lead paint in older homes, **139**
League of American Bicyclists, **231**
leakproof disposable diapers, **149**
leaks, water, **65**
LEDs (light-emitting diodes), **75**

LEED (Leadership in Energy and
Environmental Design) rating
system, **118–120**
lemon juice, **17**
light-emitting diodes (LEDs), **75**
lighting costs, reducing, **47**
lime scale, removing, **24**
linoleum floors, **136**
liquid manure handling system, **174**
litter, biodegradable, **169**
living wage, defined, **208**
local businesses, supporting, **203–205**
local community projects, **278–279**
LocalHarvest, **202**
long-distance travel, **241–245**
lotions, baby, **155**
lumber and framing (green homes),
133–134
lumens of light, **71–72**

M

mail, junk. *See* junk mail
makeup. *See* beauty products
MakeYourCosmetics.com, **219**
manual removal of garden bugs, **198**
manure on factory farms, **182**
Map My Ride (bicycling), **231**
MapQuest, **234**
meat industry pollution, **182**
mercury in CFLs, **73**
microhydro power, **128**
microloans, **285**
microwaves, baby food and, **155**
mildew and mold, removing, **23**
Mink Shoes, **214**
mirrors, cleaning, **24**
mold
and mildew, removing, **23**
in renovated homes, **139–140**
money
Money Central (MSN), **286**
saving through recycling, **102–103**
monofills (landfill), **83**
Morningstar, **286**
mortgage options, **143–144**
motor oil (cars), **233**

Try the online edition free for 45 days